SENIOR
DRAMA

EDITED BY SADLER & HAYLLAR

First published 1985 by
MACMILLAN EDUCATION AUSTRALIA PTY LTD
107 Moray Street, South Melbourne 3205
6 Clarke Street, Crows Nest 2065
Reprinted 1985, 1988, 1990, 1992, 1993 (twice)

Associated companies and representatives
throughout the world

National Library of Australia
cataloguing in publication data

Senior drama

Includes index.
ISBN 0 333 38117 3.

1. English drama. 2. College and school drama.
3. Playwriting. I. Sadler, R. K. (Rex Kevin).
II. Hayllar, T. A. S. (Thomas Albert S.)

822'.008

Set in Bembo and Univers by
Setrite Typesetters, Hong Kong
Printed in Hong Kong

Contents

Acknowledgements iv

Preface v

Coming to Terms with Drama 1

OF MICE AND MEN (John Steinbeck) **7**

    Questions 82

    Looking Back 83

THE OTHER FOOT (Ray Bradbury/Martin Walsh) **91**

    Questions 100

NAPOLEON'S PIANO (Spike Milligan) **101**

    Questions 116

FAWLTY TOWERS (John Cleese and Connie Booth) **117**

    Questions 124

BOOKSHOP (John Cleese and Graham Chapman) **125**

    Questions 130

THE TELL-TALE HEART (Edgar Allan Poe) **131**

    Questions 139

PICNIC AT HANGING ROCK (Cliff Green/Joan Lindsay) **141**

    Looking Back 236

    General Questions 240

    Technical Terms 241

Acknowledgements

The editors and publishers are grateful to the following for permission to reproduce copyright material.

Photographs reproduced on pp. 1, 3, 4 courtesy of The Melbourne Theatre Comapny.

McIntosh and Otis, Inc. for *Of Mice and Men*, © 1937 by John Steinbeck, © John Steinbeck 1965; photographs courtesy of The Melbourne Theatre Company.

Don Congdon and Associates for *The Other Foot* by Martin Walsh (dramatization of story by Ray Bradbury).

Norma Farnes for *Napoleon's Piano* by Spike Milligan (*Goon Show* script); BBC copyright photographs.

BBC Enterprises for *Fawlty Towers* by John Cleese and Connie Booth (extract from episode 'The Germans'); BBC copyright photograph.

BBC Enterprises for *Bookshop* by John Cleese and Graham Chapman (sketch from *At Last the 1948 Show*).

Grace Gibson Radio Productions for *The Tell-Tale Heart* by Edgar Allan Poe, from *Tales of the Supernatural*.

Cliff Green Productions for *Picnic at Hanging Rock* (novel © Joan Lindsay 1967, screenplay © Cliff Green 1975); photographs reproduced with permission of McElroy & McElroy Pty Ltd.

Warning: All scripts in this book are copyright and permission to perform must be obtained, with the payment of a fee in some cases. Application should be made to the appropriate source. The publishers regret that they cannot undertake to forward applications for performance.

While every care has been taken to trace and acknowledge copyright, the publishers tender their apologies for any accidental infringement where copyright has proved untraceable. They would be pleased to come to a suitable arrangement with the rightful owner in each case.

We would like to express our appreciation to our editor, Alex Skovron, for all his guidance and creativity. — R.S. and T.H.

Cover: Jan Schmoeger
Drawings: Randy Glusac

Preface

Senior Drama is a book designed to appeal to students in the senior years of high school. Tragedy, comedy, excitement, conflict and suspense are all here for the acting and the reading. Some of the plays and scripts raise social, moral and emotional issues that will help students towards a deeper understanding of their environment.

A special introductory section defines and explains dramatic terms such as setting, plot, theme, climax, characterization and dialogue. Actual production photographs have been placed throughout *Of Mice and Men* and *Picnic at Hanging Rock* to highlight the dramatic impact of respective scenes. In addition, an invaluable glossary of technical terms and abbreviations accompanies the film screenplay.

The plays and scripts have been found to be ideal for the classroom: the longer ones have large casts, and the shorter are able to be performed and discussed in a single lesson. The questions following each play or script assist understanding and interpretation. A detailed discussion of the Steinbeck play is also included.

We believe that this book will appeal to students and teachers alike, offering as it does a wide and involving range of human experiences and responses enacted within the conventions of the four dramatic media of our time — stage, radio, television and cinema.

Rex Sadler
Tom Hayllar

Coming to Terms with Drama

Plot

The dramatist arranges the events that take place in the play using the framework of a story. This pattern of events, complete in itself, is known as the plot.

Characterization

To make the play convincing and absorbing for the audience, the playwright tries to create characters that appear lifelike and interesting. He or she attempts to achieve this through the words and actions of the characters as they reveal their emotions, attitudes and beliefs. The kind of language the characters use and the manner in which they speak help to reveal what kind of people they are.

Through the mouths of other characters, the playwright may reveal to the audience additional information about a character which is not brought out through his or her own words and actions. Sometimes the playwright gives specific advice in the stage directions on how some of the characters should look, act, dress and behave. Most members of the audience would be unfamiliar with the stage directions in the script, and it would be the task of the director to ensure that these are brought to life in the scene being enacted.

Here are some questions to ask yourself about the characters as you are reading the plays in this book:

(1) Are the characters true to life?
(2) Which characters are the most memorable? Why?
(3) Do the characters change during the play? How?

Just from looking as the scene on page 1, from the play *The Last of the Knucklemen*, what comments would you make about the characters?

Motivation

The audience requires that a character's motivations—the things that cause that character to act in a certain way—be clear and consistent.

Exposition

In the exposition or opening scenes of the play, the playwright, through the dialogue of the characters, aims to explain to the audience as quickly as possible what has happened *up to* the time at which the action of the play takes place. The playwright provides whatever information the audience needs to enable it to understand the rest of the play.

Setting

The setting of a play is the place and time in which the action occurs. For example, the setting for Shakespeare's *Julius Caesar* is Rome, and also Sardis and Philippi, in the years 44−42 BC; while that of his *Macbeth* is medieval Scotland. The setting helps to reinforce the overall mood of a play.

Dialogue

The dialogue is the conversation amongst the characters in the play. Good dialogue fits the character who is speaking as naturally as do that character's dress and actions.

Theme

The theme of the play is the central idea that runs through it. Very often the theme makes important comments on human behaviour. For a deeper understanding of a play you should ask yourself these two questions:

(1) What message was the playwright trying to communicate?
(2) How did the playwright get this message across?

Conflict

The great dramatist George Bernard Shaw once said, 'No conflict, no drama'. There are certainly many kinds of conflict in drama. The main character in a play will not escape being subjected to one kind of conflict or another. It may be a conflict with one of the other characters, or quite possibly it may be an *internal* conflict. The character may be struggling against opposing ideas and beliefs, or may even be at odds with the society or the environment. As the play develops and the main character tries to solve these problems and resolve the conflict, suspense is created for the audience.

Suspense

Suspense comes from the building up of tension in a particular situation or a number of situations. As the plot progresses, the audience is kept in doubt about the outcome. The playwright arouses expectations in the minds of the audience about what the future holds for the characters. This element of anxious uncertainty is heightened until the *climax* is reached.

Suspense may rely on a number of factors. It may depend on conflict among the characters themselves, or on the struggle of a character against the circumstances intervening between that character and a goal that must be attained. The setting itself may help to create suspense. A haunted house, a wet, dark and windy night, a gloomy

cellar, a museum of wax dummies, the morgue, the graveyard—all
have been used many times by dramatists to create suspense.

Suspense can be found in many kinds of situation. In the thrill of
the chase, the audience wonders whether the hero, or the villain, will
be able to evade capture; James Bond scripts abound in high-powered
chase scenes of this kind. In warfare, the audience wonders who will
win the crucial battle. In a murder mystery, everyone tries to guess
who actually did commit the murder. And so on.

Climax

The climax is the point in the play at which the interest-level is at its
peak. Every other action in the play has led to this moment. The
climax sometimes comes at the very end of the play, but usually it is
followed by further action.

Dénouement

The action following the climax is called the dénouement. This is the
'unknotting' or working-out of the plot. It is the time when the
playwright can explain, through the characters, how and why everything turned out as it did.

Structure

This is the underlying pattern of development of the play. The following simple diagram will give you some idea of the structure of a play.

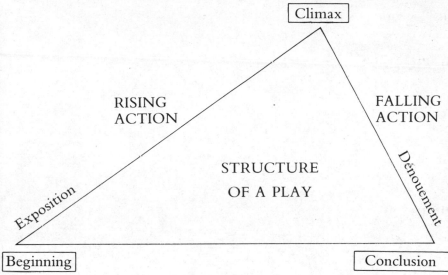

Of Mice and Men

John Steinbeck

This powerful and tragic story made its appearance in 1937, in the form of a novelette. It was dramatized by the author, John Steinbeck, in the same year.

CAST

George	Curley's Wife
Lennie	Slim
Candy	Carlson
The Boss	Whit
Curley	Crooks

Time: The present.
Place: An agricultural valley in Southern California.

ACT ONE

SCENE I

Thursday night.
A sandy bank of the Salinas River sheltered with willows—one giant sycamore right, upstage.
The stage is covered with dry leaves. The feeling of the stage is sheltered and quiet.
Stage is lit by a setting sun.
Curtain rises on an empty stage. A sparrow is singing. There is a distant sound of ranch dogs barking aimlessly and one clear quail call. The quail call turns to a warning call and there is a beat of the flock's wings. Two figures are seen entering the stage in single file, with GEORGE, *the short man, coming*

in ahead of LENNIE. *Both men are carrying blanket rolls. They approach the water. The small man throws down his blanket roll, the large man follows and then falls down and drinks from the river, snorting as he drinks.*

George (*irritably*) Lennie, for God's sake, don't drink so much. (*Leans over and shakes* LENNIE.) Lennie, you hear me! You gonna be sick like you was last night.

Lennie (*dips his whole head under, hat and all. As he sits upon the bank, his hat drips down the back.*) That's good. You drink some, George. You drink some too.

George (*kneeling and dipping his finger in the water*) I ain't sure it's good water. Looks kinda scummy to me.

Lennie (*imitates, dipping his finger also*) Look at them wrinkles in the water, George. Look what I done.

George (*drinking from his cupped palm*) Tastes all right. Don't seem to be runnin' much, though. Lennie, you oughtn' to drink water when it ain't running. (*hopelessly*) You'd drink water out of a gutter if you was thirsty. (*He throws a scoop of water into his face and rubs it around with his hand, pushes himself back and embraces his knees.* LENNIE, *after watching him, imitates him in every detail.*)

George (*beginning tiredly and growing angry as he speaks*) God damn it, we could just as well of rode clear to the ranch. That bus driver didn't know what he was talkin' about. 'Just a little stretch down the highway,' he says. 'Just a little stretch'—damn near four miles. I bet he didn't want to stop at the ranch gate....I bet he's too damn lazy to pull up. Wonder he ain't too lazy to stop at Soledad at all! (*mumbling*) Just a little stretch down the road.

Lennie (*timidly*) George?

George Yeh...what you want?

Lennie Where we goin', George?

George (*jerks down his hat furiously*) So you forgot that already, did you? So I got to tell you again! Jeez, you're a crazy bastard!

Lennie (*softly*) I forgot. I tried not to forget, honest to God, I did!

George Okay, okay, I'll tell you again.... (*with sarcasm*) I ain't got nothin' to do. Might just as well spen' all my time tellin' you things. You forgit 'em and I tell you again.

Lennie (*continuing on from his last speech*) I tried and tried, but it didn't do no good. I remember about the rabbits, George!

George The hell with the rabbits! You can't remember nothing but them rabbits. You remember settin' in that gutter on Howard Street and watchin' that blackboard?

Lennie (*delightedly*) Oh, sure! I remember that ... but ... wha'd we do then? I remember some girls come by, and you says—

George The hell with what I. says! You remember about us goin' in Murray and Ready's and they give us work cards and bus tickets?

Lennie (*confidently*) Oh, sure, George...I remember that now. (*Puts his hand into his side coat-pocket; his confidence vanishes. Very gently.*)...George?

George Huh?

Lennie (*staring at the ground in despair*) I ain't got mine. I musta lost it.

George You never had none. I got both of 'em here. Think I'd let you carry your own work card?

Lennie (*with tremendous relief*) I thought I put it in my side pocket. (*Puts his hand in his pocket again.*)

George (*looking sharply at him; and as he looks,* LENNIE *brings his hand out of his pocket.*) Wha'd you take out of that pocket?

Lennie (*cleverly*) Ain't a thing in my pocket.

George I know there ain't. You got it in your hand now. What you got in your hand?

Lennie I ain't got nothing, George! Honest!

George Come on, give it here!

Lennie (*holds his closed hand away from* GEORGE) It's on'y a mouse!

George A mouse? A live mouse?

Lennie No ... just a dead mouse. (*worriedly*) I didn't kill it. Honest. I found it. I found it dead.

George Give it here!

Lennie Leave me have it, George.

George (*sternly*) Give it here! (LENNIE *reluctantly gives him the mouse.*) What do you want of a dead mouse, anyway?

Lennie (*in a propositional tone*) I was petting it with my thumb while we walked along.

George Well, you ain't pettin' no mice while you walk with me. Now let's see if you can remember where we're going. (GEORGE *throws it across the water into the brush.*)

Lennie (*looks startled and then in embarrassment hides his face against his knees*) I forgot again.

George Jesus Christ! (*resignedly*) Well, look, we are gonna work on a ranch like the one we come from up north.

Lennie Up north?

George In Weed!

Lennie Oh, sure I remember—in Weed.

George (*still with exaggerated patience*) That ranch we're goin' to is right down there about a quarter mile. We're gonna go in and see the boss.

Lennie (*repeats as a lesson*) And see the boss!

George Now, look! I'll give him the work tickets, but you ain't gonna say a word. You're just gonna stand there and not say nothing.

Lennie Not say nothing!

George If he finds out what a crazy bastard you are, we won't get no job. But if he sees you work before he hears you talk, we're set. You got that?

Lennie Sure, George ... sure, I got that.

George Okay. Now when we go in to see the boss, what you gonna do?

Lennie (*concentrating*) I ... I ... I ain't gonna say nothing ... jus' gonna stand there.

George (*greatly relieved*) Good boy, that's swell! Now say that over two or three times so you sure won't forget it.

Lennie (*drones softly under his breath*) I ain't gonna say nothing...I ain't gonna say nothing....(*Trails off into a whisper.*)

George And you ain't gonna do no bad things like you done in Weed neither.

Lennie (*puzzled*) Like I done in Weed?

George So you forgot that too, did you?

Lennie (*triumphantly*) They run us out of Weed!

George (*disgusted*) Run us out, hell! We run! They was lookin' for us, but they didn't catch us.

Lennie (*happily*) I didn't forget that, you bet.

George (*lies back on the sand, crosses his hands under his head. And again* LENNIE *imitates him.*) God, you're a lot of trouble! I could get along so easy and nice, if I didn't have you on my tail. I could live so easy!

Lennie (*hopefully*) We gonna work on a ranch, George.

George All right, you got that. But we're gonna sleep here tonight, because...I want to. I want to sleep out. (*The light is going fast, dropping into evening. A little wind whirls into the clearing and blows leaves. A dog howls in the distance.*)

Lennie Why ain't we goin' on to the ranch to get some supper? They got supper at the ranch.

George No reason at all. I just like it here. Tomorrow we'll be goin' to work. I seen thrashing machines on the way down; that means we'll be buckin' grain bags. Bustin' a gut liftin' up them bags. Tonight I'm gonna lay right here an' look up! Tonight there ain't a grain bag or a boss in the world. Tonight, the drinks is on the . . . house. Nice house we got here, Lennie.

Lennie (*gets up on his knees and looks down at* GEORGE, *plaintively*) Ain't we gonna have no supper?

George Sure we are. You gather up some dead willow sticks. I got three cans of beans in my bindle. I'll open 'em up while you get a fire ready. We'll eat 'em cold.

Lennie (*companionably*) I like beans with ketchup.

George Well, we ain't got no ketchup. You go get the wood, and don't you fool around none. Be dark before long. (LENNIE *lumbers to his feet and disappears into the brush.* GEORGE *gets out the bean cans, opens two of them, suddenly turns his head and listens. A little sound of splashing comes from the direction that* LENNIE *has taken.* GEORGE *looks after him; shakes his head.* LENNIE *comes back carrying a few small willow sticks in his hand.*) All right, give me that mouse.

Lennie (*with elaborate pantomime of innocence*) What, George? I ain't got no mouse.

George (*holding out his hand*) Come on! Give it to me! You ain't puttin' nothing over. (LENNIE *hesitates, backs away, turns and looks as if he were going to run. Coldly.*) You gonna give me that mouse or do I have to take a sock at you?

Lennie Give you what, George?

George You know goddamn well, what! I want that mouse!

Lennie (*almost in tears*) I don't know why I can't keep it. It ain't nobody's mouse. I didn' steal it! I found it layin' right beside the road. (GEORGE *snaps his fingers sharply, and* LENNIE *lays the mouse in his hand.*) I wasn't doin' nothing bad with it. Just stroking it. That ain't bad.

George (*stands up and throws the mouse as far as he can into the brush, then he steps to the pool, and washes his hands*) You crazy fool! Thought you could get away with it, didn't you? Don't you think I could see your feet was wet where you went in the water to get it? (LENNIE *whimpers like a puppy.*) Blubbering like a baby. Jesus Christ, a big guy like you! (LENNIE *tries to control himself, but his lips quiver and his face works with an effort.* GEORGE *puts his hand on* LENNIE's *shoulder for a moment.*) Aw, Lennie, I ain't takin' it away just for meanness. That mouse ain't fresh. Besides, you broke it pettin' it. You get a mouse that's fresh and I'll let you keep it a little while.

Lennie I don't know where there is no other mouse. I remember a lady used to give 'em to me. Ever' one she got she used to give it to me, but that lady ain't here no more.

George Lady, huh! ... Give me them sticks there ... Don't even remember who that lady was. That was your own Aunt Clara. She stopped givin' 'em to you. You always killed 'em.

Lennie (*sadly and apologetically*) They was so little. I'd pet 'em and pretty soon they bit my fingers and then I pinched their head a little bit and then they was dead...because they was so little. I wish we'd get the rabbits pretty soon, George. They ain't so little.

George The hell with the rabbits! Come on, let's eat. (*The light has continued to go out of the scene so that when* GEORGE *lights the fire, it is the major light on the stage.* GEORGE *hands one of the open cans of beans to* LENNIE.) There's enough beans for four men.

Lennie (*sitting on the other side of the fire, speaks patiently*) I like 'em with ketchup.

George (*explodes*) Well, we ain't got any. Whatever we ain't got, that's what you want. God Almighty, if I was alone, I could live so easy. I could go get a job of work and no trouble. No mess...and when the end of the month come, I could take my fifty bucks and go into town and get whatever I want. Why, I could stay in a cat-house all night. I could eat any place I want. Order any damn thing.

Lennie (*plaintively, but softly*) I didn't want no ketchup.

George (*continuing violently*) I could do that every damn month. Get a gallon of whiskey or set in a pool room and play cards or shoot pool. (LENNIE *gets up to his knees and looks over the fire, with frightened face.*) And what have I got? (*disgustedly*) I got you. You can't keep a job and you lose me every job I get!

Lennie (*in terror*) I don't mean nothing, George.

George Just keep me shovin' all over the country all the time. And that ain't the worst—you get in trouble. You do bad things and I got to get you out. It ain't bad people that raises hell. It's dumb ones. (*He shouts.*) You crazy son-of-a-bitch, you keep me in hot water all the time. (LENNIE *is trying to stop* GEORGE's *flow of words with his hands. Sarcastically.*) You just wanta feel that girl's dress. Just wanta pet it like it was a mouse. Well, how the hell'd she know you just wanta feel her dress? How'd she know you'd just hold onto it like it was a mouse?

Lennie (*in panic*) I didn't mean to, George!

George Sure you didn't mean to. You didn't mean for her to yell bloody hell, either. You didn't mean for us to hide in the irrigation ditch all day with guys out lookin' for us with guns. Alla time it's something you didn't mean. God damn it, I wish I could put you in a cage with a million mice and let them pet *you*. (GEORGE's *anger leaves him suddenly. For the first time he seems to see the expression of terror on* LENNIE's *face. He looks down ashamedly at the fire, and manoeuvres some beans onto the blade of his pocket-knife and puts them into his mouth.*)

Lennie (*after a pause*) George! (GEORGE *purposely does not answer him.*) George?

George What do you want?

Lennie I was only foolin', George. I don't want no ketchup. I wouldn't eat no ketchup if it was right here beside me.

George (*with a sullenness of shame*) If they was some here you could have it. And if I had a thousand bucks I'd buy ya a bunch of flowers.

Lennie I wouldn't eat no ketchup, George. I'd leave it all for you. You could cover your beans so deep with it, and I wouldn't touch none of it.

George (*refusing to give in from his sullenness, refusing to look at* LENNIE) When I think of the swell time I could have without you, I go nuts. I never git no peace!

Lennie You want I should go away and leave you alone?

George Where the hell could you go?

Lennie Well, I could...I could go off in the hills there. Some place I could find a cave.

George Yeah, how'd ya eat? You ain't got sense enough to find nothing to eat.

Lennie I'd find things. I don't need no nice food with ketchup. I'd lay out in the sun and nobody would hurt me. And if I found a mouse—why, I could keep it. Wouldn't nobody take it away from me.

George (*at last he looks up*) I been mean, ain't I?

Lennie (*presses his triumph*) If you don't want me, I can go right in them hills, and find a cave. I can go away any time.

George No. Look! I was just foolin' ya. 'Course I want you to stay with me. Trouble with mice is you always kill 'em. (*He pauses.*) Tell you what I'll do, Lennie. First chance I get I'll find you a pup. Maybe you wouldn't kill it. That would be better than mice. You could pet it harder.

Lennie (*still avoiding being drawn in*) If you don't want me, you only gotta say so. I'll go right up on them hills and live by myself. And I won't get no mice stole from me.

George I want you to stay with me. Jesus Christ, somebody'd shoot you for a coyote if you was by yourself. Stay with me. Your Aunt Clara wouldn't like your runnin' off by yourself, even if she is dead.

Lennie George?

George Huh?

Lennie (*craftily*) Tell me—like you done before.

George Tell you what?

Lennie About the rabbits.

George (*near to anger again*) You ain't gonna put nothing over on me!

Lennie (*pleading*) Come on, George...tell me! Please! Like you done before.

George You get a kick out of that, don't you? All right, I'll tell you. And then we'll lay out our beds and eat our dinner.

Lennie Go on, George. (*Unrolls his bed and lies on his side, supporting his head on one hand.* GEORGE *lays out his bed and sits cross-legged on it.* GEORGE *repeats the next speech rhythmically, as though he had said it many times before.*)

George Guys like us that work on ranches is the loneliest guys in the world. They ain't got no family. They don't belong no place. They come to a ranch and work up a stake and then they go in to town and blow their stake. And then the first thing you know they're poundin' their tail on some other ranch. They ain't got nothin' to look ahead to.

Lennie (*delightedly*) That's it, that's it! Now tell how it is with us.

George (*still almost chanting*) With us it ain't like that. We got a future. We got somebody to talk to that gives a damn about us. We don't have to sit in no barroom blowin' in our jack, just because we got no place else to go. If them other guys gets in jail, they can rot for all anybody gives a damn.

Lennie (*who cannot restrain himself any longer. Bursts into speech.*) But not us! And why? Because...because I got you to look after me...and you got me to look after you...and that's why! (*He laughs.*) Go on, George!

George You got it by heart. You can do it yourself.

Lennie No, no. I forget some of the stuff. Tell about how it's gonna be.

George Some other time.

Lennie No, tell how it's gonna be!

George Okay. Some day we're gonna get the jack together and we're gonna have a little house, and a couple of acres and a cow and some pigs and . . .

Lennie (*shouting*) And live off the fat of the land! And have rabbits. Go on, George! Tell about what we're gonna have in the garden. And about the rabbits in the cages. Tell about the rain in the winter...and about the stove and how thick the cream is on the milk, you can hardly cut it. Tell about that, George!

George Why don't you do it yourself—you know all of it!

Lennie It ain't the same if I tell it. Go on now. How I get to tend the rabbits.

George (*resignedly*) Well, we'll have a big vegetable patch and a rabbit hutch and chickens. And when it rains in the winter we'll just say to hell with goin' to work. We'll build up a fire in the stove, and set around it and listen to the rain comin' down on the roof—Nuts! (*Begins to eat with his knife.*) I ain't got time for no more. (*He falls to eating.* LENNIE *imitates him, spilling a few beans from his mouth with every bite.* GEORGE, *gesturing with his knife.*) What you gonna say tomorrow when the boss asks you questions?

Lennie (*stops chewing in the middle of a bite, swallows painfully. His face contorts with thought.*) I...I ain't gonna say a word.

George Good boy. That's fine. Say, maybe you're gittin' better. I bet I can let you tend the rabbits...specially if you remember as good as that!

Lennie (*choking with pride*) I can remember, by God!

George (*as though remembering something, points his knife at* LENNIE's *chest*) Lennie, I want you to look around here. Think you can remember this place? The ranch is 'bout a quarter mile up that way. Just follow the river and you can get here.

Lennie (*looking around carefully*) Sure, I can remember here. Didn't I remember 'bout not gonna say a word?

George 'Course you did. Well, look, Lennie, if you just happen to get in trouble, I want you to come right here and hide in the brush.

Lennie (*slowly*) Hide in the brush.

George Hide in the brush until I come for you. Think you can remember that?

Lennie Sure I can, George. Hide in the brush till you come for me!

George But you ain't gonna get in no trouble. Because if you do I won't let you tend the rabbits.

Lennie I won't get in no trouble. I ain't gonna say a word.

George You got it. Anyways, I hope so. (GEORGE *stretches out on his blankets. The light dies slowly out of the fire until only the faces of the two men can be seen.* GEORGE *is still eating from his can of beans.*) It's gonna be nice sleeping here. Lookin' up...and the leaves...Don't build no more fire. We'll let her die. Jesus, you feel free when you ain't got a job—if you ain't hungry. (*They sit silently for a few moments. A night owl is heard for off. From across the river there comes the sound of a coyote howl and on the heels of the howl all the dogs in the country start to bark.*)

Lennie (*from almost complete darkness*) George?

George What do you want?

Lennie Let's have different color rabbits, George.

George Sure. Red rabbits and blue rabbits and green rabbits. Millions of 'em!

Lennie Furry ones, George. Like I seen at the fair in Sacramento.

George Sure. Furry ones.

Lennie 'Cause I can jus' as well go away, George, and live in a cave.

George (*amiably*) Aw, shut up.

Lennie (*after a long pause*) George?

George What is it?

Lennie I'm shutting up, George. (*A coyote howls again.*)

SCENE II

Late Friday morning.
The interior of a bunkhouse.
Walls, white-washed board and bat. Floors unpainted.
There is a heavy square table with upended boxes around it used for chairs.
Over each bunk there is a box nailed to the wall which serves as two shelves on which are the private possessions of the working men.
On top of each bunk there is a large noisy alarm clock ticking madly.
The sun is streaking through the windows. Note: Articles in the boxes on wall are soap, talcum powder, razors, pulp magazines, medicine bottles, combs, and from nails on the sides of the boxes a few neckties.
There is a hanging light from the ceiling over the table, with a round dim reflector on it.
The curtain rises on an empty stage. Only the ticking of the many alarm clocks is heard. CANDY, GEORGE *and* LENNIE *are first seen passing the open window of the bunkhouse.*

Candy This is the bunkhouse here. Door's around this side. (*The latch on the door rises and* CANDY *enters, a stoop-shouldered old man. He is dressed in blue jeans and a denim coat. He carries a big push broom in his left hand. His right hand is gone at the wrist. He grasps things with his right arm between arm and side. He walks into the room followed by* GEORGE *and* LENNIE. *Conversationally.*) The boss was expecting you last night. He was sore as hell when you wasn't here to go out this morning. (*Points with his handless arm.*) You can have them two beds there.

George I'll take the top one. . .I don't want you falling down on me. (*Steps over to the bunk and throws his blankets down. He looks into the nearly emtpy box shelf over it, then picks up a small yellow can.*) Say, what the hell's this?

Candy I don't know.

George Says 'positively kills lice, roaches and other scourges'. What the hell kinda beds you givin' us, anyway? We don't want no pants rabbits.

Candy (*shifts his broom, holding it between his elbow and his side, takes the can in his left hand and studies the label carefully*) Tell you what . . . last guy that had this bed was a blacksmith. Helluva nice fellow. Clean a guy as you'd want to meet. Used to wash his hands even *after* he et.

George (*with gathering anger*) Then how come he got pillow-pigeons? (LENNIE *puts his blanket on his bunk and sits down, watching* GEORGE *with his mouth slightly open.*)

Candy Tell you what. This here blacksmith, name of Whitey, was the kinda guy that would put that stuff around even if there wasn't no bugs. Tell you what he used to do. He'd peel *his* boiled potatoes and take out every little spot before he et it, and if there was a red splotch on an egg, he'd scrape it off. Finally quit about the food. That's the kind of guy Whitey was. Clean. Used to dress up Sundays even when he wasn't goin' no place. Put on a necktie even, and then set in the bunkhouse.

George (*skeptically*) I ain't so sure. What da' ya say he quit for?

Candy (*puts the can in his pocket, rubs his bristly white whiskers with his knuckles*) Why . . . he just quit the way a guy will. Says it was the food. Didn't give no other reason. Just says 'give me my time' one night, the way any guy would. (GEORGE *lifts his bed tick and looks underneath, leans over and inspects the sacking carefully.* LENNIE *does the same with his bed.*)

George (*half satisfied*) Well, if there's any grey-backs in this bed, you're gonna hear from me! (*He unrolls his blankets and puts his razor and bar of soap and comb and bottle of pills, his liniment and leather wristband in the box.*)

Candy I guess the boss'll be out here in a minute to write your name in. He sure was burned when you wasn't here this morning. Come right in when we was eatin' breakfast and says, 'Where the hell's them new men?' He give the stable buck hell, too. Stable buck's a nigger.

George Nigger, huh!

Candy Yeah. (*Continues.*) Nice fellow too. Got a crooked back where a horse kicked him. Boss gives him hell when he's mad. But the stable buck don't give a damn about that.

George What kinda guy is the boss?

Candy Well, he's a pretty nice fella for a boss. Gets mad sometimes. But he's pretty nice. Tell you what. Know what he done Christmas? Brung a gallon of whiskey right in here and says, 'Drink hearty, boys, Christmas comes but once a year!'

George The hell he did! A whole gallon?

Candy Yes, sir. Jesus, we had fun! They let the nigger come in that night. Well, sir, a little skinner name Smitty took after the nigger. Done pretty good too. The guys wouldn't let him use his feet so the nigger got him. If he could a used his feet Smitty says he would have killed the nigger. The guys says on account the nigger got a crooked back Smitty can't use his feet. (*He smiles in reverie at the memory.*)

George Boss the owner?

Candy Naw! Superintendent. Big land company ... Yes, sir, that night ... he comes right in here with a whole gallon ... he set right over there and says, 'Drink hearty, boys,' ... he says.... (*The door opens. Enter the* BOSS. *He is a stocky man, dressed in blue jean trousers, flannel shirt, a black unbuttoned*

vest and a black coat. He wears a soiled brown Stetson hat, a pair of high-heeled boots and spurs. Ordinarily he puts his thumbs in his belt. CANDY, *shuffling towards the door, rubbing his whiskers with his knuckles as he goes.*) Them guys just come. (CANDY *exits and shuts the door behind him.*)

Boss I wrote Murray and Ready I wanted two men this morning. You got your work slips?

George (*digs in his pockets, produces two slips, and hands them to the* BOSS) Here they are.

Boss (*reading the slips*) Well, I see it wasn't Murray and Ready's fault. It says right here on the slip, you was to be here for work this morning.

George Bus driver give us a bum steer. We had to walk ten miles. That bus driver says we was here when we wasn't. We couldn't thumb no rides. (GEORGE *scowls meaningly at* LENNIE *and* LENNIE *nods to show that he understands.*)

Boss Well, I had to send out the grain teams short two buckers. It won't do any good to go out now until after dinner. You'd get lost. (*Pulls out his time book, opens it to where a pencil is stuck between the leaves. Licks his pencil carefully.*) What's your name?

George George Milton.

Boss George Milton. (*writing*) And what's yours?

George His name's Lennie Small.

Boss Lennie Small. (*writing*) Le's see, this is the twentieth. Noon the twentieth...(*Makes positive mark. Closes the book and puts it in his pocket.*) Where you boys been workin'?

George Up around Weed.

Boss (*to* LENNIE) You too?

George Yeah. Him too.

Boss (*to* LENNIE) Say, you're a big fellow, ain't you?

George Yeah, he can work like hell, too.

Boss He ain't much of a talker, though, is he?

George No, he ain't. But he's a hell of a good worker. Strong as a bull.

Lennie (*smiling*) I'm strong as a bull. (GEORGE *scowls at him and* LENNIE *drops his head in shame at having forgotten.*)

Boss (*sharply*) You are, huh? What can you do?

George He can do anything.

Boss (*addressing* LENNIE) What can you do? (LENNIE, *looking at* GEORGE, *gives a high nervous chuckle.*)

George (*quickly*) Anything you tell him. He's a good skinner. He can wrestle grain bags, drive a cultivator. He can do anything. Just give him a try.

Boss (*turning to* GEORGE) Then why don't you let *him* answer? (LENNIE *laughs.*) What's he laughing about?

George He laughs when he gets excited.

Boss Yeah?

George (*loudly*) But he's a goddamn good worker. I ain't saying he's bright, because he ain't. But he can put up a four hundred pound bale.

Boss (*hooking his thumbs in his belt*) Say, what you sellin'?

George Huh?

Boss I said what stake you got in this guy? You takin' his pay away from him?

George No. Of course I ain't!

Boss Hell, I never seen one guy take so much trouble for another guy. I just like to know what your percentage is.

George He's my...cousin. I told his ole lady I'd take care of him. He got kicked in the head by a horse when he was a kid. He's all right.... Just ain't bright. But he can do anything you tell him.

Boss (*turning half away*) Well, God knows he don't need no brains to buck barley bags. (*He turns back.*) But don't you try to put nothing over, Milton. I got my eye on you. Why'd you quit in Weed?

George (*promptly*) Job was done.

Boss What kind of job?

George Why...we was diggin' a cesspool.

Boss (*after a pause*) All right. But don't try to put nothing over 'cause you can't get away with nothing. I seen wise guys before. Go out with the grain teams after dinner. They're out pickin' up barley with the thrashin' machines. Go out with Slim's team.

George Slim?

Boss Yeah. Big, tall skinner. You'll see him at dinner. (*Up to this time the* BOSS *has been full of business. He has been calm and suspicious. In the following lines he relaxes, but gradually, as though he wanted to talk but felt always the burden of his position. He turns toward the door, but hesitates and allows a little warmth into his manner.*) Been on the road long?

George (*obviously on guard*) We was three days in 'Frisco lookin' at the boards.

Boss (*with heavy jocularity*) Didn't go to no night clubs, I 'spose?

George (*stiffly*) We was lookin' for a job.

Boss (*attempting to be friendly*) That's a great town if you got a little jack, Frisco.

George (*refusing to be drawn in*) We didn't have no jack for nothing like that.

Boss (*realizes there is no contact to establish; grows rigid with his position again*) Go out with the grain teams after dinner. When my hands work hard they get pie and when they loaf they bounce down the road on their can. You ask anybody about me. (*He turns and walks out of bunkhouse.*)

George (*turns to* LENNIE) So you wasn't gonna say a word! You was gonna leave your big flapper shut. I was gonna do the talkin'. . . . You goddamn near lost us the job!

Lennie (*stares hopelessly at his hands*) I forgot.

George You forgot. You always forget. Now, he's got his eye on us. Now, we gotta be careful and not make no slips. You keep your big flapper shut after this.

Lennie He talked like a kinda nice guy towards the last.

George (*angrily*) He's the boss, ain't he? Well, he's the boss first an' a nice guy afterwards. Don't you have nothin' to do with no boss, except do your work and draw your pay. You can't never tell whether you're talkin' to the nice guy or the boss. Just keep your goddamn mouth shut. Then you're all right.

Lennie George?

George What you want now?

Lennie I wasn't kicked in the head with no horse, was I, George?

George Be a damn good thing if you was. Save everybody a hell of a lot of trouble!

Lennie (*flattered*) You says I was your cousin.

George Well, that was a goddamn lie. And I'm glad it was. Why, if I was a relative of yours—(*He stops and listens, then steps to the front door, and looks out.*) Say, what the hell you doin', listenin'?

Candy (*comes slowly into the room. By a rope, he leads an ancient drag-footed, blind sheep dog. Guides it from running into a table leg, with the rope. Sits down on a box, and presses the hind quarters of the old dog down.*) Naw ... I wasn't listenin'.... I was just standin' in the shade a minute, scratchin' my dog. I jest now finished swamping out the washhouse.

George You was pokin' your big nose into our business! I don't like nosey guys.

Candy (*looks uneasily from* GEORGE *to* LENNIE *and then back*) I jest come there...I didn't hear nothing you guys was sayin'. I ain't interested in nothing you was sayin'. A guy on a ranch don't never listen. Nor he don't ast no questions.

George (*slightly mollified*) Damn right he don't! Not if the guy wants to stay workin' long. (*His manner changes.*) That's a helluva ole dog.

Candy Yeah. I had him ever since he was a pup. God, he was a good

sheep dog, when he was young. (*Rubs his cheek with his knuckles.*) How'd you like the boss?

George Pretty good! Seemed all right.

Candy He's a nice fella. You got ta take him right, of course. He's runnin' this ranch. He don't take no nonsense.

George What time do we eat? Eleven-thirty? (CURLEY *enters. He is dressed in working clothes. He wears brown high-heeled boots and has a glove on his left hand.*)

Curley Seen my ole man?

Candy He was here just a minute ago, Curley. Went over to the cookhouse, I think.

Curley I'll try to catch him. (*Looking over at the new men, measuring them. Unconsciously bends his elbow and closes his hand and goes into a slight crouch. He walks gingerly close to* LENNIE.) You the new guys my ole man was waitin' for?

George Yeah. We just come in.

Curley How's it come you wasn't here this morning?

George Got off the bus too soon.

Curley (*again addressing* LENNIE) My ole man got to get the grain out. Ever bucked barley?

George (*quickly*) Hell, yes. Done a lot of it.

Curley I mean him. (*To* LENNIE.) Ever bucked barley?

George Sure he has.

Curley (*irritatedly*) Let the big guy talk!

George 'Spose he don't want ta talk?

Curley (*pugnaciously*) By Christ, he's gotta talk when he's spoke to. What the hell you shovin' into this for?

George (*stands up and speaks coldly*) Him and me travel together.

Curley Oh, so it's that way?

George (*tense and motionless*) What way?

Curley (*letting the subject drop*) And you won't let the big guy talk? Is that it?

George He can talk if he wants to tell you anything. (*He nods slightly to* LENNIE.)

Lennie (*in a frightened voice*) We just come in.

Curley Well, next time you answer when you're spoke to, then.

George He didn't do nothing to you.

Curley (*measuring him*) You drawin' cards this hand?

George (*quietly*) I might.

Curley (*stares at him for a moment, his threat moving to the future*) I'll see you get a chance to ante, anyway. (*He walks out of the room.*)

George (*after he has made his exit*) Say, what the hell's he got on his shoulder? Lennie didn't say nothing to him.

Candy (*looks cautiously at the door*) That's the boss's son. Curley's pretty handy. He done quite a bit in the ring. The guys say he's pretty handy.

George Well, let 'im be handy. He don't have to take after Lennie. Lennie didn't do nothing to him.

Candy (*considering*) Well...tell you what, Curley's like a lot a little guys. He hates big guys. He's alla time pickin' scraps with big guys. Kinda like he's mad at 'em because *he* ain't a big guy. You seen little guys like that, ain't you—always scrappy?

George Sure, I seen plenty tough little guys. But this here Curley better not make no mistakes about Lennie. Lennie ain't handy, see, but this Curley punk's gonna get hurt if he messes around with Lennie.

Candy (*skeptically*) Well, Curley's pretty handy. You know, it never did seem right to me. 'Spose Curley jumps a big guy and licks him. Everybody says what a game guy Curley is. Well, 'spose he jumps 'im and gits licked, everybody says the big guy oughta pick somebody his own size. Seems like Curley ain't givin' nobody a chance.

George (*watching the door*) Well, he better watch out for Lennie. Lennie ain't no fighter. But Lennie's strong and quick and Lennie don't know no rules. (*Walks to the square table, and sits down on one of the boxes. Picks up scattered cards and pulls them together and shuffles them.*)

Candy Don't tell Curley I said none of this. He'd slough me! He jus' don't give a damn. Won't ever get canned because his ole man's the boss!

George (*cuts the cards. Turns over and looks at each one as he throws it down.*) This guy Curley sounds like a son-of-a-bitch to me! I don't like mean little guys!

Candy Seems to me like he's worse lately. He got married a couple of weeks ago. Wife lives over in the boss's house. Seems like Curley's worse'n ever since he got married. Like he's settin' on a ant-hill an' a big red ant come up an' nipped 'im on the turnip. Just feels so goddamn miserable he'll strike at anything that moves. I'm kinda sorry for 'im.

George Maybe he's showin' off for his wife.

Candy You seen that glove on his left hand?

George Sure I seen it!

Candy Well, that glove's full of vaseline.

George Vaseline? What the hell for?

Candy Curley says he's keepin' that hand soft for his wife.

George That's a dirty kind of a thing to tell around.

Candy I ain't quite so sure. I seen such funny things a guy will do to try to be nice. I ain't sure. But you jus' wait till you see Curley's wife!

George (*begins to lay out a solitaire hand, speaks casually*) Is she purty?

Candy Yeah. Purty, but—

George (*studying his cards*) But what?

Candy Well, she got the eye.

George (*still playing at his solitaire hand*) Yeah? Married two weeks an' got the eye? Maybe that's why Curley's pants is fulla ants.

Candy Yes, sir, I seen her give Slim the eye. Slim's a jerkline skinner. Hell of a nice fella. Well, I seen her give Slim the eye. Curley never seen it. And I seen her give a skinner named Carlson the eye.

George (*pretending a very mild interest*) Looks like we was gonna have fun!

Candy (*stands up*) Know what I think? (*Waits for an answer.* GEORGE *doesn't answer.*) Well, I think Curley's married himself a tart.

George (*casually*) He ain't the first. Black queen on a red king. Yes, sir...there's plenty done that!

Candy (*moves towards the door, leading his dog out with him*) I got to be settin' out the wash basins for the guys. The teams'll be in before long. You guys gonna buck barley?

George Yeah.

Candy You won't tell Curley nothing I said?

George Hell, no!

Candy (*just before he goes out the door, he turns back*) Well, you look her over, mister. You see if she ain't a tart! (*He exits.*)

George (*continuing to play out his solitaire. He turns to* LENNIE.) Look, Lennie, this here ain't no set-up. You gonna have trouble with that Curley guy. I seen that kind before. You know what he's doin'. He's kinda feelin' you out. He figures he's got you scared. And he's gonna take a sock at you, first chance he gets.

Lennie (*frightened*) I don't want no trouble. Don't let him sock me, George!

George I hate them kind of bastards. I seen plenty of 'em. Like the ole guy says: 'Curley don't take no chances. He always figures to win.' (*Thinks for a moment.*) If he tangles with you, Lennie, we're goin' get the can. Don't make no mistake about that. He's the boss's kid. Look, you try to keep away from him, will you? Don't never speak to him. If he comes in here you move clear to the other side of the room. Will you remember that, Lennie?

Lennie (*mourning*) I don't want no trouble. I never done nothing to him!

George Well, that won't do you no good, if Curley wants to set himself up for a fighter. Just don't have nothing to do with him. Will you remember?

Lennie Sure, George...I ain't gonna say a word. (*Sounds of the teams coming in from the fields, jingling of harness, croak of heavy laden axles, men talking to and cussing the horses. Crack of a whip and from a distance a voice calling.*)

Slim's voice Stable buck! Hey! Stable buck!

George Here come the guys. Just don't say nothing.

Lennie (*timidly*) You ain't mad, George?

George I ain't mad at you. I'm mad at this here Curley bastard! I wanted we should get a little stake together. Maybe a hundred dollars. You keep away from Curley.

Lennie Sure I will. I won't say a word.

George (*hesitating*) Don't let 'im pull you in—but—if the son-of-a-bitch socks you—let him have it!

Lennie Let him have what, George?

George Never mind.... Look, if you get in any kind of trouble, you remember what I told you to do.

Lennie If I get in any trouble, you ain't gonna let me tend the rabbits?

George That's not what I mean. You remember where we slept last night. Down by the river?

Lennie Oh, sure I remember. I go there and hide in the brush until you come for me.

George That's it. Hide till I come for you. Don't let nobody see you. Hide in the brush by the river. Now say that over.

Lennie Hide in the brush by the river. Down in the brush by the river.

George If you get in trouble.

Lennie If I get in trouble.
    (*A brake screeches outside and a call: 'Stable buck, oh, stable buck!'
    'Where the hell's that goddamn nigger?' Suddenly* CURLEY'S WIFE *is
    standing in the door. Full, heavily rouged lips. Wide-spaced, made-
    up eyes, her fingernails are bright red, her hair hangs in little rolled
    clusters like sausages. She wears a cotton house dress and red mules,
    on the insteps of which are little bouquets of red ostrich feathers.*
    GEORGE *and* LENNIE *look up at her.*)

Curley's wife I'm lookin' for Curley!

George (*looks away from her*) He was in here a minute ago but he went along.

Curley's wife (*puts her hands behind her back and leans against the door frame so that her body is thrown forward*) You're the new fellas that just come, ain't you?

George (*suddenly*) Yeah.

Curley's wife (*bridles a little and inspects her fingernails*) Sometimes Curley's in here.

George (*brusquely*) Well, he ain't now!

Curley's wife (*playfully*) Well, if he ain't, I guess I'd better look some place else. (LENNIE *watches her, fascinated.*)

George If I see Curley I'll pass the word you was lookin' for him.

Curley's wife Nobody can't blame a person for lookin'.

George That depends what she's lookin' for.

Curley's wife (*a little wearily, dropping her coquetry*) I'm jus' lookin' for somebody to talk to. Don't you never jus' want to talk to somebody?

Slim (*offstage*) Okay! Put that lead pair in the north stalls.

Curley's wife (*to* SLIM, *offstage*) Hi, Slim!

Slim (*voice offstage*) Hello.

Curley's wife I—I'm trying to find Curley.

Slim's voice (*offstage*) Well, you ain't tryin' very hard. I seen him goin' in your house.

Curley's wife I—I'm tryin' to find Curley.... I gotta be goin'! (*She exits hurriedly.*)

George (*looking around at* LENNIE) Jesus, what a tramp! So, that's what Curley picks for a wife. God Almighty, did you smell that stink she's got on? I can still smell her. Don't have to see *her* to know she's around.

Lennie She's purty!

George Yeah. And she's sure hidin' it. Curley got his work ahead of him.

Lennie (*still staring at the doorway where she was*) Gosh, she's purty!

George (*turning furiously at him*) Listen to me, you crazy bastard. Don't you even look at that bitch. I don't care what she says or what she does. I seen 'em poison before, but I ain't never seen no piece of jail bait worse than her. Don't you even smell near her!

Lennie I never smelled, George!

George No, you never. But when she was standin' there showin' her legs, you wasn't lookin' the other way neither!

Lennie I never meant no bad things, George. Honest I never.

George Well, you keep away from her. You let Curley take the rap. He let himself in for it. (*disgustedly*) Glove full of vaseline. I bet he's eatin' raw eggs and writin' to patent-medicine houses.

Lennie (*cries out*) I don't like this place. This ain't no good place. I don't like this place!

George Listen—I don't like it here no better than you do. But we gotta keep it till we get a stake. We're flat. We gotta get a stake. (*Goes back to the table, thoughtfully.*) If we can get just a few dollars in the poke we'll shove off and go up to the American River and pan gold. Guy can make a couple dollars a day there.

Lennie (*eagerly*) Let's go, George. Let's get out of here. It's mean here.

George (*shortly*) I tell you we gotta stay a little while. We gotta get a stake. (*The sounds of running water and rattle of basins are heard.*) Shut up now, the guys'll be comin' in! (*pensively*) Maybe we ought to wash up...But hell, we ain't done nothin' to get dirty.

Slim (*enters. He is a tall, dark man in blue jeans and a short denim jacket. He carries a crushed Stetson hat under his arm and combs his long dark damp hair straight back. He stands and moves with a kind of majesty. He finishes combing his hair. Smoothes out his crushed hat, creases it in the middle and puts it on. In a gentle voice.*) It's brighter'n a bitch outside. Can't hardly see nothing in here. You the new guys?

George Just come.

Slim Goin' to buck barley?

George That's what the boss says.

Slim Hope you get on my team.

George Boss said we'd go with a jerk-line skinner named Slim.

Slim That's me.

George You a jerk-line skinner?

Slim (*in self-disparagement*) I can snap 'em around a little.

George (*terribly impressed*) That kinda makes you Jesus Christ on this ranch, don't it?

Slim (*obviously pleased*) Oh, nuts!

George (*chuckles*) Like the man says, 'The boss tells you what to do. But if you want to know how to do it, you got to ask the mule skinner.' The man says any guy that can drive twelve Arizona jack rabbits with a jerk line can fall in a toilet and come up with a mince pie under each arm.

Slim (*laughing*) Well, I hope you get on my team. I got a pair a punks that don't know a barley bag from a blue ball. You guys ever bucked any barley?

George Hell, yes. I ain't nothin' to scream about, but that big guy there can put up more grain alone than most pairs can.

Slim (*looks approvingly at* GEORGE) You guys travel around together?

George Sure. We kinda look after each other. (*Points at* LENNIE *with his thumb.*) He ain't bright. Hell of a good worker, though. Hell of a nice fella too. I've knowed him for a long time.

Slim Ain't many guys travel around together. I don't know why. Maybe everybody in the whole damn world is scared of each other.

George It's a lot nicer to go 'round with a guy you know. You get used to it an' then it ain't no fun alone any more. (*Enter* CARLSON. *A big-stomached, powerful man. His head still drips water from scrubbing and dousing.*)

Carlson Hello, Slim! (*He looks at* GEORGE *and* LENNIE.)

Slim These guys just come.

Carlson Glad to meet ya! My name's Carlson.

George I'm George Milton. This here's Lennie Small.

Carlson Glad to meet you. He ain't very small. (*Chuckles at his own joke.*) He ain't small at all. Meant to ask you, Slim, how's your bitch? I seen she wasn't under your wagon this morning.

Slim She slang her pups last night. Nine of 'em. I drowned four of 'em right off. She couldn't feed that many.

Carlson Got five left, huh?

Slim Yeah. Five. I kep' the biggest.

Carlson What kinda dogs you think they gonna be?

Slim I don't know. Some kind of shepherd, I guess. That's the most kind I seen around here when she's in heat.

Carlson (*laughs*) I had an airedale an' a guy down the road got one of them little white floozy dogs, well, she was in heat and the guy locks her up. But my airedale, named Tom he was, he et a woodshed clear down to the roots to get to her. Guy come over one day, he's sore as hell, he says, 'I wouldn't mind if my bitch had pups, but Christ Almighty, this morning she slang a litter of Shetland ponies....' (*Takes off his hat and scratches his head.*) Got five pups, huh! Gonna keep all of 'em?

Slim I don't know, gotta keep 'em awhile, so they can drink Lulu's milk.

Carlson (*thoughtfully*) Well, looka here, Slim, I been thinkin'. That dog of Candy's is so goddamn old he can't hardly walk. Stinks like hell. Every time Candy brings him in the bunkhouse, I can smell him two or three days. Why don't you get Candy to shoot his ol' dog, and give him one of them pups to raise up? I can smell that dog a mile off. Got no teeth. Can't eat. Candy feeds him milk. He can't chew nothing else. And leadin' him around on a string so he don't bump into things...(*The triangle outside begins to ring wildly. Continues for a few moments, then stops suddenly.*) There she goes! (*Outside there is a burst of voices as a group of men go by.*)

Slim (*to* LENNIE *and* GEORGE) You guys better come on while they's still somethin' to eat. Won't be nothing left in a couple of minutes. (*Exit* SLIM *and* CARLSON, LENNIE *watches* GEORGE *excitedly.*)

Lennie George!

George (*rumpling his cards into a pile*) Yeah, I heard 'im, Lennie ... I'll ask 'im!

Lennie (*excitedly*) A brown and white one.

George Come on, let's get dinner. I don't know whether he's got a brown and white one.

Lennie You ask him right away, George, so he won't kill no more of 'em!

George Sure! Come on now—le's go. (*They start for the door.*)

Curley (*bounces in, angrily*) You seen a girl around here?

George (*coldly*) 'Bout half an hour ago, mebbe.

Curley Well, what the hell was she doin'?

George (*insultingly*) She *said* she was lookin' for you.

Curley (*measures both men with his eyes for a moment*) Which way did she go?

George I don't know. I didn't watch her go. (CURLEY *scowls at him a moment and then turns and hurries out the door.*) You know, Lennie, I'm scared I'm gonna tangle with that bastard myself. I hate his guts! Jesus Christ, come on! They won't be a damn thing left to eat.

Lennie Will you ask him about a brown and white one? (*They exeunt.*)

ACT TWO

SCENE I

About seven-thirty Friday evening.
Same bunkhouse interior as in last scene.
The evening light is seen coming in through the window, but it is quite dark in the interior of the bunkhouse.
From outside comes the sound of a horseshoe game. Thuds on the dirt and occasional clangs as a shoe hits the peg. Now and then voices are raised in approval or derision: 'That's a good one.'...'Goddamn right it's a good one.' ... 'Here goes for a ringer. I need a ringer.' ... 'Goddamn near got it, too.'
SLIM and GEORGE come into the darkening bunkhouse together. SLIM reaches up and turns on the tin-shaded electric light. Sits down on a box at the table. GEORGE takes his place opposite.

Slim It wasn't nothing. I would of had to drown most of them pups anyway. No need to thank me about that.

George Wasn't much to you, mebbe, but it was a hell of a lot to him. Jesus Christ, I don't know how we're gonna get him to sleep in here. He'll want to stay right out in the barn. We gonna have trouble keepin' him from gettin' right in the box with them pups.

Slim Say, you sure was right about him. Maybe he ain't bright—but I never seen such a worker. He damn near killed his partner buckin' barley. He'd take his end of that sack (*a gesture*) pretty near kill his partner. God Almighty, I never seen such a strong guy.

George (*proudly*) You just tell Lennie what to do and he'll do it if it don't take no figuring. (*Outside the sound of the horseshoe game goes on: 'Son of a bitch if I can win a goddamn game.' ... 'Me neither. You'd think them shoes was anvils.'*)

Slim Funny how you and him string along together.

George What's so funny about it?

Slim Oh, I don't know. Hardly none of the guys ever travels around together. I hardly never seen two guys travel together. You know how the hands are. They come in and get their bunk and work a month and then they quit and go on alone. Never seem to give a damn about nobody. Jest seems kinda funny. A cuckoo like him and a smart guy like you travelling together.

George I ain't so bright neither or I wouldn't be buckin' barley for my fifty and found. If I was bright, if I was even a little bit smart, I'd have my own place and I'd be bringin' in my own crops 'stead of doin' all the work and not gettin' what comes up out of the ground. (*He falls silent for a moment.*)

Slim A guy'd like to do that. Sometimes I'd like to cuss a string of mules that was my own mules.

George It ain't so funny, him and me goin' round together. Him and me was both born in Auburn. I knowed his aunt. She took him when he was a baby and raised him up. When his aunt died Lennie jus' come along with me, out workin'. Got kinda used to each other after a little while.

Slim Uh huh.

George First I used to have a hell of a lot of fun with him. Used to play jokes on him because he was too dumb to take care of himself. But, hell, he was too dumb even to know when he had a joke played on him. (*sarcastically*) Hell, yes, I had fun! Made me seem goddamn smart alongside of him.

Slim I seen it that way.

George Why, he'd do any damn thing I tole him. If I tole him to walk over a cliff, over he'd go. You know that wasn't so damn much fun after a while. He never got mad about it, neither. I've beat hell out of him and he could bust every bone in my body jest with his hands. But he never lifted a finger against me.

Slim (*braiding a bull whip*) Even if you socked him, wouldn't he?

George No, by God! I tell you what made me stop playing jokes. One day a bunch of guys was standin' aroun' up on the Sacramento river. I was feelin' pretty smart. I turns to Lennie and I says, 'Jump in'.

Slim What happened?

George He jumps. Couldn't swim a stroke. He damn near drowned. And he was so nice to me for pullin' him out. Clean forgot I tole him to jump in. Well, I ain't done nothin' like that no more. Makes me kinda sick tellin' about it.

Slim He's a nice fella. A guy don't need no sense to be a nice fella. Seems to be sometimes it's jest the other way round. Take a real smart guy, he ain't hardly ever a nice fella.

George (*stacking the scattered cards and getting his solitaire game ready again*) I ain't got no people. I seen guys that go round on the ranches alone. That ain't no good. They don't have no fun. After a while they get mean.

Slim (*quietly*) Yeah, I seen 'em get mean. I seen 'em get so they don't want to talk to nobody. Some ways they got to. You take a bunch of guys all livin' in one room an' by God they got to mind their own business. 'Bout the only private thing a guy's got is where he come from and where he's goin'.

George 'Course Lennie's a goddamn nuisance most of the time. But you get used to goin' round with a guy and you can't get rid of him. I mean you get used to him an' you can't get rid of bein' used to him. I'm sure drippin' at the mouth. I ain't told nobody all this before.

Slim Do you want to git rid of him?

George Well, he gets in trouble all the time. Because he's so goddamn dumb. Like what happened in Weed. (*He stops, alarmed at what he has said.*) You wouldn't tell nobody?

Slim (*calmly*) What did he do in Weed?

George You wouldn't tell?—No, 'course you wouldn't.

Slim What did he do?

George Well, he seen this girl in a red dress. Dumb bastard like he is he wants to touch everything he likes. Jest wants to feel of it. So he reaches out to feel this red dress. Girl lets out a squawk and that gets Lennie all mixed up. He holds on 'cause that's the only thing he can think to do.

Slim The hell!

George Well, this girl squawks her head off. I'm right close and I hear all the yellin', so I comes a-running. By that time Lennie's scared to death. You know, I had to sock him over the head with a fence picket to make him let go.

Slim So what happens then?

George (*carefully building his solitaire hand*) Well, she runs in and tells the law she's been raped. The guys in Weed start out to lynch Lennie. So there we sit in an irrigation ditch, under water all

the rest of that day. Got only our heads stickin' out of water, up under the grass that grows out of the side of the ditch. That night we run outa there.

Slim Didn't hurt the girl none, huh?

George Hell, no, he jes' scared her.

Slim He's a funny guy.

George Funny! Why, one time, you know what that big baby done! He was walking along a road—(*Enter* LENNIE *through the door. He wears his coat over his shoulder like a cape and walks hunched over.*) Hi, Lennie. How do you like your pup?

Lennie (*breathlessly*) He's brown and white jus' like I wanted. (*Goes directly to his bunk and lies down. Face to the wall and knees drawn up.*)

George (*puts down his cards deliberately*) Lennie!

Lennie (*over his shoulder*) Huh? What you want, George?

George (*sternly*) I tole ya, ya couldn't bring that pup in here.

Lennie What pup, George? I ain't got no pup. (GEORGE *goes quickly over to him, grabs him by the shoulder and rolls him over. He picks up a tiny puppy from where* LENNIE *has been concealing it against his stomach.*)

Lennie (*quickly*) Give him to me, George.

George You get right up and take this pup to the nest. He's got to sleep with his mother. Ya want ta kill him? Jes' born last night and ya take him out of the nest. Ya take him back or I'll tell Slim not to let you have him.

Lennie (*pleadingly*) Give him to me, George. I'll take him back. I didn't mean no bad thing, George. Honest I didn't. I jus' want to pet him a little.

George (*giving the pup to him*) All right, you get him back there quick. And don't you take him out no more. (LENNIE *scuttles out of the room.*)

Slim Jesus, he's just like a kid, ain't he?

George Sure he's like a kid. There ain't no more harm in him than a kid neither, except he's so strong. I bet he won't come in here to sleep tonight. He'll sleep right alongside that box in the barn. Well, let him. He ain't doin' no harm out there. (*The light has faded out outside and it appears quite dark outside. Enter*

CANDY *leading his old dog by a string.*)

Candy Hello, Slim. Hello, George. Didn't neither of you play horseshoes?

Slim I don't like to play every night.

Candy (*goes to his bunk and sits down, presses the old blind dog to the floor beside him*) Either you guys got a slug of whiskey? I got a gut ache.

Slim I ain't. I'd drink it myself if I had. And I ain't got no gut ache either.

Candy Goddamn cabbage give it to me. I knowed it was goin' to before I ever et it. (*Enter* CARLSON *and* WHIT.)

Carlson Jesus, how that nigger can pitch shoes!

Slim He's plenty good.

Whit Damn right he is.

Carlson Yeah. He don't give nobody else a chance to win. (*Stops and sniffs the air. Looks around until he sees* CANDY's *dog.*) God Almighty, that dog stinks. Get him outa here, Candy. I don't know nothing that stinks as bad as ole dogs. You got to get him outa here.

Candy (*lying down on his bunk, reaches over and pats the ancient dog, speaks softly*) I been round him so much I never notice how he stinks.

Carlson Well, I can't stand him in here. That stink hangs round even after he's gone. (*Walks over and stands looking down at the dog.*) Got no teeth. All stiff with rheumatism. He ain't no good to you, Candy. Why don't you shoot him?

Candy (*uncomfortably*) Well, hell, I had him so long! Had him since he was a pup. I herded sheep with him. (*proudly*) You wouldn't think it to look at him now. He was the best damn sheep dog I ever seen.

George I knowed a guy in Weed that had an airedale that could herd sheep. Learned it from the other dogs.

Carlson (*sticking to his point*) Lookit, Candy. This ole dog jus' suffers itself all the time. If you was to take him out and shoot him—right in the back of the head ... (*Leans over and points.*)...right there, why he never'd know what hit him.

Candy (*unhappily*) No, I couldn't do that. I had him too long.

Carlson (*insisting*) He don't have no fun no more. He stinks like hell. Tell you what I'll do. I'll shoot him for you. Then it won't be you that done it.

Candy (*sits up on the bunk, rubbing his whiskers nervously, speaks plaintively*) I had him from a pup.

Whit Let 'im alone, Carl. It ain't a guy's dog that matters. It's the way the guy feels about the dog. Hell, I had a mutt once I wouldn't a traded for a field trial pointer.

Carlson (*being persuasive*) Well, Candy ain't being nice to him, keeping him alive. Lookit, Slim's bitch got a litter right now. I bet you Slim would give ya one of them pups to raise up, wouldn't ya, Slim?

Slim (*studying the dog*) Yeah. You can have a pup if you want to.

Candy (*helplessly*) Mebbe it would hurt. (*after a moment's pause, positively*) And I don't mind taking care of him.

Carlson Aw, he'd be better off dead. The way I'd shoot him he wouldn't feel nothin'. I'd put the gun right there. (*Points with his toe.*) Right back of the head.

Whit Aw, let 'im alone, Carl.

Carlson Why, hell, he wouldn't even quiver.

Whit Let 'im alone. (*He produces a magazine.*) Say, did you see this? Did you see this in the book here?

Carlson See what?

Whit Right there. Read that.

Carlson I don't want to read nothing. . . . It'd be all over in a minute, Candy. Come on.

Whit Did you see it, Slim? Go on, read it. Read it out loud.

Slim What is it?

Whit Read it.

Slim (*reads slowly*) 'Dear Editor: I read your mag for six years and I think it is the best on the market. I like stories by Peter Rand. I think he is a whing-ding. Give us more like the Dark Rider. I don't write many letters. Just thought I would tell you I think your mag is the best dime's worth I ever spen'.' (*Looks up questioningly.*) What you want me to read that for?

Whit Go on, read the name at the bottom.

Slim (*reading*) 'Yours for Success, William Tenner.' (*Looks up at* WHIT.) What ya want me to read that for?

Carlson Come on, Candy—what you say?

Whit (*taking the magazine and closing it impressively. Talks to cover* CARLSON.) You don't remember Bill Tenner? Worked here about three months ago?

Slim (*thinking*) Little guy? Drove a cultivator?

Whit That's him. That's the guy.

Carlson (*has refused to be drawn into this conversation*) Look, Candy. If you want me to, I'll put the old devil outa his misery right now and get it over with. There ain't nothing left for him. Can't eat, can't see, can't hardly walk. Tomorrow you can pick one of Slim's pups.

Slim Sure...I got a lot of 'em.

Candy (*hopefully*) You ain't got no gun.

Carlson The hell, I ain't. Got a Luger. It won't hurt him none at all.

Candy Mebbe tomorrow. Let's wait till tomorrow.

Carlson I don't see no reason for it. (*Goes to his bunk, pulls a bag from underneath, takes a Luger pistol out.*) Let's get it over with. We can't sleep with him stinking around in here. (*He snaps a shell into the chamber, sets the safety and puts the pistol into his hip pocket.*)

Slim (*as* CANDY *looks toward him for help*) Better let him go, Candy.

Candy (*looks at each person for some hope.* WHIT *makes a gesture of protest and then resigns himself. The others look away, to avoid responsibility. At last, very softly and hopelessly.*) All right. Take him.

(*He doesn't look down at the dog at all. Lies back on his bunk and crosses his arms behind his head and stares at the ceiling.* CARLSON *picks up the string, helps the dog to its feet.*)

Carlson Come, boy. Come on, boy. (*to* CANDY, *apologetically*) He won't even feel it. (CANDY *does not move nor answer him.*) Come on, boy. That's the stuff. Come on. (*He leads the dog toward the door.*)

Slim Carlson?

Carlson Yeah.

Slim (*curtly*) Take a shovel.

Carlson Oh, sure, I get you.

> (*Exit* CARLSON *with the dog.* GEORGE *follows to the door, shuts it carefully and sets the latch.* CANDY *lies rigidly on his bunk. The next scene is one of silence and quick staccato speeches.*)

Slim (*loudly*) One of my lead mules got a bad hoof. Got to get some tar on it. (*There is a silence.*)

George (*loudly*) Anybody like to play a little euchre?

Whit I'll lay out a few with you. (*They take places opposite each other at the table but* GEORGE *does not shuffle the cards. He ripples the edge of the deck. Everybody looks over at him. He stops. Silence again.*)

Slim (*compassionately*) Candy, you can have any of them pups you want. (*There is no answer from* CANDY. *There is a little gnawing noise on the stage.*)

George Sounds like there was a rat under there. We ought to set a trap there. (*Deep silence again.*)

Whit (*exasperated*) What the hell is takin' him so long? Lay out some cards, why don't you? We ain't gonna get no euchre played this way.

> (GEORGE *studies the backs of the cards. And after a long silence there is a shot in the distance. All the men start a bit, look quickly at* CANDY. *For a moment he continues to stare at the ceiling and then rolls slowly over and faces the wall.* GEORGE *shuffles the cards noisily and deals them.*)

George Well, let's get to it.

Whit (*still to cover the moment*) Yeah...I guess you guys really come here to work, huh?

George How do you mean?

Whit (*chuckles*) Well, you come on a Friday. You got two days to work till Sunday.

George I don't see how you figure.

Whit You do if you been round these big ranches much. A guy that wants to look over a ranch comes in Saturday afternoon. He gets Saturday night supper, three meals on Sunday and he can quit Monday morning after breakfast without turning a hand. But you come to work on Friday noon. You got ta put in a day and a half no matter how ya figure it.

George (*quietly*) We're goin' stick around awhile. Me and Lennie's gonna roll up a stake. (*Door opens and the Negro stable buck puts in his head. A lean-faced Negro with pained eyes.*)

Crooks Mr Slim.

Slim (*who has been watching* CANDY *the whole time*) Huh? Oh, hello, Crooks, what's the matter?

Crooks You tole me to warm up tar for that mule's foot. I got it warm now.

Slim Oh, sure, Crooks. I'll come right out and put it on.

Crooks I can do it for you if you want, Mr Slim.

Slim (*standing up*) Naw, I'll take care of my own team.

Crooks Mr Slim.

Slim Yeah.

Crooks That big new guy is messing round your pups in the barn.

Slim Well, he ain't doin' no harm. I give him one of them pups.

Crooks Just thought I'd tell ya. He's takin' 'em out of the nest and handling 'em. That won't do 'em no good.

Slim Oh, he won't hurt 'em.

George (*looks up from his cards*) If that crazy bastard is foolin' round too much jus' kick him out. (SLIM *follows the stable buck out.*)

Whit (*examining his cards*) Seen the new kid yet?

George What kid?

Whit Why, Curley's new wife.

George (*cautiously*) Yeah, I seen her.

Whit Well, ain't she a lulu?

George I ain't seen that much of her.

Whit Well, you stick around and keep your eyes open. You'll see plenty of her. I never seen nobody like her. She's just workin' on everybody all the time. Seems like she's even workin' on the stable buck. I don't know what the hell she wants.

George (*casually*) Been any trouble since she got here? (*Obviously neither man is interested in the card game.* WHIT *lays down his hand and* GEORGE *gathers the cards in and lays out a solitaire hand.*)

Whit I see what you mean. No, they ain't been no trouble yet. She's only been here a couple of weeks. Curley's got yellow jackets in his drawers, but that's all so far. Every time the guys is around she shows up. She's lookin' for Curley. Or she thought she left somethin' layin' around and she's lookin' for that. Seems like she can't keep away from guys. And Curley's runnin' round like a cat lookin' for a dirt road. But they ain't been no trouble.

George Ranch with a bunch of guys on it ain't no place for a girl. Specially like her.

Whit If she's give you any ideas you ought to come in town with us guys tomorrow night.

George Why, what's doin'?

Whit Just the usual thing. We go in to old Susy's place. Hell of a nice place. Old Susy is a laugh. Always cracking jokes. Like she says when we come up on the front porch last Saturday night: Susy opens the door and she yells over her shoulder: 'Get your coats on, girls, here comes the sheriff.' She never talks dirty neither. Got five girls there.

George What does it set you back?

Whit Two and a half. You can get a shot of whiskey for fifteen cents. Susy got nice chairs to set in too. If a guy don't want to flop, why, he can just set in them chairs and have a couple or three shots and just pass the time of day. Susy don't give a damn. She ain't rushin' guys through, or kicking them out if they don't want to flop.

George Might go in and look the joint over.

Whit Sure. Come along. It's a hell of a lot of fun—her crackin' jokes all the time. Like she says one time, she says: 'I've knew people that if they got a rag rug on the floor and a kewpie doll lamp on the phonograph they think they're runnin' a parlor house.' That's Gladys's house she's talkin' about. And Susy says: 'I know what you boys want,' she says: 'My girls is clean,' she says. 'And there ain't no water in my whiskey,' she says. 'If any you guys want to look at a kewpie doll lamp and take your chance of gettin' burned, why, you know where to go.' She says: 'They's guys round here walkin' bowlegged because they liked to look at a kewpie doll lamp.'

George Gladys runs the other house, huh?

Whit Yeah. (*Enter* CARLSON. CANDY *looks at him.*)

Carlson God, it's a dark night. (*Goes to his bunk; starts cleaning his pistol.*)

Whit We don't never go to Gladys's. Gladys gits three bucks, and two bits a shot and she don't crack no jokes. But Susy's place is clean and she got nice chairs. A guy can set in there like he lived there. Don't let no Manila Goo-Goos in, neither.

George Aw, I don't know. Me and Lennie's rollin' up a stake. I might go in and set and have a shot, but I ain't puttin' out no two and a half.

Whit Well, a guy got to have some fun sometimes. (*Enter* LENNIE. LENNIE *creeps to his bunk and sits down.*)

George Didn't bring him back in, did you, Lennie?

Lennie No, George, honest I didn't. See?

Whit Say, how about this euchre game?

George Okay. I didn't think you wanted to play. (*Enter* CURLEY *excitedly.*)

Curley Any you guys seen my wife?

Whit She ain't been here.

Curley (*looks threateningly about the room*) Where the hell's Slim?

George Went out in the barn. He was goin' put some tar on a split hoof.

Curley How long ago did he go?

George Oh, five, ten minutes. (CURLEY *jumps out the door.*)

Whit (*standing up*) I guess maybe I'd like to see this. Curley must be spoilin' or he wouldn't start for Slim. Curley's handy, goddamn handy. But just the same he better leave Slim alone.

George Thinks Slim's with his wife, don't he?

Whit Looks like it. 'Course Slim ain't. Least I don't think Slim is. But I like to see the fuss if it comes off. Come on, le's go.

George I don't want to git mixed up in nothing. Me and Lennie got to make a stake.

Carlson (*finishes cleaning gun, puts it in his bag and stands up*) I'll look her over. Ain't seen a good fight in a hell of a while. (WHITE *and* CARLSON *exeunt.*)

George You see Slim out in the barn?

Lennie Sure. He tole me I better not pet that pup no more, like I said.

George Did you see that girl out there?

Lennie You mean Curley's girl?

George Yeah. Did she come in the barn?

Lennie (*cautiously*) No—anyways I never seen her.

George You never seen Slim talkin' to her?

Lennie Uh-uh. She ain't been in the barn.

George Okay. I guess them guys ain't gonna see no fight. If they's any fightin', Lennie, ya get out of the way and stay out.

Lennie I don't want no fight. (GEORGE *lays out his solitaire hand.* LENNIE *picks up a face card and studies it. Turns it over and studies it again.*) Both ends the same. George, why is it both ends the same?

George I don't know. That jus' the way they make 'em. What was Slim doin' in the barn when you seen him?

Lennie Slim?

George Sure, you seen him in the barn. He tole you not to pet the pups so much.

Lennie Oh. Yeah. He had a can of tar and a paint brush. I don't know what for.

George You sure that girl didn't come in like she come in here today?

Lennie No, she never come.

George (*sighs*) You give me a good whorehouse every time. A guy can go in and get drunk and get it over all at once and no messes. And he knows how much it's goin' set him back. These tarts is jus' buckshot to a guy. (LENNIE *listens with admiration, moving his lips, and* GEORGE *continues.*) You remember Andy Cushman, Lennie? Went to grammar school same time as us?

Lennie The one that his ole lady used to make hot cakes for the kids?

George Yeah. That's the one. You can remember if they's somepin to eat in it. (*Scores up some cards in his solitaire playing.*) Well, Andy's in San Quentin right now on account of a tart.

Lennie George?

George Huh?

Lennie How long is it goin' be till we git that little place to live on the fat of the land?

George I don't know. We gotta get a big stake together. I know a little place we can get cheap, but they ain't givin' it away. (CANDY *turns over and watches* GEORGE.)

Lennie Tell about that place, George.

George I jus' tole you. Jus' last night.

Lennie Go on, tell again.

George Well, it's ten acres. Got a windmill. Got a little shack on it and a chicken run. Got a kitchen orchard. Cherries, apples, peaches, 'cots and nuts. Got a few berries. There's a place for alfalfa and plenty water to flood it. There's a pig pen....

Lennie (*breaking in*) And rabbits, George?

George I could easy build a few hutches. And you could feed alfalfa to them rabbits.

Lennie Damn right I could. (*excitedly*) You goddamn right I could.

George (*his voice growing warmer*) And we could have a few pigs. I'd build a smoke-house. And when we kill a pig we could smoke the hams. When the salmon run up the river we can catch a hundred of 'em. Every Sunday we'd kill a chicken or rabbit. Mebbe we'll have a cow or a goat. And the cream is so goddamn thick you got to cut it off the pan with a knife.

Lennie (*watching him with wide eyes, softly*) We can live off the fat of the land.

George Sure. All kinds of vegetables in the garden, and if we want a little whiskey we can sell some eggs or somethin'. And we wouldn't sleep in no bunkhouse. Nobody could can us in the middle of a job.

Lennie (*begging*) Tell about the house, George.

George Sure. We'd have a little house. And a room to ourselves. And it ain't enough land so we'd have to work too hard. Mebbe six, seven hours a day only. We wouldn't have to buck no barley eleven hours a day. And when we put in a crop, why we'd be there to take that crop up. We'd know what come of our planting.

Lennie (*eagerly*) And rabbits. And I'd take care of them. Tell how I'd do that, George.

George Sure. You'd go out in the alfalfa patch and you'd have a sack. You'd fill up the sack and bring it in and put it in the rabbit cages.

Lennie They'd nibble and they'd nibble, the way they do. I seen 'em.

George Every six weeks or so them does would throw a litter. So we'd have plenty rabbits to eat or sell. (*Pauses for inspiration.*) And we'd keep a few pigeons to go flying round and round the windmill, like they done when I was a kid. (*Seems entranced.*) And it'd be our own. And nobody could can us. If we don't like a guy we can say: 'Get to hell out,' and by God he's got to do it. And if a friend come along, why, we'd have an extra bunk. Know what we'd say? We'd say, 'Why don't you spen' the night?' And by God he would. We'd have a setter dog and a couple of striped cats. (*Looks sharply at* LENNIE.) But you gotta watch out them cats don't get the little rabbits.

Lennie (*breathing hard*) You jus' let 'em try. I'll break their goddamn necks. I'll smash them cats flat with a stick. I'd smash 'em flat with a stick. That's what I'd do. (*They sit silently for a moment.*)

Candy (*at the sound of his voice, both* LENNIE *and* GEORGE *jump as though caught in some secret*) You know where's a place like that?

George (*solemnly*) S'pose I do, what's that to you?

Candy You don't need to tell me where it's at. Might be any place.

George (*relieved*) Sure. That's right, you couldn't find it in a hundred years.

Candy (*excitedly*) How much they want for a place like that?

George (*grudgingly*) Well, I could get it for six hundred bucks. The ole people that owns it is flat bust. And the ole lady needs medicine. Say, what's it to you? You got nothing to do with us!

Candy (*softly*) I ain't much good with only one hand. I lost my hand right here on the ranch. That's why they didn't can me. They give me a job swampin'. And they give me two hundred and fifty dollars 'cause I lost my hand. An' I got fifty more saved up right in the bank right now. That's three hundred. And I got forty more comin' the end of the month. Tell you what...(*He leans forward eagerly.*) S'pose I went in with you guys? That's three hundred and forty bucks I'd put in. I ain't much good, but I could cook and tend the chickens and hoe the garden some. How'd that be?

George (*his eyes half closed, uncertainly*) I got to think about that. We was always goin' to do it by ourselves. Me an' Lennie. I never thought of nobody else.

Candy I'd make a will. Leave my share to you guys in case I kicked off. I ain't got no relations nor nothing. You fellas got any money? Maybe we could go there right now.

George (*disgustedly*) We got ten bucks between us. (*He thinks.*) Say, look. If me and Lennie work a month and don't spend nothing at all, we'll have a hundred bucks. That would be four forty. I bet we could swing her for that. Then you and Lennie could go get her started and I'd get a job and make up the rest. You could sell eggs and stuff like that. (*They look at each other in amazement. Reverently.*) Jesus Christ, I bet we could swing her. (*His voice is full of wonder.*) I bet we could swing 'er.

Candy (*scratches the stump of his wrist nervously*) I got hurt four years ago. They'll can me pretty soon. Jest as soon as I can't swamp out no bunkhouses they'll put me on the county. Maybe if I give you guys my money, you'll let me hoe in the garden, even when I ain't no good at it. And I'll wash dishes and little chicken stuff like that. But hell, I'll be on our own place. I'll be let to work on our own place. (*miserably*) You seen what they done to my dog. They says he wasn't no good to himself nor nobody else. But when I'm that way nobody'll shoot me. I wish somebody would. They won't do nothing like that. I won't have no place to go and I can't get no more jobs.

George (*stands up*) We'll do 'er! God damn, we'll fix up that little ole place and we'll go live there. (*wonderingly*) S'pose they was a carnival, or a circus come to town or a ball game or any damn thing. (CANDY *nods in appreciation.*) We'd just go to her. We wouldn't ask nobody if we could. Just say we'll go to her, by God, and we would. Just milk the cow and sling some grain to the chickens and go to her.

Lennie And put some grass to the rabbits. I wouldn't forget to feed them. When we gonna to do it, George?

George (*decisively*) In one month. Right squack in one month. Know what I'm gonna do? I'm goin' write to them ole people that owns the place that we'll take 'er. And Candy'll send a hundred dollars to bind her.

Candy (*happily*) I sure will. They got a good stove there?

George Sure, got a nice stove. Burns coal or wood.

Lennie I'm gonna take my pup. I bet by Christ he likes it there. (*The window, centre backstage, swings outward.* CURLEY's WIFE *looks in. They do not see her.*)

George (*quickly*) Now don't tell nobody about her. Jus' us three and nobody else. They'll liable to can us so we can't make no stake. We'll just go on like we was a bunch of punks. Like we was gonna buck barley the rest of our lives. And then all of a sudden, one day, bang! We get our pay and scram out of here.

Candy I can give you three hundred right now.

Lennie And not tell nobody. We won't tell nobody, George.

George You're goddamn right we won't. (*There is a silence and then* GEORGE *speaks irritably*.) You know, seems to me I can almost smell that carnation stuff that goddamn tart dumps on herself.

Curley's wife (*in the first part of the speech by* GEORGE *she starts to step out of sight but at the last words her face darkens with anger. At her first words everybody in the room looks around at her and remains rigid during the tirade*) Who you callin' a tart! I come from a nice home. I was brung up by nice people. Nobody never got to me before I was married. I was straight. I tell you I was good. (*a little plaintively*) I was. (*angrily again*) You know Curley. You know he wouldn't stay with me if he wasn't sure. I tell you Curley is sure. You got no right to call me a tart.

George (*sullenly*) If you ain't a tart, what you always hangin' round guys for? You got a house an' you got a man. We don't want no trouble from you.

Curley's wife (*pleadingly*) Sure I got a man. He ain't never home. I got nobody to talk to. I got nobody to be with. Think I can just sit home and do nothin' but cook for Curley? I want to see somebody. Just see 'em an' talk to 'em. There ain't no women. I can't walk to town. And Curley don't take me to no dances now. I tell you I jus' want to talk to somebody.

George (*boldly*) If you're just friendly what you givin' out the eye for an' floppin' your can around?

Curley's wife (*sadly*) I just wanta be nice.

(*The sound of approaching voices: 'You don't have to get mad about it, do you?'...'I ain't mad, but I just don't want no more questions, that's all. I just don't want no more questions.'*)

George Get goin'. We don't want no trouble.

(CURLEY'S WIFE *looks from the window and closes it silently and disappears. Enter* SLIM, *followed by* CURLEY, CARLSON *and* WHIT. SLIM'S *hands are black with tar.* CURLEY *hangs close to his elbow.*)

Curley (*explaining*) Well, I didn't mean nothing, Slim. I jus' ast you.

Slim Well, you been askin' too often. I'm gettin' goddamn sick of it. If you can't look after your own wife, what you expect me to do about it? You lay off of me.

Curley I'm jus' tryin' to tell you I didn't mean nothing. I just thought you might of saw her.

Carlson Why don't you tell her to stay to hell home where she belongs? You let her hang around the bunkhouses and pretty soon you're goin' to have somethin' on your hands.

Curley (*whirls on* CARLSON) You keep out of this 'less you want ta step outside.

Carlson (*laughing*) Why you goddamn punk. You tried to throw a scare into Slim and you couldn't make it stick. Slim throwed a scare into you. You're yellow as a frog's belly. I don't care if you're the best boxer in the country, you come for me and I'll kick your goddamn head off.

Whit (*joining in the attack*) Glove full of vaseline!

Curley (*glares at him, then suddenly sniffs the air, like a hound*) By God, she's been in here. I can smell—By God, she's been in here. (*to* GEORGE) You was here. The other guys was outside. Now, God damn you—you talk.

George (*looks worried. He seems to make up his mind to face an inevitable situation. Slowly takes off his coat, and folds it almost daintily. Speaks in an unemotional monotone.*) Somebody got to beat the hell outa you. I guess I'm elected. (LENNIE *has been watching, fascinated. He gives his high, nervous chuckle.*)

Curley (*whirls on him*) What the hell you laughin' at?

Lennie (*blankly*) Huh?

Curley (*exploding with rage*) Come on, you big bastard. Get up on your feet. No big son-of-a-bitch is gonna laugh at me. I'll show you who's yellow.

(LENNIE *looks helplessly at* GEORGE. *Gets up and tries to retreat upstage.* CURLEY *follows slashing at him. The others mass themselves in front of the two contestants: 'That ain't no way, Curley—he ain't done nothing to you.'...'Lay off him, will you, Curley. He ain't no fighter.'...'Sock him back, big guy! Don't be afraid of him!'... 'Give him a chance, Curley. Give him a chance.'*)

Lennie (*crying with terror*) George, make him leave me alone, George.

George Get him, Lennie. Get him! (*There is a sharp cry. The gathering of men opens and* CURLEY *is flopping about, his hand lost in* LENNIE's *hand.*) Let go of him, Lennie. Let go! (*'He's got his hand!'...'Look at that, will you?'...'Jesus, what a guy!'* LENNIE *watches in terror the flopping man he holds.* LENNIE's *face is covered with blood.* GEORGE *slaps* LENNIE *in the face again and again.* CURLEY *is weak and shrunken.*) Let go his hand, Lennie. Slim, come help me, while this guy's got any hand left. (*Suddenly* LENNIE *lets go. He cowers away from* GEORGE.)

Lennie You told me to, George. I heard you tell me to. (CURLEY *has dropped to the floor.* SLIM *and* CARLSON *bend over him and look at his hand.* SLIM *looks over at* LENNIE *with horror.*)

Slim We got to get him to a doctor. It looks to me like every bone in his hand is busted.

Lennie (*crying*) I didn't wanta. I didn't wanta hurt 'im.

Slim Carlson, you get the candy wagon out. He'll have to go into Soledad and get his hand fixed up. (*Turns to the whimpering* LENNIE.) It ain't your fault. This punk had it comin' to him. But Jesus—he ain't hardly got no hand left.

George (*moving near*) Slim, will we git canned now? Will Curley's ole man can us now?

Slim I don't know. (*Kneels down beside* CURLEY.) You got your sense enough to listen? (CURLEY *nods.*) Well, then you listen. I think you got your hand caught in a machine. If you don't tell nobody what happened, we won't. But you jest tell and try to get this guy canned and we'll tell everybody. And then will you get the laugh! (*Helps* CURLEY *to his feet.*) Come on now. Carlson's goin' to take you in to a doctor. (*Starts for the door, turns back to* LENNIE.) Le's see your hands. (LENNIE *sticks out both hands.*) Christ Almighty!

George Lennie was just scairt. He didn't know what to do. I tole you nobody ought never to fight him. No, I guess it was Candy I tole.

Candy (*solemnly*) That's just what you done. Right this morning when Curley first lit into him. You says he better not fool with Lennie if he knows what's good for him. (*They all leave the stage except* GEORGE *and* LENNIE *and* CANDY.)

George (*to* LENNIE, *very gently*) It ain't your fault. You don't need to be scairt no more. You done jus' what I tole you to. Maybe you better go in the washroom and clean up your face. You look like hell.

Lennie I didn't want no trouble.

George Come on—I'll go with you.

Lennie George?

George What you want?

Lennie Can I still tend the rabbits, George?

(*They exeunt together, side by side, through the door of the bunkhouse.*)

SCENE II

Ten o'clock Saturday evening.
The room of the stable buck, a lean-to off the barn. There is a plank door upstage centre; a small square window centre right. On one side of the door a leather working bench with tools racked behind it, and on the others racks with broken and partly mended harnesses, collars, hames, traces, etc. At the left upstage Crooks's bunk. Over it two shelves. On one a great number of medicines in cans and bottles. And on the other a number of tattered books and

a big alarm clock. In the corner right upstage a single-barrelled shotgun and on the floor beside it a pair of rubber boots. A large pair of gold spectacles hang on a nail over Crooks's bunk.

The entrance leads into the barn proper. From that direction and during the whole scene come the sounds of horses eating, stamping, jingling their halter chains and now and then whinnying.

Two empty nail kegs are in the room to be used as seats. Single unshaded small-candlepower carbon light hanging from its own cord.

As the curtain rises, we see CROOKS *sitting on his bunk rubbing his back with liniment. He reaches up under his shirt to do this. His face is lined with pain. As he rubs he flexes his muscles and shivers a little.*

LENNIE *appears in the open doorway, nearly filling the opening. Then* CROOKS, *sensing his presence, raises his eyes, stiffens and scowls.*

LENNIE *smiles in an attempt to make friends.*

Crooks (*sharply*) You got no right to come in my room. This here's my room. Nobody got any right in here but me.

Lennie (*fawning*) I ain't doin' nothing. Just come in the barn to look at my pup, and I seen your light.

Crooks Well, I got a right to have a light. You go on and get out of my room. I ain't wanted in the bunkhouse and you ain't wanted in my room.

Lennie (*ingenuously*) Why ain't you wanted?

Crooks (*furiously*) 'Cause I'm black. They play cards in there. But I can't play because I'm black. They say I stink. Well, I tell you all of you stink to me.

Lennie (*helplessly*) Everybody went into town. Slim and George and everybody. George says I got to stay here and not get into no trouble. I seen your light.

Crooks Well, what do you want?

Lennie Nothing...I seen your light. I thought I could jus' come in and set.

Crooks (*stares at* LENNIE *for a moment, takes down his spectacles and adjusts them over his ears; says in a complaining tone*) I don't know what you're doin' in the barn anyway. You ain't no skinner. There's no call for a bucker to come into the barn at all. You've got nothing to do with the horses and mules.

Lennie (*patiently*) The pup. I come to see my pup.

Crooks Well, God damn it, go and see your pup then. Don't go no place where you ain't wanted.

Lennie (*advances a step into the room, remembers and backs to the door again*) I looked at him a little. Slim says I ain't to pet him very much.

Crooks (*the anger gradually going out of his voice*) Well, you been taking him out of the nest all the time. I wonder the ole lady don't move him some place else.

Lennie (*moving into the room*) Oh, she don't care. She lets me.

Crooks (*scowls and then gives up*) Come on in and set awhile. Long as you won't get out and leave me alone, you might as well set down. (*A little more friendly.*) All the boys gone into town, huh?

Lennie All but old Candy. He jus' sets in the bunkhouse sharpening his pencils. And sharpening and figurin'.

Crooks (*adjusting his glasses*) Figurin'? What's Candy figurin' about?

Lennie 'Bout the land. 'Bout the little place.

Crooks You're nuts. You're crazy as a wedge. What land you talkin' about?

Lennie The land we're goin' to get. And a little house and pigeons.

Crooks Just nuts. I don't blame the guy you're travelling with for keeping you out of sight.

Lennie (*quietly*) It ain't no lie. We're gonna do it. Gonna get a little place and live on the fat of the land.

Crooks (*settling himself comfortably on his bunk*) Set down. Set down on that nail keg.

Lennie (*hunches over on the little barrel*) You think it's a lie. But it ain't no lie. Ever' word's the truth. You can ask George.

Crooks (*puts his dark chin on his palm*) You travel round with George, don't you?

Lennie (*proudly*) Sure, me and him goes ever' place together.

Crooks (*after a pause, quietly*) Sometimes he talks and you don't know what the hell he's talkin' about. Ain't that so? (*Leans forward.*) Ain't that so?

Lennie Yeah. Sometimes.

Crooks Just talks on. And you don't know what the hell it's all about.

Lennie How long you think it'll be before them pups will be old enough to pet?

Crooks (*laughs again*) A guy can talk to you and be sure you won't go blabbin'. A couple of weeks and them pups will be all right. (*musing*) George knows what he's about. Just talks and you don't understand nothing. (*Mood gradually changes to excitement.*) Well, this is just a nigger talkin' and a busted-back nigger. It don't mean nothing, see. You couldn't remember it anyway. I seen it over and over— a guy talking to another guy and it don't make no difference if he don't hear or understand. The thing is they're talkin'. (*He pounds his knee with his hand.*) George can tell you screwy things and it don't matter. It's just the talkin'. It's just bein' with another guy, that's all. (*His voice becomes soft and malicious.*) S'pose George don't come back no more? S'pose he took a powder and just ain't comin' back. What you do then?

Lennie (*trying to follow* CROOKS) What? What?

Crooks I said s'pose George went into town tonight and you never heard of him no more. (*Presses forward.*) Just s'pose that.

Lennie (*sharply*) He won't do it. George wouldn't do nothing like that. I been with George a long time. He'll come back tonight. ...(*Doubt creeps into his voice.*) Don't you think he will?

Crooks (*delighted with his torture*) Nobody can tell what a guy will do. Let's say he wants to come back and can't. S'pose he gets killed or hurt so he can't come back.

Lennie (*in terrible apprehension*) I don't know. Say, what you doin' anyway? It ain't true. George ain't got hurt.

Crooks (*cruelly*) Want me to tell you what'll happen? They'll take you to the booby hatch. They'll tie you up with a collar like a dog. Then you'll be jus' like me. Livin' in a kennel.

Lennie (*furious, walks over towards* CROOKS) Who hurt George?

Crooks (*recoiling from him with fright*) I was just supposin'. George ain't hurt. He's all right. He'll be back all right.

Lennie (*standing over him*) What you supposin' for? Ain't nobody goin' to s'pose any hurt to George.

Crooks (*trying to calm him*) Now set down. George ain't hurt. Go on now, set down.

Lennie (*growling*) Ain't nobody gonna talk no hurt to George.

Crooks (*very gently*) Maybe you can see now. You got George. You know he's comin' back. S'pose you didn't have nobody. S'pose you couldn't go in the bunkhouse and play rummy, 'cause you was black. How would you like that? S'pose you had to set out here and read books. Sure, you could play horseshoes until it got dark, but then you got to read books. Books ain't no good. A guy needs somebody . . . to be near him. (*His tone whines.*) A guy goes nuts if he ain't got nobody. Don't make no difference who it is as long as he's with you. I tell you a guy gets too lonely, he gets sick.

Lennie (*reassuring himself*) George gonna come back. Maybe George come back already. Maybe I better go see.

Crooks (*more gently*) I didn't mean to scare you. He'll come back. I was talkin' about myself.

Lennie (*miserably*) George won't go away and leave me. I know George won't do that.

Crooks (*continuing dreamily*) I remember when I was a little kid on my ole man's chicken ranch. Had two brothers. They was always near me, always there. Used to sleep right in the same room. Right in the same bed, all three. Had a strawberry patch. Had an alfalfa patch. Used to turn the chickens out in the alfalfa on a sunny morning. Me and my brothers would set on the fence and watch 'em—white chickens they was.

Lennie (*interested*) George says we're gonna have alfalfa.

Crooks You're nuts.

Lennie We are too gonna get it. You ask George.

Crooks (*scornfully*) You're nuts. I seen hundreds of men come by on the road and on the ranches, bindles on their back and that same damn thing in their head. Hundreds of 'em. They come and they quit and they go on. And every damn one of 'em is got a little piece of land in his head. And never a goddamn one of 'em gets it. Jus' like heaven. Everybody wants a little piece of land. Nobody never gets to heaven. And nobody gets no land.

Lennie We are too.

Crooks It's jest in your head. Guys all the time talkin' about it, but it's jest in your head. (*The horses move restlessly. One of them whinnies.*) I guess somebody's out there. Maybe Slim. (*Pulls himself painfully upright and moves toward the door. Calls.*) That you, Slim?

Candy (*from outside*) Slim went in town. Say, you seen Lennie?

Crooks You mean the big guy?

Candy Yes. Seen him around any place?

Crooks (*goes back to his bunk and sits down, says shortly*) He's in here.

Candy (*stands in the doorway, scratching his wrist. Makes no attempt to enter.*) Look, Lennie, I been figuring something out. About the place.

Crooks (*irritably*) You can come in if you want.

Candy (*embarrassed*). I don't know. 'Course, if you want me to ...

Crooks Oh, come on in. Everybody's comin' in. You might just as well. Gettin' to be a goddamn race track. (*He tries to conceal his pleasure.*)

Candy (*still embarrassed*) You've got a nice cozy little place in here. Must be nice to have a room to yourself this way.

Crooks Sure. And a manure pile under the window. All to myself. It's swell.

Lennie (*breaking in*) You said about the place.

Candy You know, I been here a long time. An' Crooks been here a long time. This is the first time I ever been in his room.

Crooks (*darkly*) Guys don't come in a colored man's room. Nobody been here but Slim.

Lennie (*insistently*) The place. You said about the place.

Candy Yeah. I got it all figured out. We can make some real money on them rabbits if we go about it right.

Lennie But I get to tend 'em. George says I get to tend 'em. He promised.

Crooks (*brutally*) You guys is just kiddin' yourselves. You'll talk about it a hell of a lot, but you won't get no land. You'll be a swamper here until they take you out in a box. Hell, I seen too many guys.

Candy (*angrily*) We're gonna do it. George says we are. We got the money right now.

Crooks Yeah. And where is George now? In town in a whorehouse. That's where your money's goin'. I tell you I seen it happen too many times.

Candy George ain't got the money in town. The money's in the bank. Me and Lennie and George. We gonna have a room to ourselves. We gonna have a dog and chickens. We gonna have green corn and maybe a cow.

Crooks (*impressed*) You say you got the money?

Candy We got most of it. Just a little bit more to get. Have it all in one month. George's got the land all picked out too.

Crooks (*exploring his spine with his hands*) I've never seen a guy really do it. I seen guys nearly crazy with loneliness for land, but every time a whorehouse or a blackjack game took it away from 'em. (*Hesitates and then speaks timidly.*) If you guys would want a hand to work for nothin'—just his keep, why I'd come and lend a hand. I ain't so crippled I can't work like a son-of-a-bitch if I wanted to.

George (*strolls through the door, hands in pockets, leans against the wall, speaks in a half-satiric, rather gentle voice*) You couldn't go to bed like I told you, could you, Lennie? Hell, no—you got to get out in society an' flap your mouth. Holdin' a convention out here.

Lennie (*defending himself*) You was gone. There wasn't nobody in the bunkhouse. I ain't done no bad things, George.

George (*still casually*) Only time I get any peace is when you're asleep. If you ever get walkin' in your sleep I'll chop off your head like a chicken. (*Chops with his hand.*)

Crooks (*coming to* LENNIE's *defence*) We was jus' settin' here talkin'. Ain't no harm in that.

George Yeah. I heard you. (*A weariness has settled on him.*) Got to be here ever' minute, I guess. Got to watch ya. (*to* CROOKS) It ain't nothing against you, Crooks. We just wasn't gonna tell nobody.

Candy (*tries to change subject*) Didn't you have no fun in town?

George Oh! I set in a chair and Susy was crackin' jokes an' the guys was startin' to raise a little puny hell. Christ Almighty—I never been this way before. I'm jus' gonna set out a dime and a nickel for a shot an' I think what a hell of a lot of bulk carrot seed you can get for fifteen cents.

Candy Not in them damn little envelopes—but bulk seed—you sure can.

George So purty soon I come back. I can't think of nothing else. Them guys slingin' money around got me jumpy.

Candy Guy got to have *some* fun. I was to a parlor house in Bakersfield once. God Almighty, what a place. Went upstairs on a red carpet. They was big pitchers on the wall. We set in big sof' chairs. They was cigarettes on the table—an' they was *free*. Purty soon a Jap come in with drinks on a tray an' them *drinks* was free. Take all you want. (*in a reverie*) Purty soon the girls come in an' they was jus' as polite an' nice an' quiet an' purty. Didn't seem like hookers. Made ya kinda scared to ask 'em....That was a long time ago.

George Yeah? An' what'd them sof' chairs set you back?

Candy Fifteen bucks.

George (*scornfully*) So ya got a cigarette an' a whiskey an' a look at a purty dress an' it cost ya twelve and a half bucks extra. You shot a week's pay to walk on that red carpet.

Candy (*still entranced with his memory*) A week's pay? Sure. But I worked weeks all my life. I can't remember none of them weeks. But...that was nearly twenty years ago. And I can remember that. Girl I went with was named Arline. Had on a pink silk dress.

George (*turns suddenly and looks out the door into the dark barn, speaks savagely*) I s'pose ya lookin' for Curley? (CURLEY's WIFE *appears in the door.*) Well, Curley ain't here.

Curley's wife (*determined now*) I know Curley ain't here. I wanted to ast Crooks somepin'. I didn't know you guys was here.

Candy Didn't George tell you before—we don't want nothing to do with you. You know damn well Curley ain't here.

Curley's wife I know where Curley went. Got his arm in a sling an' he went anyhow. I tell ya I come out to ast Crooks somepin'.

Crooks (*apprehensively*) Maybe you better go along to your own house. You hadn't ought to come near a colored man's room. I don't want no trouble. You don't want to ask me nothing.

Candy (*rubbing his wrist stump*) You got a husband. You got no call to come foolin' around with other guys, causin' trouble.

Curley's wife (*suddenly angry*) I try to be nice an' polite to you lousy bindle bums—but you're too good. I tell ya I could of went with shows. An'—an' a guy wanted to put me in pitchers right in Hollywood. (*Looks about to see how she is impressing them. Their eyes are hard.*) I come out here to ast somebody somepin' an'—

Candy (*stands up suddenly and knocks his nail keg over backwards, speaks angrily*) I had enough. You ain't wanted here. We tole you, you ain't. Callin' us bindle stiffs. You got floozy idears what us guys amounts to. You ain't got sense enough to see us guys ain't bindle stiffs. S'pose you could get us *canned*—s'pose you *could*. You think we'd hit the highway an' look for another two-bit job. You don't know we got our own ranch to go to an' our own house an' fruit trees. An' we got friends. That's what we got. Maybe they was a time when we didn't have nothing, but that ain't so no more.

Curley's wife You damn ol' goat. If you had two bits, you'd be in Soledad gettin' a drink an' suckin' the bottom of the glass.

George Maybe she could ask Crooks what she come to ask an' then get the hell home. I don't think she come to ask nothing.

Curley's wife What happened to Curley's hand? (CROOKS *laughs.* GEORGE *tries to shut him up.*) So it wasn't no machine. Curley didn't act like he was tellin' the truth. Come on, Crooks—what happened?

Crooks I wasn't there. I didn't see it.

Curley's wife (*eagerly*) What happened? I won't let on to Curley. He says he caught his han' in a gear. (CROOKS *is silent.*) Who done it?

George Didn't nobody do it.

Curley's wife (*turns slowly to* GEORGE) So *you* done it. Well, he had it comin'.

George I didn't have no fuss with Curley.

Curley's wife (*steps near him, smiling*) Maybe now you ain't scared of him no more. Maybe you'll talk to me sometimes now. Ever'body was scared of him.

George (*speaks rather kindly*) Look! I didn't sock Curley. If he had trouble, it ain't none of our affair. Ask Curley about it. Now listen. I'm gonna try to tell ya. We tole you to get the hell out and it don't do no good. So I'm gonna tell you another way. Us guys got somepin' we're gonna do. If you stick around you'll gum up the works. It ain't your fault. If a guy steps on a round pebble an' falls an' breaks his neck, it ain't the pebble's fault, but the guy wouldn't of did it if the pebble wasn't there.

Curley's wife (*puzzled*) What you talkin' about pebbles? If you didn't sock Curley, who did? (*She looks at the others, then steps quickly over to* LENNIE.) Where'd you get them bruises on your face?

George I tell you he got his hand caught in a machine.

Lennie (*looks anxiously at* GEORGE, *speaks miserably*) He caught his han' in a machine.

George So now get out of here.

Curley's wife (*goes close to* LENNIE, *speaks softly and there is a note of affection in her voice*) So...it was you. Well...maybe you're dumb like they say...an' maybe...you're the only guy on the ranch with guts. (*She puts her hand on* LENNIE's *shoulder. He looks up in her face and a smile grows on his face. She strokes his shoulder.*) You're a nice fella.

George (*suddenly leaps at her ferociously, grabs her shoulder and whirls her around*) Listen...you! I tried to give you a break. Don't you walk into nothing! We ain't gonna let you mess up what we're gonna do. You let this guy alone an' get the hell out of here.

Curley's wife (*defiant but slightly frightened*) You ain't tellin' me what to do. (*The* BOSS *appears in the door, stands legs spread, thumbs hooked over his belt.*) I got a right to talk to anybody I want to.

George Why, you—(GEORGE, *furiously, steps close—his hand is raised to strike her. She cowers a little.* GEORGE *stiffens, seeing* BOSS, *frozen in position. The others see* BOSS *too. Girl retreats slowly.* GEORGE's *hand drops slowly to his side—he takes two slow backward steps. Hold the scene for a moment.*)

ACT THREE

SCENE I

Mid-afternoon Sunday.

One end of a great barn. Backstage the hay slopes up sharply against the wall. High in the upstage wall is a large hay window. On each side are seen the hay racks, behind which are the stalls with the horses in them. Throughout this scene the horses can be heard in their stalls, rattling their halter chains and chewing at the hay.

The entrance is downstage right.

The boards of the barn are not close together. Streaks of afternoon sun come between the boards, made visible by dust in the air. From outside comes the clang of horseshoes on the playing peg, shouts of men encouraging or jeering.

In the barn there is a feeling of quiet and humming and lazy warmth. Curtain rises on LENNIE *sitting in the hay, looking down at a little dead puppy in front of him. He puts out his big hand and strokes it clear from one end to the other.*

Lennie (*softly*) Why do you got to get killed? You ain't so little as mice. I didn' bounce you hard. (*Bends the pup's head up and looks in its face.*) Now maybe George ain't gonna let me tend no rabbits if he finds out you got killed. (*He scoops a little hollow and lays the puppy in it out of sight and covers it over with hay. He stares at the mound he has made.*) This ain't no bad thing like I got to hide in the brush. I'll tell George I found it dead. (*He unburies the pup and inspects it. Twists its ears and works his fingers in its fur. Sorrowfully.*) But he'll know. George always knows. He'll say: 'You done it. Don't try to put nothin' over on me.' And he'll say: 'Now just for that you don't get to tend no—you-know-whats.' (*His anger rises. Addresses the pup.*) God damn you. Why do you got to get killed? You ain't so little as mice. (*Picks up the pup and hurls it from him and turns his back on it. He sits bent over his knees moaning to himself.*) Now he won't let me. . . . Now he won't let me. (*Outside there is a clang of horseshoes on the iron stake and a little chorus of cries.* LENNIE *gets up and brings the pup back and lays it in the hay and sits down. He mourns.*) You wasn't big enough. They tole me and tole me you wasn't. I didn't know you'd get killed so easy. Maybe George won't care. This here goddamn little son-of-a-bitch wasn't nothin' to George.

Candy (*voice from behind the stalls*) Lennie, where you at? (LENNIE *frantically buries the pup under the hay.* CANDY *enters excitedly.*) Thought I'd find ya here. Say . . . I been talkin' to Slim. It's okay. We ain't gonna get the can. Slim been talkin' to the boss. Slim tol' the boss you guys is good buckers. The boss got to move that grain. 'Member what hell the boss give us las' night? He tol' Slim he got his eye on you an' George. But you ain't gonna get the can. Oh! an' say. The boss give Curley's wife hell, too. Tole her never to go near the men no more. Give her worse hell than you an' George. (*For the first time notices* LENNIE's *dejection.*) Ain't you glad?

Lennie Sure.

Candy You ain't sick?

Lennie Uh-uh!

Candy I got to go tell George. See you later.

(*Exits.* LENNIE, *alone, uncovers the pup. Lies down in the hay and sinks deep in it. Puts the pup on his arm and strokes it.* CURLEY's WIFE *enters secretly. A little mound of hay conceals* LENNIE *from her. In her hand she carries a small suitcase, very cheap. She crosses the barn and buries the case in the hay. Stands up and looks to see whether it can be seen.* LENNIE *watching her quietly tries to cover the pup with hay. She sees the movement.*)

Curley's wife What—what you doin' here?

Lennie (*sullenly*) Jus' settin' here.

Curley's wife You seen what I done.

Lennie Yeah! you brang a valise.

Curley's wife (*comes near to him*) You won't tell—will you?

Lennie (*still sullen*) I ain't gonna have nothing to do with you. George tole me. I ain't to talk to you or nothing. (*Covers the pup a little more.*)

Curley's wife George give you all your orders?

Lennie Not talk nor nothing.

Curley's wife You won't tell about that suitcase? I ain't gonna stay here no more. Tonight I'm gonna get out. Come here an' get my stuff an' get out. I ain't gonna be run over no more. I'm gonna go in pitchers. (*Sees* LENNIE's *hand stroking the pup under the hay.*) What you got there?

Lennie Nuthing. I ain't gonna talk to you. George says I ain't.

Curley's wife Listen. The guys got a horseshoe tenement out there.

It's on'y four o'clock. Them guys ain't gonna leave that tenement. They got money bet. You don't need to be scared to talk to me.

Lennie (*weakening a little*) I ain't supposed to.

Curley's wife (*watching his buried hand*) What you got under there?

Lennie (*his woe comes back to him*) Jus' my pup. Jus' my little ol' pup. (*Sweeps the hay aside.*)

Curley's wife Why! He's dead.

Lennie (*explaining sadly*) He was so little. I was jus' playin' with him—an' he made like he's gonna bite me—an' I made like I'm gonna smack him—an'—I done it. An' then he was dead.

Curley's wife (*consoling*) Don't you worry none. He was just a mutt. The whole country is full of mutts.

Lennie It ain't that so much. George gonna be mad. Maybe he won't let me—what he said I could tend.

Curley's wife (*sits down in the hay beside him, speaks soothingly*) Don't you worry. Them guys got money bet on that horseshoe tenement. They ain't gonna leave it. And tomorra I'll be gone. I ain't gonna let them run over me. (*In the following scene it is apparent that neither is listening to the other and yet as it goes on, as a happy tone increases, it can be seen that they are growing closer together.*)

Lennie We gonna have a little place an' raspberry bushes.

Curley's wife I ain't meant to live like this. I come from Salinas. Well, a show come through an' I talked to a guy that was in it. He says I could go with the show. My ol' lady wouldn't let me, 'cause I was on'y fifteen. I wouldn't be no place like this if I had went with that show, you bet.

Lennie Gonna take a sack an' fill it up with alfalfa an'—

Curley's wife (*hurrying on*) 'Nother time I met a guy an' he was in pitchers. Went out to the Riverside Dance Palace with him. He said he was gonna put me in pitchers. Says I was a natural. Soon's he got back to Hollywood he was gonna write me about it. (*Looks impressively at* LENNIE.) I never got that letter. I think my ol' lady stole it. Well, I wasn't gonna stay no place where they stole your letters. So I married Curley. Met *him* out to the Riverside Dance Palace too.

Lennie I hope George ain't gonna be mad about this pup.

Curley's wife I ain't tol' this to nobody before. Maybe I oughtn' to. I don't like Curley. He ain't a nice fella. I might a stayed with him but last night him an' his ol' man both lit into me. I don't have to stay here. (*Moves closer and speaks confidentially.*) Don't tell nobody till I get clear away. I'll go in the night an' thumb a ride to Hollywood.

Lennie We gonna get out a here purty soon. This ain't no nice place.

Curley's wife (*ecstatically*) Gonna get in the movies an' have nice clothes—all them nice clothes like they wear. An' I'll set in them big hotels and they'll take pitchers of me. When they have them openings I'll go an' talk in the radio...an' it won't cost me nothing 'cause I'm in the pitcher. (*Puts her hand on* LENNIE's *arm for a moment.*) All them nice clothes like they wear...because this guy says I'm a natural.

Lennie We gonna go way ... far away from here.

Curley's wife 'Course, when I run away from Curley, my ol' lady won't never speak to me no more. She'll think I ain't decent. That's what she'll say. (*defiantly*) Well, we really ain't decent, no matter how much my ol' lady tries to hide it. My ol' man was a drunk. They put him away. There! Now I told.

Lennie George an' me was to the Sacramento Fair. One time I fell in the river an' George pulled me out an' saved me, an' then we went to the Fair. They got all kinds of stuff there. We seen long-hair rabbits.

Curley's wife My ol' man was a sign-painter when he worked. He used to get drunk an' paint crazy pitchers an' waste paint. One night when I was a little kid, him an' my ol' lady had an awful fight. They was always fightin'. In the middle of the night he come into my room, and he says, 'I can't stand this no more. Let's you an' me go away.' I guess he was drunk. (*Her voice takes on a curious wondering tenderness.*) I remember in the night—walkin' down the road, and the trees was black. I was pretty sleepy. He picked me up, an' he carried me on his back. He says, 'We gonna live together. We gonna live together because you're my own little girl, an' not no stranger. No arguin' and fightin',' he says, 'because you're my little daughter.' (*Her voice becomes soft.*) He says, 'Why you'll bake little cakes for me, and I'll paint pretty pitchers all over the wall.' (*sadly*) In the morning they caught us ... an' they put him away. (*Pause.*) I wish we'd a' went.

Lennie Maybe if I took this here pup an' throwed him away George wouldn't never know.

Curley's wife They locked him up for a drunk, and in a little while he died.

Lennie Then maybe I could tend the rabbits without no trouble.

Curley's wife Don't you think of nothing but rabbits? (*Sound of horseshoe on metal.*) Somebody made a ringer.

Lennie (*patiently*) We gonna have a house and a garden, an' a place for alfalfa. And I take a sack and get it all full of alfalfa, and then I take it to the rabbits.

Curley's wife What makes you so nuts about rabbits?

Lennie (*moves close to her*) I like to pet nice things. Once at a fair I seen some of them long-hair rabbits. And they was nice, you bet. (*despairingly*) I'd even pet mice, but not when I could get nothin' better.

Curley's wife (*giggles*) I think you're nuts.

Lennie (*earnestly*) No, I ain't. George says I ain't. I like to pet nice things with my fingers. Soft things.

Curley's wife Well, who don't? Everybody likes that. I like to feel silk and velvet. You like to feel velvet?

Lennie (*chuckling with pleasure*) You bet, by God. And I had some too. A lady give me some. And that lady was—my Aunt Clara. She give it right to me....(*measuring with his hands*)

'Bout this big a piece. I wish I had that velvet right now. (*He frowns.*) I lost it. I ain't seen it for a long time.

Curley's wife (*laughing*) You're nuts. But you're a kinda nice fella. Jus' like a big baby. A person can see kinda what you mean. When I'm doin' my hair sometimes I jus' set there and stroke it, because it's so soft. (*Runs her fingers over the top of her head.*) Some people got kinda coarse hair. You take Curley, his hair's just like wire. But mine is soft and fine. Here, feel. Right here. (*Takes* LENNIE's *hand and puts it on her head.*) Feel there and see how soft it is. (LENNIE's *fingers fall to stroking her hair.*) Don't you muss it up.

Lennie Oh, that's nice. (*Strokes harder.*) Oh, that's nice.

Curley's wife Look out now, you'll muss it. (*angrily*) You stop it now, you'll mess it all up. (*She jerks her head sideways and* LENNIE's *fingers close on her hair and hang on. In a panic.*) Let go. (*She screams.*) You let go. (*She screams again. His other hand closes over her mouth and nose.*)

Lennie (*begging*) Oh, please don't do that. George'll be mad. (*She struggles violently to be free. A soft screaming comes from under* LENNIE's *hand. Crying with fright.*) Oh, please don't do none of that. George gonna say I done a bad thing. (*He raises his hand from her mouth and a hoarse cry escapes. Angrily.*) Now don't. I don't want you to yell. You gonna get me in trouble just like George says you will. Now don't you do that. (*She struggles more.*) Don't you go yellin'. (*He shakes her violently. Her neck snaps sideways and she lies still. Looks down at her and cautiously removes his hand from over her mouth.*) I don't wanta hurt you. But George will be mad if you yell. (*When she doesn't answer he bends closely over her. He lifts her arm and lets it drop. For a moment he seems bewildered.*) I done a bad thing. I done another bad thing. (*He paws up the hay until it partly covers her. The sound of the horseshoe game comes from the outside. And for the first time* LENNIE *seems conscious of it. He crouches down and listens.*) Oh, I done a real bad thing. I shouldn't a did that. George will be mad. And...he said...and hide in the brush till he comes. That's what he said. (*He picks up the puppy from beside the girl.*) I'll throw him away. It's bad enough like it is.

(*He puts the pup under his coat, creeps to the barn wall and peers out between the cracks and then he creeps around to the end of the manger and disappears. The stage is vacant except for* CURLEY's WIFE. *She lies in the hay half covered up and she looks very young and peaceful. Her rouged cheeks and red lips make her seem alive and sleeping slightly. For a moment the stage is absolutely silent. Then the horses stamp on the other side of the feeding rack. The halter chains clink and from outside men's voices come loud and clear.*)

Candy (*offstage*) Lennie! Oh, Lennie, you in there? (*He enters.*) I been figurin' some more, Lennie. Tell you what we can do. (*Sees* CURLEY'S WIFE *and stops. Rubs his white whiskers.*) I didn't know you was here. You was tol' not to be here. (*He steps near her.*) You oughtn't to sleep out here. (*He is right beside her and looks down.*) Oh, Jesus Christ! (*Goes to the door and calls softly.*) George, George! Come here...George!

George (*enters*) What do you want?

Candy (*points at* CURLEY'S WIFE) Look.

George What's the matter with her? (*Steps up beside her.*) Oh, Jesus Christ! (*Kneels beside her and feels her heart and her wrist. Finally stands up slowly and stiffly. From this time on through the rest of the scene* GEORGE *is wooden.*)

Candy What done it?

George (*coldly*) Ain't you got any ideas? (CANDY *looks away.*) I should of knew. I guess way back in my head I did.

Candy What we gonna do now, George? What we gonna do now?

George (*answering slowly and dully*) Guess ... we gotta ... tell ... the guys. Guess we got to catch him and lock him up. We can't let him get away. Why, the poor bastard would starve. (*He tries to reassure himself.*) Maybe they'll lock him up and be nice to him.

Candy (*excitedly*) You know better'n that, George. You know Curley's gonna want to get him lynched. You know how Curley is.

George Yeah.... Yeah...that's right. I know Curley. And the other guys too. (*He looks back at* CURLEY'S WIFE.)

Candy (*pleadingly*) You and me can get that little place, can't we, George? You and me can go there and live nice, can't we? Can't we? (CANDY *drops his head and looks down at the hay to indicate that he knows.*)

George (*shakes his head slowly*) It was somethin' me and him had. (*softly*) I think I knowed it from the very first. I think I knowed we'd never do her. He used to like to hear about it so much. I got fooled to thinkin' maybe we would. (CANDY *starts to speak but doesn't.*)

(*as though repeating a lesson*) I'll work my month and then I'll take my fifty bucks. I'll stay all night in some lousy cat-house or I'll set in a pool room until everybody goes home. An' then—I'll come back an' work another month. And then I'll have fifty bucks more.

Candy He's such a nice fellow. I didn't think he'd a done nothing like this.

George (*gets a grip on himself and straightens his shoulders*) Now listen. We gotta tell the guys. I guess they've gotta bring him in. They ain't no way out. Maybe they won't hurt him. I ain't gonna let 'em hurt Lennie. (*sharply*) Now you listen. The guys might think I was in on it. I'm gonna go in the bunkhouse. Then in a minute you come out and yell like you just seen her. Will you do that? So the guys won't think I was in on it?

Candy Sure, George. Sure, I'll do that.

George Okay. Give me a couple of minutes then. And then you yell your head off. I'm goin' now. (GEORGE *exits.*)

Candy (*watches him go, looks helplessly back at* CURLEY'S WIFE; *his next words are in sorrow and in anger*) You goddamn tramp. You done it, didn't you? Everybody knowed you'd mess things up. You just wasn't no good. (*His voice shakes.*) I could of hoed in the garden and washed dishes for them guys....(*Pauses for a moment and then goes into a sing-song repeating the old words.*) If there was a circus or a baseball game...we would o' went to her...just said to hell with work and went to her. And they'd been a pig and chickens...and in the winter a little fat stove. An' us jus' settin' there...settin' there....(*His eyes blind with tears and he goes weakly to the entrance of the barn. Tries for a moment to break a shout out of his throat before he succeeds.*) Hey, you guys! Come here! Come here!

(*Outside the noise of the horseshoe game stops. The sound of discussion and then the voices come closer: 'What's the matter?' ... 'Who's that?' ... 'It's Candy.' ... 'Something must have happened.' Enter* SLIM *and* CARLSON, *young* WHIT *and* CURLEY, CROOKS *in the back, keeping out of attention range. And last of all* GEORGE. GEORGE *has put on his blue denim coat and buttoned it. His black hat is pulled down low over his eyes. 'What's the matter?'...'What's happened?'*)

(*A gesture from* CANDY. *The men stare at* CURLEY'S WIFE. SLIM *goes over to her, feels her wrist and touches her cheek with his fingers. His hand goes under her slightly twisted neck.* CURLEY *comes near.*

For a moment he seems shocked. Looks around helplessly and suddenly he comes to life.)

Curley I know who done it. That big son-of-a-bitch done it. I know he done it. Why, everybody else was out there playing horseshoes. (*working himself into a fury*) I'm gonna get him. I'm gonna get my shotgun. Why, I'll kill the big son-of-a-bitch myself. I'll shoot him in the guts. Come on, you guys. (*He runs out of the barn.*)

Carlson I'll go get my Luger. (*He runs out too.*)

Slim (*quietly to* GEORGE) I guess Lennie done it all right. Her neck's busted. Lennie could o' did that. (GEORGE *nods slowly. Half-questioning.*) Maybe like that time in Weed you was tellin' me about. (GEORGE *nods. Gently.*) Well, I guess we got to get him. Where you think he might o' went?

George (*struggling to get words out*) I don't know.

Slim I guess we gotta get him.

George (*stepping close and speaking passionately*) Couldn't we maybe bring him in and lock him up? He's nuts, Slim, he never done this to be mean.

Slim If we could only keep Curley in. But Curley wants to shoot him. (*He thinks.*) And s'pose they lock him up, George, and strap him down and put him in a cage, that ain't no good.

George I know. I know.

Slim I think there's only one way to get him out of it.

George I know.

Carlson (*enters running*) The bastard stole my Luger. It ain't in my bag.

Curley (*enters carrying a shotgun in his good hand. Officiously.*) All right, you guys. The nigger's got a shotgun. You take it, Carlson.

Whit Only cover around here is down by the river. He might have went there.

Curley Don't give him no chance. Shoot for his guts, that'll double him over.

Whit I ain't got a gun.

Curley Go in and tell my old man. Get a gun from him. Let's go now. (*Turns suspiciously on* GEORGE.) You're comin' with us, fella!

George Yeah. I'll come. But listen, Curley, the poor bastard's nuts. Don't shoot him, he didn't know what he was doin'.

Curley Don't shoot him! He's got Carlson's Luger, ain't he?

George (*weakly*) Maybe Carlson lost his gun.

Carlson I seen it this morning. It's been took.

Slim (*looking down at* CURLEY'S WIFE) Curley, maybe you better stay here with your wife. (*The light is fading into evening.* CURLEY *hesitates. Seems almost to weaken, then he hardens again.*)

Curley Naw, I'm gonna shoot the guts out of that big bastard, I'm gonna get him myself. Come on, you guys.

Slim (*to* CANDY) You stay here then, Candy. The rest of us better get goin'. (*They walk out,* SLIM *and* GEORGE *last. Exeunt all but* CANDY. *He squats in the hay, watching the face of* CURLEY'S WIFE.)

Candy Poor bastard.

SCENE II

Evening.
The riverbank again.
Light from the setting sun shines on the low brown hills. Among the trees by the river, the shade is deep with evening feeling.

Sounds: distant barking of dogs and the quiet call of quail.

The curtain rises on an empty stage.

There is a sudden whistle of evening wind that stirs the trees and scuds the leaves on the ground.

The stage is still again. LENNIE *enters as silently as a bear. He is bent over and wary. On stage he looks behind him. Then he takes from under his coat the dead pup, lays it on the ground and, going to the river, lies on his stomach and drinks.*

He returns to the dead pup, sits down beside it.

Lennie George gonna give me hell...I bet. I...won't tell him. I'll bury him. (*Begins to scoop a hole in the sand in front of him. Softly.*) But I didn't forget, you bet. I come right here. Hide in the brush an' wait for George. (*Works carefully at his little grave, shaping the hole. At last he picks up the pup and lays it in the hole. Mourning.*) He gonna give me hell. He gonna wish he was alone. (*Adjusts the puppy in the hole, turning it around to make it fit better. Defiantly.*) Well ... I can go right up in the hills an' find a cave. 'Course I wouldn't never have no ketchup. (*Begins packing sand down carefully about the pup, patting it as he does in beat with his words.*) I'll—go—away—go—away. (*Every word a pat. Fills the grave carefully, smooths the sand over it.*) There now. (*Gathers leaves and scatters them over the place. Gets up on his knees and cocks his head to inspect the job.*) Now. I won't never tell George. (*Sinks back to a sitting position.*) He'll know. He always knows.

(*Far-off sound of voices approaching. They come closer during the scene. Suddenly there is the clicking warning of a cock-quail and then the drum of the flock's wings.* GEORGE *enters silently, but hurriedly.*)

George (*in a hoarse whisper*) Get in the tules—quick.

Lennie I ain't done nothing, George. (*The voices are very close.*)

George (*frantically*) Get in the tules—damn you. (*Voices are nearly there.* GEORGE *half pushes* LENNIE *down among the tules. The tops rustle showing his crawling progress.*)

Whit (*offstage*) There's George. (*Enters.*) Better not get so far ahead. You ain't got a gun. (*Enter* SLIM, CARLSON, BOSS, CURLEY, *and three other ranch-hands. They are armed with shotguns and rifles.*)

Carlson He musta come this way. Them prints in the sand was aimed this way.

Slim (*has been regarding* GEORGE) Now look. We ain't gonna find him stickin' in a bunch this way. We got to spread out.

Curley Brush is pretty thick here. He might be lying in the brush. (*Steps toward the tules.* GEORGE *moves quickly after him.*)

Slim (*Seeing the move speaks quickly*) Look—(*pointing*)—up there's the county road an' open fields an' over there's the highway. Le's spread out an' cover the brush.

Boss Slim's right. We got to spread.

Slim We better drag up to the roads an' then drag back.

Curley 'Member what I said—shoot for his guts.

Slim Okay, move out. Me an' George'll go up to the county road. You guys gets the highway an' drag back.

Boss If we get separated, we'll meet here. Remember this place.

Curley All I care is getting the bastard.

(*The men move offstage right, talking.* SLIM *and* GEORGE *move slowly upstage listening to the voices that grow fainter and fainter.*)

Slim (*softly to* GEORGE) Where is he? (GEORGE *looks him in the eyes for a long moment. Finally trusts him and points with his thumb toward the tules.*)

Slim You want—I should—go away?

(GEORGE *nods slowly, looking at the ground.* SLIM *starts away, comes back, tries to say something, instead puts his hand on* GEORGE'S *shoulder for a second, and then hurries off upstage.*)

George (*moves woodenly toward the bank and the tule clump and sits down*) Lennie! (*The tules shiver again and* LENNIE *emerges dripping.*)

Lennie Where's them guys goin'? (*Long pause.*)

George Huntin'.

Lennie Whyn't we go with 'em? I like huntin'. (*Waits for an answer.* GEORGE *stares across the river.*) Is it 'cause I done a bad thing?

George It don't make no difference.

Lennie Is that why we can't go huntin' with them guys?

George (*woodenly*) It don't make no difference....Sit down, Lennie. Right there. (*The light is going now. In the distance there are shouts of men.* GEORGE *turns his head and listens to the shouts.*)

Lennie George!

George Yeah?

Lennie Ain't you gonna give me hell?

George Give ya hell?

Lennie Sure....Like you always done before. Like—'If I didn't have you I'd take my fifty bucks...'

George (*softly as if in wonder*) Jesus Christ, Lennie, you can't remember nothing that happens. But you remember every word I say!

Lennie Well, ain't you gonna say it?

George (*reciting*) 'If I was alone I—could live—so easy. (*His voice is monotonous.*) I could get a job and not have no mess....'

Lennie Go on, go on! 'And when the end of the month come...'

George 'And when the end of the month come, I could take my fifty bucks and go to—a cat-house....'

Lennie (*eagerly*) Go on, George, ain't you gonna give me no more hell?

George No!

Lennie I can go away. I'll go right off in the hills and find a cave if you don't want me.

George (*speaks as though his lips were stiff*) No, I want you to stay here with me.

Lennie (*craftily*) Then tell me like you done before.

George Tell you what?

Lennie 'Bout the other guys and about us!

George (*recites again*). 'Guys like us got no families. They got a little stake and then they blow it in. They ain't got nobody in the world that gives a hoot in hell about 'em!'

Lennie (*happily*) 'But not *us*.' Tell about us now.

George 'But not us.'

Lennie 'Because...'

George 'Because I got you and...'

Lennie (*triumphantly*) 'And I got you. We got each other,' that's what, that gives a hoot in hell about us. (*A breeze blows up the*

leaves and then they settle back again. There are the shouts of men again. This time closer.)

George (*takes off his hat; shakily*) Take off your hat, Lennie. The air feels fine!

Lennie (*removes his hat and lays it on the ground in front of him*) Tell how it's gonna be. (*Again the sound of men.* GEORGE *listens to them.*)

George Look acrost the river, Lennie, and I'll tell you like you can almost see it. (LENNIE *turns his head and looks across the river.*) 'We gonna get a little place...' (*Reaches in his side pocket and brings out* CARLSON's *Luger. Hand and gun lie on the ground behind* LENNIE's *back. He stares at the back of* LENNIE's *head at the place where spine and skull are joined. Sounds of men's voices talking offstage.*)

Lennie Go on! (GEORGE *raises the gun, but his hand shakes and he drops his hand on to the ground.*) Go on! How's it gonna be? 'We gonna get a little place....'

George (*thickly*) 'We'll have a cow. And we'll have maybe a pig and chickens—and down the flat we'll have a ... little piece of alfalfa....'

Lennie (*shouting*) 'For the rabbits!'

George 'For the rabbits!'

Lennie 'And I get to tend the rabbits?'

George 'And you get to tend the rabbits!'

Lennie (*giggling with happiness*) 'And live on the fat o' the land!'

George Yes. (LENNIE *turns his head. Quickly.*) Look over there, Lennie. Like you can really see it.

Lennie Where?

George Right acrost that river there. Can't you almost see it?

Lennie (*moving*) Where, George?

George It's over there. You keep lookin', Lennie. Just keep lookin'.

Lennie I'm lookin', George. I'm lookin'.

George That's right. It's gonna be nice there. Ain't gonna be no trouble, no fights. Nobody ever gonna hurt nobody, or steal from 'em. It's gonna be—nice.

Lennie I can see it, George. I can see it! Right over there! I can see it! (GEORGE *fires.* LENNIE *crumples; falls behind the brush. The voices of the men in the distance.*)

CURTAIN

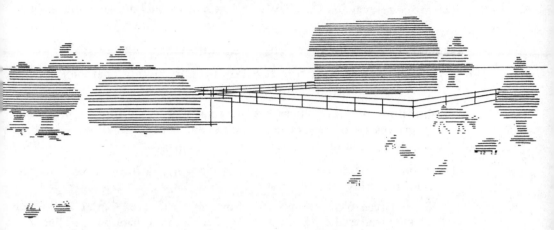

Questions

(1) Explain and comment on the relationship between George and Lennie.

(2) How relevant is the play's title, *Of Mice and Men*, to the events of the play?

(3) What is 'the dream'? Why is it important in the play?

(4) Briefly describe the role of each of the following characters in the play: (a) Candy (b) Curley (c) Curley's wife (d) Crooks.

(5) Slim is the only character in the play who understands and approves of the relationship between George and Lennie. What are your feelings towards Slim?

(6) What is prophetic about the following comment by George about Curley:

> Sure, I seen plenty tough little guys. But this here Curley better not make no mistakes about Lennie. Lennie ain't handy, see, but this Curley punk's gonna get hurt if he messes around with Lennie.

(7) The blind old dog that Candy leads around on a string is finally taken outside and shot. What is symbolic about the dog and the way it meets its end?

(8) How is the suspense built up in the last act of the play?

(9) Why do you think George shoots Lennie?

(10) Conflict is present in all drama. Describe one or two incidents in the play which involve conflict.

Of Mice and Men — Looking Back

Title

The title, *Of Mice and Men*, comes from the poem 'To a Mouse' by the great Scottish poet Robert Burns: 'The best laid schemes o' mice an' men / Gang aft a-gley' (i.e. often go wrong).

Setting

The play's action moves through several settings. It begins on a sandy bank of the Salinas River (a river that flows through agricultural country in southern California); shifts to the interior of a ranch bunk-house and a barn on the same ranch; and, for the final scene, returns to the riverbank. Thus, the action comes full circle, ending where it began in the natural setting of the riverbank. This serves to emphasize the brutality and deviousness of the ranch world, where, instead of being fulfilled, George and Lennie's dream of independence is shattered and their relationship destroyed.

Plot

Act 1, Scene I

The play opens with George and Lennie, two agricultural workers, on their way to a ranch job. As they prepare to eat and sleep on a bank of the Salinas River before going on to the ranch, the audience is made aware of the special relationship that exists between George and his huge but childlike companion, Lennie. Despite Lennie's size and strength, he needs caring for as if he were a child. Even his simple day-to-day needs must be supervised by George to make sure that he comes to no harm:

> GEORGE *(irritably)* Lennie, for God's sake, don't drink so much. *(Leans over and shakes* LENNIE.) Lennie, you hear me! You gonna be sick like you was last night.
>
> LENNIE *(dips his whole head under, hat and all. As he sits upon the bank, his hat drips down the back.)* That's good. You drink some, George. You drink some too.
>
> GEORGE *(drinking from his cupped palm)* Tastes all right. Don't seem to be runnin' much, though. Lennie, you oughtn' to drink water when it ain't running. *(hopelessly)* You'd drink water out of a gutter if you was thirsty.

Lennie has a passion for soft, furry things such as mice—which invariably die from the petting Lennie gives them. He cannot control the strength in his large, powerful hands.

George is concerned to prepare Lennie for the job ahead. When they meet the ranch boss, Lennie is to leave all the talking to George. George sarcastically recalls the time when they had worked in the town of Weed and Lennie had 'petted' a girl's dress so powerfully that they had had to flee the place.

> ...You just wanta feel that girl's dress. Just wanta pet it like it was a mouse. Well, how the hell'd she know you just wanta feel her dress? How'd she know you'd just hold onto it like it was a mouse?

George bitterly reminds Lennie that if he didn't have to look after him he (George) could get a job anywhere.

> ...I could live so easy. I could go get a job of work and no trouble. No mess ... and when the end of the month come, I could take my fifty bucks and go into town and get whatever I want. Why, I could stay in a cat-house all night. I could eat any place I want. Order any damn thing.

However, when he realizes that Lennie is as upset as a terrified child, George relents and calms him with the dream they share—a place of their own, where they could be independent; where they could watch their crops grow; where Lennie could keep rabbits to pet to his heart's content....

Act 1, Scene II

In this second scene of the play, set in the bunkhouse of the ranch, most of the other characters are introduced and significant tensions develop.

George is revealed as a shrewd judge of people and situations who clearly sees the threat of trouble posed by the aggressive Curley and his provocative wife. He is now even more insistent that Lennie should remain silent and not become involved:

> If he tangles with you, Lennie, we're goin' get the can. Don't make no mistake about that. He's the boss's kid. Look, you try to keep away from him, will you? Don't never speak to him. If he comes in here you move clear to the other side of the room. Will you remember that, Lennie?

In this scene we also meet the old man Candy—crippled and without hope—who cleans out the ranch buildings. His old, smelly dog soon becomes a focus for the attentions of the brutal ranch-hand, Carlson. By contrast, Slim is the admired natural leader of the men: he 'stands and moves with a kind of majesty'.

Act 2, Scene I

Here, right in the middle of the play, a number of conflicts between characters occur which foreshadow the play's final tragedy.

Carlson bullies Candy into letting him take his old dog outside. There is a period of suspense as the characters in the bunkhouse make smalltalk while waiting for the shot that will kill the old dog. The gun used—Carlson's Luger—is the gun that will later be used to kill Lennie.

The dream is reaffirmed between George and Lennie, and Candy makes the dream a real possibility by offering to put in his savings to buy 'the little place'. Then George reveals that he has an actual place in mind.

A crisis develops when Curley, provoked by his wife's absence, becomes determined to fight somebody and finally whirls on Lennie. Lennie, his uncontrollable strength finally unleashed, crushes Curley's hand. The audience now clearly foresees the fatal possibilities of such strength. At the end of the scene, the audience, along with Lennie, realizes that the dream and the plan of 'a little place of their own' has been seriously undermined:

> LENNIE I didn't want no trouble.
>
> GEORGE Come on—I'll go with you.
>
> LENNIE George?
>
> GEORGE What you want?
>
> LENNIE Can I still tend the rabbits, George?

Act 2, Scene II

Crooks is a man who has suffered injustice and indignity because he is a black in a white man's world. This scene explores some of the practical aspects of his plight. For instance, he has to humble himself when Curley's wife walks into his room.

There is also a pause in the action in this scene—almost a gathering of the suspense before the final rush to doom. However, while the suspense gathers, the audience is presented with a further erosion of the dream. Crooks brutally tells Lennie:

> You guys is just kiddin' yourselves. You'll talk about it a hell of a lot, but you won't get no land. You'll be a swamper here until they take you out in a box. Hell, I seen too many guys.

Act 3, Scene I

Lennie has killed his pup in the same way as he killed his mouse and crushed Curley's hand—through the simple overuse of his strength. Next, Curley's wife appears and she insists on talking to Lennie.

Ironically, both the girl and Lennie talk about their dreams of the future—hers in Hollywood and Lennie's on the farm; and both dreams are impossible of fulfilment because both of the dreamers will soon be dead.

Inevitably, Lennie begins to stroke the girl's hair; inevitably she dies at his hands when she panics and screams and Lennie tries to stifle her cries:

> ...I don't want you to yell. You gonna get me in trouble just like George says you will. Now don't you do that. (*She struggles more.*) Don't you go yellin'. (*He shakes her violently. Her neck snaps sideways and she lies still. Looks down at her and cautiously removes his hand from over her mouth.*) I don't wanta hurt you. But George will be mad if you yell....

Lennie, dimly realizing that he has done a terrible thing and fearing George's anger, leaves the barn and the ranch and makes for the place on the riverbank where he and George had camped.

The ranch-hands set out to find Lennie. Curley is intent on shooting him. George, realizing that Lennie will never be brought in alive, steals Carlson's Luger.

Act 3, Scene II

The climax of the play comes when George shoots Lennie, even as he is telling him 'how it's gonna be', with Lennie persuaded that he can see their little place across the river:

GEORGE It's over there. You keep lookin', Lennie. Just keep lookin'.

LENNIE I'm lookin', George. I'm lookin'.

GEORGE That's right. It's gonna be nice there. Ain't gonna be no trouble, no fights. Nobody ever gonna hurt nobody, or steal from 'em. It's gonna be—nice.

LENNIE I can see it, George. I can see it! Right over there! I can see it! (GEORGE *fires.* LENNIE *crumples; falls behind the brush. The voices of the men in the distance.*)

Characters

LENNIE

He is a tireless worker with great size and strength. However, his mind is childlike in its simplicity and innocence.

Lennie is devoted to George and relies on him for direction in his actions, thoughts and attitudes. Lennie's obsession is to pet furry creatures. He also likes to stroke the prettily coloured dresses of women, and their soft hair.

In the play's first scene we are told that Lennie had caused trouble for George and himself in Weed when he had stroked and then clutched and pulled at a girl's pretty red dress till she had begun to scream in terror; this had made him hang on to the dress even more tightly, until George had got to him and forced him to let go and run. They were pursued by townspeople, who believed that Lennie had tried to rape the girl.

Lennie and George share the dream of a small place of their own where they could live and watch their own crops grow. Lennie would be in charge of the rabbits on this dream farm. However, as a condition for the eventual fulfilment of their dream, Lennie must keep out of trouble and leave all the talking to George.

Amongst the ranch-hands of Soledad, Lennie's abnormalities cannot be hidden and he soon faces aggression from Curley (the boss's son) and temptation from his wife. Inevitably, Lennie, unconscious of the immense strength in his hands, kills Curley's wife as his attempt to stroke her hair goes terribly wrong.

GEORGE

In contrast to Lennie, George is 'a smart little guy'. Like Lennie he is an agricultural worker, but unlike Lennie he has the wit and the will to plan to buy a little place where both of them could live and work for themselves. However, he has promised Lennie's Aunt Clara that he would look after Lennie, who unwittingly often gets them into trouble and forces them to move on before they can put any kind of 'stake' together.

Sometimes, as we have seen, George openly expresses the opinion that without the burden of his care for Lennie he could lead a life of successful independence and self-indulgence. However, George also realizes that without Lennie the idea of settling down on a farm would never materialize. He needs Lennie just as Lennie needs him.

George is the play's only truly developing character. We see him change from optimism at the possibility of the dream coming true to frustration and hopelessness when it is destroyed. In their attitude to the dream, George and Lennie complement each other. While Lennie is able to identify with the dream as if it were reality, only George is able to bring it to life with his imaginative powers of description. Lennie *believes* in the reality of the dream, while George can only *hope*. And when George is forced to kill Lennie, he destroys the dream's 'reality' and thus his own hope of ever grasping it.

CANDY

The old stable-hand is treated with indifference by the ranch workers because he is old and crippled. The only thing that keeps him from complete loneliness is his smelly old dog—and even this is taken from him.

However, he too is fired with enthusiasm by the dream and offers to put his life's savings into the project. When the dream is shattered by the discovery of the dead girl Lennie has killed, Candy too tastes true despair:

CANDY (*pleadingly*) You and me can get that little place, can't we, George? You and me can go there and live nice, can't we? Can't we? (CANDY *drops his head and looks down at the hay to indicate that he knows.*)

GEORGE (*shakes his head slowly*) It was somethin' me and him had. (*softly*) I think I knowed it from the very first. I think I knowed we'd never do her. He used to like to hear about it so much. I got fooled to thinkin' maybe we would. (CANDY *starts to speak but doesn't.*)

CROOKS
In this ranch world of Steinbeck's creation, Crooks is a misfit because he is a Negro. Yet he is dignified and intelligent and sees all too clearly the dream's true nature: some similar dream is possessed by every downtrodden person; and although it brings hope, it is also doomed, in nearly every case, to frustration.

SLIM
He is a man skilled with his hands, and the natural leader of the ranch-hands. He is fair in his opinions and judgments of others, and in this he stands in direct contrast to Curley.

CURLEY
He is the boss's son. Because of his antagonistic and aggressive behaviour, and his neglect of his wife, he is the instrument of the tragedy that befalls Lennie and George.

CURLEY'S WIFE
She is pretty and provocative, and acts like a 'tart'. Yet she is also lonely and neglected, and dreams of a career in Hollywood.

CARLSON
This ranch-hand is the embodiment of brutality and insensitivity. Callously countering each of Candy's protests, he shoots the old smelly dog with the very Luger which will later be used to shoot Lennie.

Themes

THE DREAM

One of the main themes of the play is the concept of the 'the dream'. The one shared by George and Lennie is a simple vision, concerned with a small place of their own.

> GEORGE Okay. Some day we're gonna get the jack together and we're gonna have a little house, and a couple of acres and a cow and some pigs and...
>
> LENNIE (*shouting*) And live off the fat of the land! And have rabbits. Go on, George! Tell about what we're gonna have in the garden. And about the rabbits in the cages. Tell about the rain in the winter ... and about the stove and how thick the cream is on the milk, you can hardly cut it. Tell about that, George!
>
> GEORGE Why don't you do it yourself—you know all of it!
>
> LENNIE It ain't the same if I tell it. Go on now. How I get to tend the rabbits.

Whenever any situation becomes threatening, Lennie asks George to describe 'the little place of their own' once again. Within the play, the dream functions to keep George and Lennie together and to provide them with a goal in life. However, it also possesses a wider function— that of presenting the universal element in the play. This becomes apparent when the black stable-hand, Crooks, points out:

> You're nuts. I seen hundreds of men come by on the road and on the ranches, bindles on their back and that same damn thing in their head. Hundreds of 'em. They come and they quit and they go on. And every damn one of 'em is got a little piece of land in his head. And never a goddamn one of 'em gets it. Jus' like heaven. Everybody wants a little piece of land. Nobody never gets to heaven. And nobody gets no land.

By inference, everyone who has to work for a boss has a dream of independence. The trouble with such dreams is that they are hard to fulfil. This is often because some other pleasure or temptation intervenes between the dream and its fulfilment. Lennie was tempted by the woman in Weed, while George was attracted by the 'cat-house'. On these occasions the dream faded a little.

George is also tugged away from the dream by an alternative longing—for a life free of the burden of looking after the simpleminded Lennie: 'When I think of the swell time I could have without you, I go nuts. I never git no peace!'

The dream endures to the final scene of the play, where it ends with the death of Lennie. With the dream and Lennie gone, George *is* independent, but the audience is left with little doubt that George has lost his main interest and support in life.

LONELINESS

Loneliness is another important theme that runs through the play. George expresses it clearly:

> Guys like us that work on ranches is the loneliest guys in the world. They ain't got no family. They don't belong no place. They come to a ranch and work up a stake and then they go in to town and blow their stake. And then the first thing you know they're poundin' their tail on some other ranch. They ain't got nothin' to look ahead to.

George could easily be talking about the old and tired Candy, who only has his old dog; or Crooks, who is shunned because of his race. Curley's wife is lonely too.

In the play, Steinbeck treats all the lonely types with compassion. By contrast, George and Lennie are spared loneliness because they have each other. However, loneliness must finally descend on George as well, when he is forced to kill the person he loves most.

The Other Foot

Story by **Ray Bradbury**

Dramatized by **Martin Walsh**

In *The Other Foot* Ray Bradbury uses a science-fiction setting to explore the problems of racial prejudice.

CAST

Hattie Johnson	First Man
Grant Johnson	Second Man
Alice Johnson	First Woman
Ronald Johnson	Second Woman
Willie Johnson	Kid
Elizabeth Brown	Mayor
Ralph Brown	White Man

Crowd

SCENE I

The planet Mars, sometime in the future. HATTIE JOHNSON *is working in her kitchen. She hears her three children shouting outside.*

Grant Come on, Ma! Hey, Ma, come on! You'll miss it!

Alice Hey, Ma!

Hattie I'm coming. (*She goes outside.*) Where did you hear this rumour?

Grant Up at Jones'. They say a rocket's coming, the first one in twenty years, and a white man is in it!

Ronald What's a white man?

Hattie You'll find out. Yes, indeed, you'll find out.

Ronald Tell us about one, Ma.

Hattie Well, it's been a long time. I was a little girl, you see. That was back in 1975.

Ronald Tell us what happened.

Hattie Well, first of all, they got white hands.

Alice (*laughing*) White hands!

Hattie And they got white arms.

Alice (*laughing harder*) White arms!

Hattie And white faces.

Grant White like this, Ma? (*He throws some dust on his face.*)

Hattie Whiter than that. (*She looks at the sky.*) Maybe you better go inside.

Grant Oh, Ma! We got to watch! Nothing's going to happen, is it?

Hattie I don't know. I got a feeling, is all.

Alice We just want to see the ship and maybe see that white man. What's he like, Ma?

Hattie (*shaking her head*) I don't know.

Alice Tell us some more!

Hattie Well, the white people live on Earth. That's where we all came from, twenty years ago. We just up and came to Mars. We built towns, and here we are. And no men have come up in all that time.

Grant Why didn't they come up?

Hattie Right after we got up here, Earth got in an atom war. They blew each other up. They forgot us. When they finished fighting, they didn't have any rockets. Took them until recently to build more. So here they come now, twenty years later, to visit. (*She begins to walk away.*) You wait here. I'm going down to Elizabeth Brown's house.

The home of RALPH *and* ELIZABETH BROWN. *The Brown family is getting ready to leave in the family car.* HATTIE *appears.*

Elizabeth Hey, there, Hattie! Come on along!

Hattie Where you going?

Elizabeth To see the white man!

Ralph These children never seen one.

Hattie What are you going to do with that white man?

Ralph Do? Just look at him, is all.

Hattie You sure?

Ralph What else can we do?

Hattie I don't know. I just thought there might be trouble.

Elizabeth Trouble?

Hattie You know. (*She pauses.*) You ain't going to lynch him?

Ralph (*laughing*) Bless you, child, no! We're going to shake his hand. (*A car pulls up. It's* WILLIE, *Hattie's husband.*)

Hattie Willie!

Willie (*angry*) What are you doing here? (*He looks at the others.*) You going like a bunch of fools to see that man come in?

Ralph (*smiling*) That appears to be right.

Willie Well, take your guns along. I'm on my way home for mine right now!

Hattie Willie!

Willie What right have they got coming up here this late? Why don't they leave us in peace? Why didn't they blow themselves up on that old world?

Hattie Willie, that's no Christian way to talk.

Willie I'm not feeling Christian. I'm just feeling mean. After all them years of doing what they did to our folks. My mom and dad, and your mom and dad...you remember? You remember what Greenwater, Alabama, was like? You remember how they hanged my father on Knockwood Hill and shot my mother? Or have you got a short memory?

Hattie (*sadly*) I remember.

Willie You remember Dr Phillips and Mr Burton and their big houses? My mother washed their clothes. Dad worked for them until he was old. The thanks he got was being hung by Dr Phillips and Mr Burton. Well, the shoe's on the other foot now. We'll see who gets lynched, who rides the back of streetcars, who gets segregated in shows.

Hattie Oh, Willie, you're talking trouble.

Willie Everybody's thought on this day, thinking it would never be. Well, here's the day, and we can't run away.

Hattie Ain't you going to let the white people live up here?

Willie (*smiling*) Sure. They can come up and work here. All they got to do is live in their own part of town, shine our shoes, and mop up our floors. That's all we ask. And once a week, we hang one or two of them.

Hattie You don't sound human, and I don't like it.

Willie You'll have to get used to it. Let's go find my guns and some rope.

Hattie Oh, Willie! Oh, Willie!

SCENE III

The centre of town. WILLIE JOHNSON *is on the steps of City Hall.* HATTIE *is there, too. Willie has gathered guns and ammunition. A large crowd is around him.*

Hattie Willie! What are you doing? Those people, they all have guns.

Willie I stopped at every house. I told them to get their guns, some paint, and some rope. And here we all are, the welcoming committee! Yes, sir!

(*The crowd shouts to* WILLIE. *They hold up guns and ropes.* WILLIE *holds up a rope tied in the shape of a hangman's noose. The crowd cheers.*)

Hattie Willie! Willie! Have you thought about what you're doing?

Willie That's all I have thought about for twenty years. I was sixteen when I left Earth, and I was glad to leave. There wasn't anything there for me or you or anybody like us. We've had peace here, the first time we ever drew a solid breath. Now, come on.

First man Willie, what are we going to do?

Willie Here's a gun. Here's another. (*He starts passing out guns to the crowd.*) Here's a shotgun. Here's a pistol.

Second man What's the paint for, Willie?

Willie (*smiles*) I'll show you. (*He picks up a can of yellow paint and a brush. Then he walks through the crowd to a bus on the side of the street. He climbs inside and paints a sign that says: 'For Whites—Rear Section.' Part of the crowd cheers as* WILLIE *walks back up the City Hall steps.*)

Second man Let's paint all the buses with signs like that!

Willie Any volunteers? (*Hands go up.*) Get going! (*A group leaves.*) Now who's going to rope off theatre seats, leaving the last two rows for whites? (*Hands go up.*) Go on! (*Another group leaves.*) Let's see now. Oh yes. We got to pass a law this afternoon. There will be no marriages between races!

First woman That's right!

Willie All shoeshine boys quit their jobs today!

Kid I'm quitting right now!

Willie Got to pass a minimum wage law, don't we?

First man Sure!

Willie Pay them white folks at least 10 cents an hour.

Second woman That's right! That's right!

Mayor (*pushing through the crowd*) Now look here, Willie Johnson. Get down off these steps. You're making a mob.

Willie That's the idea, Mayor.

Mayor The same thing you always hated when you were a kid. You're no better than some of those white men you yell about!

Willie This is the other shoe, Mayor, and the other foot. (WILLIE *looks at the faces around him. Some are smiling. Some look unsure. Some are drawing away.*)

Mayor You'll be sorry.

Willie We'll have an election and get a new mayor!

Kid (*pointing to sky*) Here it comes! Here it comes!

SCENE IV

A rocket sweeps across the sky. It circles over a nearby field and lands. The crowd, led by WILLIE, *rushes over. The rocket is still. Then a door slides open, and an old man steps out.*

Kid A white man! It's a white man!

> (*The* WHITE MAN *is tall and very thin. He looks old and tired. He has to lean against the side of the ship because he is so weak. He smiles weakly. The crowd is silent.*)

White man It doesn't matter who I am. I'd just be a name to you, anyhow. (*He pauses.*) It was twenty years ago that you left Earth. That's a long, long time. After you left, the War came. The Third War. It went on for a long time. Until last year. We bombed all the cities of the world. We ruined them all. And when we finished with the big cities, we went to the little cities. We bombed and buried them too. (*He pauses.*) We bombed Natchez, Mississippi.

Crowd Oh!

White man And Columbus, Georgia.

Crowd Oh, no!

White man We bombed Greenwater, Alabama.

Crowd No! No!

> (WILLIE JOHNSON's *head jerks up.* HATTIE *sees an odd look come into his eyes.*)

First man Memphis! Did they burn Memphis?

White man Memphis was blown up.

First man Fourth Street in Memphis?

White man All of it.

First woman Detroit?

White man Gone.

> (*The crowd is remembering now. After twenty years, they are re-membering the places they thought they had forgotten.*)

Second man Philadelphia?

Second woman I remember Philadelphia.

Elizabeth New York City?

Ralph I had a store in Harlem!

White man Harlem was bombed out. And all over, everything is radioactive. Farms, roads, food—radioactive. Everything.

Willie (*softly*) Greenwater, Alabama. That's where I was born.

Hattie (*to* WILLIE) Gone. All of it gone. The man said so.

White man We ruined everything, like fools. We killed millions. I don't think there are more than 500 000 people left in the world—all kinds and types. And out of all the ruin, we found enough metal to build this one rocket. And we came to Mars to seek your help.

Willie (*half aloud*) Knockwood Hill in Greenwater. I remember. (*He grips the hangman's noose.* HATTIE *puts a hand on his arm.*)

White man We've been fools. We've brought the Earth down about our heads. You have rockets here which you haven't tried to use in twenty years. I've come to ask you to use them. To come to Earth and bring the survivors to Mars. We've been stupid and evil. All the Chinese and the Indians and the Russians and the British and the Americans. We're asking to be taken in. There's room for everyone. I've seen your fields from above. Your soil is good. We'll come and work it for you. (*He pauses. There is silence.*) If you want, I'll get into my ship and go back. We won't bother you again. Or we could come here and work for you and do the things you did for us. Clean your houses. Cook your meals. Shine your shoes. Humble ourselves in the sight of God for the things we have done to ourselves, to others, to you.

> (*There is a long silence in the crowd. They stare at the* WHITE MAN. WILLIE *holds his rope. Those around him watch to see what he will do.* HATTIE *suddenly steps forward.*)

Hattie Mister! Do you know Knockwood Hill in Greenwater, Alabama?

White man Just a minute. (*He speaks to someone inside the rocket. A moment later, he is handed a photographic map.*)

Hattie You know the big oak on top of the hill, mister?

White man Yes.

Hattie Is the oak tree still there?

White man It's gone. Blown up. The hill's gone and the oak tree, too. You see? (*He hands the map to* HATTIE. WILLIE *steps forward and grabs the map.*)

Willie That's where my father was shot and hanged.

Hattie (*to* WHITE MAN) Tell me about Greenwater.

White man What do you want to know?

Hattie Dr Phillips. Is he still alive?

   (*The* WHITE MAN *again speaks to someone inside the rocket ship. He is handed the answer.*)

White man Killed in the war.

Hattie And his son?

White man Dead.

Hattie What about their house?

White man Burned. Like all the other houses.

Hattie What about the other big tree on Knockwood Hill?

White man All the trees burned.

Willie What about Mr Burton and his house?

White man No houses at all left, no people.

Willie You know Mrs Johnson's washing shack? My mother's shack? That's where my mother was shot.

White man That's gone, too. Everything's gone. You can see for yourself. (*He holds out the pictures.*)

Willie No. You don't have to show me. (*He slowly drops his rope on the ground.*)

SCENE V

WILLIE and HATTIE have driven home. They are now getting out of their car.

Hattie It's a new start for everyone.

Willie Yes.

Hattie They are taking down the new signs and cutting down the ropes in the theatres.

Willie What happens next is up to all of us. The time for being fools is over. I knew that when he talked. Now the white man is as lonely as we have always been. He's got no home now, just like we didn't have one for so long. Now everything is even. We can start all over again—on the same level.

(The children run out of the house and over to the car.)

Alice Daddy, you see the white man?

Grant You get a good look at him?

Ronald What did he look like, Daddy?

Willie Seems like for the first time today I really seen the white man. I really seen him clear.

CURTAIN

Questions

(1) The *exposition* of a play is the explanation of events that have occurred before the play begins. What past events does Scene I of *The Other Foot* make known to the audience.

(2) What examples of racial prejudice against black people in America are revealed in the play.

(3) Explain why the play is called *The Other Foot*.

(4) What was Willie's attitude to the white race before the rocket landed? Do you think his view was justified? Why?

(5) Why has the white man come to Mars?

(6) What are the white man's feelings about the destruction of the planet Earth?

(7) Did you find the character of (a) Willie (b) the white man, true to life? Explain your viewpoint.

(8) The *plot* is the story of the play. In a few sentences, outline the plot of *The Other Foot*.

(9) What does Willie mean when he says, at the end of the play, 'Seems like for the first time today I really seen the white man. I really seen him clear'?

(10) What do you think is the play's message?

Napoleon's Piano

Spike Milligan

The Goons were a radio comedy team whose zany, rapid-fire humour was backed by an incredible variety of sounds—booted feet running, explosions, bell-chimes sounding at different speeds, and so on. *Napoleon's Piano* is a typical Goon Show script in which puns, ridiculous situations and weird sound-effects are combined to form an explosively—and infectiously—humorous mixture.

Main Characters

Ned Seagoon	Harry Secombe
Grytpype-Thynne	Peter Sellers
Moriarty	Spike Milligan
Mr Henry Crun	Peter Sellers
Miss Minnie Bannister	Spike Milligan
Eccles	Spike Milligan
Major Denis Bloodnok	Peter Sellers
Justin Eidelburger	Peter Sellers
Throat	Spike Milligan
Yakamoto	Peter Sellers
Bluebottle	Peter Sellers

Others

The Ray Ellington Quartet
Max Geldray
Announcer: Wallace Greenslade (Bill)
FX—sound-effects
Grams—recorded sound

INTRODUCTION

Tricked into signing a contract to bring over to England the very piano that Napoleon played at Waterloo, Neddie Seagoon stows away on a boat to France. A chance meeting in the disreputable Café Tom with piano robbery specialist Justin Eidelburger seems to solve all Neddie's problems—but others, too, are after Napoleon's piano. With £10 000 at stake, the only solution is to sail the instrument back to England—a voyage fraught with peril...

Bill This is the BBC Home Service.

Grams OUTBREAK OF PEOPLE SIGHING.

Bill Oh come, come, dear listeners—it's not that bad—

Harry Of course not—come, Mr Greenslade, tell them the good news.

Bill Ladies and gentlemen, we now have the extraordinary talking-type wireless 'Goon Show'.

Grams SCREAMS OF ANGUISH. PEOPLE RUNNING AWAY.

Harry Mmm—is the popularity waning? Ahemm.

Spike Ho ho ho, fear not, Neddie lad—we'll jolly them up with a merry laughing-type joke show. Stand prepared for the story of 'Napoleon's Piano'.

Grams VERY OLD RECORD OF A PIANO SOLO (MARSEIL-LAISE).

Seagoon Napoleon's piano—the story starts in the bad old days, back in April 1955. It was early one morning. Breakfast had just been served at Beauleigh Manor—I was standing at the window, looking in. With the aid of a telescope, I was reading the paper on the breakfast table—when suddenly an advertisement caught my eye. It said—

Grytpype-Thynne (*distort*) Will pay anybody five pounds to remove piano from one room to another. Apply, The Bladders, Harpyapipe, Quants.

Seagoon In needle nardle noo time I was at the address and with the aid of a piece of iron and a lump of wood—I made this sound.

FX THREE KNOCKS WITH IRON KNOCKER ON SOLID OAK DOOR.

Moriarty Sapristi Knockoes—when I heard that sound I ran down the stairs and with aid of a door knob and two hinges I made *this* sound.

FX DOOR KNOB BEING HEAVILY AGITATED FOLLOWED BY FAST SQUEAKY HINGES AS DOOR OPENS.

Seagoon Ah, good morning.

Moriarty Good morning? Just a moment.

FX FURIOUS DIALLING.

Moriarty Hello, Air Ministry Roof? Weather report. Yes? Yes, thank you.

FX PHONE DOWN.

Moriarty You're perfectly right—it is a good morning.

Seagoon Thanks. My name is Neddie Seagoon.

Moriarty What a memory you have.

Seagoon Needle nardle noo. I've come to move the piano.

Moriarty (*insane laugh*) Come in.

Seagoon (*insane laugh*) Thanks.

Moriarty You must excuse the mess but we've got the Socialists in.

Grytpype-Thynne (*approach*) Oh Moriarty, can I borrow a shoe? Mine's worn out—oh you have company.

Moriarty Ahh ah—these three men are called Neddie Seagoon. He's come in answer to our ad.

Grytpype-Thynne Ohhhh—come in—sit down. Have a gorilla.

Seagoon No thanks, I'm trying to give them up.

Grytpype-Thynne Splendid. Now, Neddie, here's the money for moving the piano—there, five pounds in fivers.

Seagoon Five pounds for moving a piano? Ha ha—this is money for old rope.

Grytpype-Thynne Is it? I'd have thought you'd have bought something more useful.

Seagoon Oh no—I have simple tastes. Now, where's this piano?

Grytpype-Thynne Just a moment. First, would you sign this contract in which you guarantee to move the piano from one room to another for five pounds.

Seagoon Of course I'll sign—have you any ink?

Grytpype-Thynne Here's a fresh bottle.

Seagoon (*drinks*) ...ahhhhhhhh. Gad, I was thirsty.

Moriarty Sapristi Nuckoes—do you always drink ink?

Seagoon Only in the mating season.

Moriarty Shall we dance?

Grams OLD 1929 SCRATCHY GUY LOMBARDO RECORD OF 'LOVER' WALTZ.

Seagoon You dance divinely.

Grytpype-Thynne Next dance please! Now, Neddie, just sign the contract on the side of this horse.

Seagoon Certainly.

FX SCRATCHING OF PEN UNDER SEAGOON AS HE SPEAKS NEXT LINE.

Seagoon Neddie—Seagoon—A.G.G.

Moriarty What's A.G.G. for?

Seagoon For the kiddies to ride on...get it? A gee-gee—ha ha ha ha— (*Agonized silence.*)

Grytpype-Thynne You're sure you won't have a gorilla?

Seagoon No thanks, I've just put one out. Now, which room is this piano in?

Grytpype-Thynne Ahemm. It's in the Louvre.

Seagoon Strange place to put a piano.

Grytpype-Thynne We refer to the Louvre Museum, Paris.

Seagoon What what what what what? Ahhhh, I've been tricked—ahhhh.

FX THUD OF UNCONSCIOUS BODY HITTING GROUND.

Moriarty For the benefit of people without television—he's fainted.

Grytpype-Thynne Don't waste time—just open his jacket—get the weight of his cruel wallet off his chest—mmm—found anything in his pockets?

Moriarty Yes—a signed photograph of Neddie Seagoon, a press cutting from the Theatre, Bolton, a gramophone record of Gigli mowing the lawn, a photo of Gigli singing, and a half share in Kim Novak.

Grytpype-Thynne He's still out cold—see if *this* brings him round.

FX PENNY THROWN ON CONCRETE FLOOR.

Seagoon Thank you, lady. (*Sings.*) Comrades comrades—ever since —oh—where—where am I?

Grytpype-Thynne England!

Seagoon What number?

Grytpype-Thynne Seven A. Have a gorilla.

Seagoon No, they hurt my throat. Wait! *Now* I remember! You've trapped me into bringing back a piano from France for only five pounds.

Grytpype-Thynne You signed the contract, Neddie—now, get that piano or we suc you for breach of contract.

Seagoon Ahhhhhhhh. (*Going off.*)

FX DOOR SLAMS.

Grytpype-Thynne Gad, Moriarty, if he brings that piano back we'll be in the money. That piano is worth ten thousand pounds.

Moriarty How do you know?

Grytpype-Thynne I've seen its bank book. Do you know, that's the very piano Napoleon played at Waterloo. With the moolah we get on that we can have a holiday. (*Sings.*)

Both April in Paris—we've found a Charlie.

Bill I say—poor Neddie must have been at his wits' end! Faced with the dilemma of having to bring Napoleon's piano back from Paris, he went to the Foreign Office for advice on passports and visas.

FX BITS AND PIECES DROPPING DOWN.

Crun & Minnie (*Nattering away.*)

Crun Ohh dee deee—dee, X9?

Minnie (*off*) X9 answering—who's that calling, buddy?

Crun It's me—the Foreign Secretary. Do you know where the key to the secret documents safe is?

Minnie Yes—its with the charlady.

Crun Do you think that's wise—she has access to all the vital British secret documents.

Minnie She can't read them, buddy, she only speaks Russian.

Crun That's a bit of luck—

FX KNOCKS ON DOOR.

Crun Ohh, that might be one of England's strolling Prime Ministers of no fixed abode.

Minnie Coming, Anthonyyy—coming...

Crun Tell him we're very sorry.

Minnie Sorry for what?

Crun Oh, mmm—make something up.

FX DOOR OPENS.

Minnie Ahh, we're very sorry, Anthony, we—ohh, you're not the Prime Minister.

Seagoon Not yet, but it's just a matter of time. My name is Neddie Seagoon.

Crun Want to buy a white paper—

Seagoon No thanks, I'm trying to give them up.

Crun So are we—

Seagoon I want a few particulars. You see, I want to leave the country...

Crun He's going to Russia! Stop him, Min—get him!

Minnie Hit him, Hen...

Grams MIX IN GREAT BATTLE. ALL STOPS SUDDENLY.

Crun There! Let that be a lesson to you—get out.

Seagoon I will, but not before I hear musical saboteur Max Geldray.

Max & Orchestra 'AIN'T MISBEHAVIN'.

    (*Applause.*)

Bill Seagoon was confused—it seems that the cheapest method of getting to Paris was to stowaway to France on board a Channel steamer.

Grams SHIP'S TELEGRAPH RINGING. SEAGULLS—WASH OF SHIP'S WAKE.

Seagoon Down in the dark hold I lay—alone—so I thought...

Eccles (*off—sings*) I talk to der trees—dat's why they put me away...

Seagoon The singer was a tall ragged idiot—he carried a plasticine gramophone, and wore a metal trilby.

Eccles Hello, shipmate. Where you goin'?

Seagoon Nowhere. I think it's safer to stay on the ship until we reach Calais.

Eccles You going to Calais?

Seagoon Yes.

Eccles What a coincidence. Dat's where the ship's going—ain't you lucky.

Seagoon Here—have a gorilla.

Eccles Oh, thanks!

Grams GORILLA FIGHTING ANOTHER GORILLA (IF YOU CAN'T GET THE RIGHT SOUND TRY TWO LIONS). ALL STOPS ABRUPTLY.

Eccles Hey—dese gorillas are strong. Have one of my monkeys—they're milder.

Seagoon And so for the rest of the voyage we sat quietly smoking our monkeys. At Calais I left the idiot singer. By sliding down the ship's rope in French I avoided detection. Late that night I checked into a French hotel. Next morning I sat in my room eating my breakfast when suddenly through the window a fork on the end of a long pole appeared—it tried to spear my kipper.

Bloodnok (*off—strained*) Aeiough.

Seagoon Who the blazes are you, sir?

Bloodnok Aeioughhh—oh, oh, I'm sorry, I was fishing.

Seagoon Fishing? This is the thirty-fourth floor.

Bloodnok Oh, the river must have dropped.

Seagoon Who are you, sir?

Bloodnok I've got it on a bit of paper here—ah yes—Major Denis Bloodnok, late of the Third Disgusting Fusiliers—OBE, MT, MT, MT, MT, and MT.

Seagoon What are all those MTs for?

Bloodnok I get tuppence on each of 'em—aeioughhh.

Seagoon You're acting suspiciously suspicious—I've a good mind to call the manager.

Bloodnok Call him—I am unafraid!

Seagoon Mmmm—no! Why should *I* call him?

Bloodnok Then *I* will—manager?

FX DOOR OPENS.

Spike (*French*) Oui, monsieur?

Bloodnok Throw this man out.

Seagoon Ahhhhh. (*Thrown out.*)

FX DOOR SLAMS.

Bloodnok Now for breakfast—see, kippers—toast de da dee deeee. What's this coming through the window—flatten me krurker and nosh me schlappers—it's a fork, on a pole, and its trying to take the kipper off me plate—I say, who's that?

Seagoon I'm sorry, I was just fishing.

Bloodnok What, you! I've a good mind to call the manager.

Seagoon Go on then, call him.

Bloodnok No, why should I?

Seagoon Then I'll call him. (Watch me turn the tables, listeners.) Manager?

FX DOOR OPENS.

Spike Oui, Monsieur?

Bloodnok Throw this man out of my room.

Seagoon Ahhhh. (*Thrown out.*)

FX DOOR SLAMS.

Seagoon Alone in Paris—I went down the notorious Café Tom. Proprietor: Maurice Ponk.

Grams 'SOUS LES TOITS DE PARIS'.

Seagoon Inside, the air was filled with gorilla smoke—I was looking for a man who might specialize in piano robberies from the Louvre.

FX WHOOSH.

Eidelburger Gute evenung. You are looking for a man who might specialize in piano robberies from the Louvre?

Seagoon How do you know?

Eidelburger I was listening on the radio and I heard you say it.

Seagoon Good—pull up a chair. Sit down.

Eidelburger No thanks—I'd rather stand.

Seagoon Very well, stand on a chair. Garcon!

Throat Oui?

Seagoon Two glasses of English port-type cooking sherry, and vite.

Throat Two glasses of sherry and vite coming up.

Seagoon Now—name?

Eidelburger I am Justin Eidelburger.

Seagoon Oh. Have a gorilla.

Eidelburger No zanks—I only smoke baboons.

Seagoon This piano we must steal, it's the one Napoleon played at Waterloo.

Eidelburger That will be a very sticky job.

Seagoon Why?

Eidelburger It's just been varnished—he ha, zer German joke.

Seagoon Zer English silence.

Eidelburger Now, Mr Snzeegroon—meet me outside the Louvre at midnight on the stroke of two.

Seagoon Right.

Seagoon True to my word, I was there dead on three.

Eidelburger You're late.

Seagoon I'm sorry—my legs were slow.

Eidelburger You must buy another pair. Zis here is my oriental assistant, Yakamoto.

Yakamoto I am very honoured to meet you. Oh boy.

Seagoon What does this oriental creep know about piano thieving?

Eidelburger Nothing—he's just here to lend colour to the scene. Now, Neddie, this is a map-plan of the Louvre and the surrounding streets.

FX LONG UNFOLDING.

Seagoon You take one end.

FX UNFOLDING. THE MAP BEING UNFOLDED CONTINUES FOR A WHOLE MINUTE.

Seagoon It's big, isn't it?

Eidelburger (*in the distance*) Yes, it is! This bit here shows the Rue de la Paix.

Seagoon Good heavens, you're miles away—walk straight up that street—take the second on the left—I'll be waiting for you.

FX TAXI PULLS UP.

Eidelburger I took a taxi—it was too far. Now—we disperse and meet again in the Hall of Mirrors, when the clock strikes twinge. At midnight we strike.

FX BIG BEN STRIKES TWELVE — AT VARYING SPEEDS.

Seagoon Shhhhhh.

Eidelburger Is that you, Seagoon?

Seagoon Yes.

Eidelburger Good.

FX HAND BELL.

Bill (*French*) Every bodee out, closing time—everyone back to zere own bed.

Seagoon Quick, hide behind this pane of glass.

Eidelburger But you can see through it.

Seagoon Not if you close your eyes.

Eidelburger Gerblunden, you're right—are all your family clever?

Seagoon Only the Crustaceans.

Bill Everybody out—and that goes for you idiots with your eyes shut behind that sheet of glass.

Seagoon You fool, you can't see us.

Bill Yes, I can—get out or I'll call the police.

Eidelburger Why, you anti-Bismarck swine, I shoot you.

Seagoon No, not through the glass—you'll break it. First I'll make a hole in it.

FX PANE OF GLASS SHATTERING TO PIECES.

Seagoon *Now* shoot through that.

FX PISTOL SHOT.

Bill You've killed me—now I'll get the sack. Ooooooo—ohhhh—ohhhhh—I die—I fall to the ground—ahhh meee—ahh my—ohhh ohhh I die, killed by death!

Seagoon Never mind—swallow this tin of Lifo guaranteed to return you to life—recommended by all corpses and Wilfred Pickles. Forward, Ray Ellington and his music!

Quartet 'BLOODSHOT EYES'. (*Applause.*)

Bill Part Two—in which our heroes are discovered creeping up to the piano.

Eidelburger Shhh, Neddie—there's someone under Napoleon's piano, trying to lift it by himself.

Seagoon He must be mad.

Eccles (*sings*) I talk to der trees. . .

Seagoon I was right. Eccles, what are you doing out after feeding time?

Eccles I signed a contract that fooled me into taking dis piano back to England.

Seagoon What? You must be an idiot to sign a contract like that—now, help me get this piano back to England. Together, lift!

Omnes (*Grunts, groans.*)

Seagoon No, no, it's too heavy—put it down.

Eccles Here, it's lighter when you let go.

Seagoon I have an idea—we'll saw the legs off. Eccles, give me that special piano-leg saw that you just happen to be carrying. Now...

FX SAWING.

Eccles (*sings over sawing*) I talk to der trees—dat's why dey put me away—

Seagoon There! I've sawn all four legs off.

Eidelburger Strange—first time I've known of a piano with four legs.

Eccles Hey—I keep falling down—ohhhhhh.

Seagoon Sorry, Eccles—here, swallow this tin of Leggo, the wonder leg-grower recommended by all good centipedes.

Bill Sweating and struggling, they managed to get Napoleon's piano into the cobbled court.

Seagoon (*dry*) Which was more than Napoleon ever did.

Bloodnok Halt—hand over le piano in the name of France!

Seagoon Bloodnok, take off that kilt, we know you're not French.

Bloodnok One step nearer and I'll strike with this fork on the end of a pole.

Seagoon You do, and I'll attack with this kipper.

Bloodnok I've a good mind to call the manager.

Seagoon Call the manager.

Bloodnok No, why should I—

Seagoon Very well, I'll call him (I'll get him this time). Manager?

FX DOOR OPENS.

Spike Oui, Monsieur?

Seagoon Throw this man out.

Spike (*Raspberry*.)

FX DOOR SHUTS.

Seagoon Nurse? Put the screen around that bed.

Bloodnok Seagoon, you must let me have that piano—you see, I foolishly signed a contract that forces me to—

Seagoon Yes, yes, we know—we're all in the same boat. We have no money, so the only way to get the piano back to England is to float it back. All together into the English Channel—hurl.

FX PAUSE—SPLASH.

Seagoon All aboard—cast off.

Orchestra SEASCAPE MUSIC.

Grams HEAVY SEAS. GULLS.

Seagoon The log of Napoleon's Piano. December the third—Second week in English Channel. Very seasick—no food—no water. Bloodnok down with the lurgi. Eccles up with the lark.

Bloodnok Ohhh—Seagoon—take over the keyboard, I can't steer any more.

Seagoon Eccles? Take over the keyboard.

Eccles I can't. I haven't brought my music.

Seagoon You'll have to busk for the next three miles.

Bloodnok Wait! Great galloping crabs, look in the sky.

Grams HELICOPTER.

Bloodnok It's a recording of a helicopter—saved!

Seagoon By St George—saved—yes. For those of you who haven't got television, they're lowering a man on a rope.

Bluebottle Yes, it is I, Sea Ranger Bluebontle. Signals applause.

Grams APPLAUSE.

Bluebottle Cease—I have drunk my fill of the clapping.

Seagoon Little stinking Admiral, you have arrived in the nick of time.

Bluebottle Silence—I must do my duty—hurriedly runs up cardboard Union Jack. I now claim this island for the British Empire and Lord Beaverbrook, the British patriot—thinks, I wonder why he lives in France. Three cheers for the Empire—hip hip hooray—hip hip . . .

Seagoon Have you come to save us?

Bluebottle Hooray! Rockall is now British—cements in brass plate—steps back to salute.

Grams SPLASH.

Bluebottle Help! I'm in the dreaded drowning-type water.

Seagoon Here, grab this fork on the end of a pole.

Bluebottle It's got a kipper on it.

Seagoon Yes, you *must* keep your strength up.

Bluebottle But I'm drowning.

Seagoon There's no need to go hungry as well. Take my hand.

Bluebottle Why? Are you a stranger in paradise?

Seagoon Heave. . .for those without television, I've pulled him back on the piano.

Bluebottle Piano? This is not a piano—this is Rockall.

Seagoon This is Napoleon's piano.

Bluebottle No, no—this is Rockall—we have tooked it because it is in the area of the rocket testing range.

Seagoon I've never heard. . .

FX ROCKET WHOOSH. EXPLOSION.

Bill What do you think, dear listeners—were they standing on Rockall or was it Napoleon's piano? Send your suggestions to anybody but us. For those who would have preferred a happy ending, here it is.

FX DOOR OPENS.

Harry Gwendeloine?? Gwendoline.

Peter John, John darling—

Harry I've found work, darling. I've got a job.

Peter Oh John, I'm so glad for you—what is it?

Harry All I've got to do is to move a piano from one room to another.

Moriarty (*Mad laugh.*)

Orchestra SIGNATURE TUNE: UP AND DOWN FOR:

Bill That was The Goon Snow—a BBC recorded programme featuring Peter Sellers, Harry Secombe and Spike Milligan with the Ray Ellington Quartet and Max Geldray. The Orchestra was conducted by Wally Stott. Script by Spike Milligan. Announcer: Wallace Greenslade. The programme produced by Peter Eton.

Orchestra SIGNATURE TUNE TO END.

(*Applause.*)

Max & Orchestra 'CRAZY RHYTHM' PLAYOUT.

Questions

(1) Goon Show humour lies in the crazy dialogue, the weird sound-effects and the impossible situations. How is humour contributed by each of these elements in the opening twelve lines of *Napoleon's Piano*?

(2) The Goon Shows have been called 'the ultimate in pure radio'. Why are they better suited to the medium of radio than to that of television?

(3) A simple but contrived misunderstanding between Grytpype-Thynne and Seagoon underlies the whole anguishing movement of Napoleon's piano from France to England. What is this misunderstanding?

(4) The repetition of an idiotic offer is another Goon device for producing humour. What examples of this kind of repetition can you find in the script of *Napoleon's Piano*?

(5) The Goon Shows as a whole have been called 'contagious verbal slapstick'. What is meant by this? In your opinion, is this an adequate characterization of the Goons? Give reasons for your answer.

Fawlty Towers

John Cleese and Connie Booth

Fawlty Towers has provided John Cleese with his popular comedy TV role as Basil Fawlty, owner of the horrendously mismanaged Fawlty Towers Hotel. The final part of the script for the episode 'The Germans', reproduced here, finds Basil Fawlty still suffering the after-effects of being knocked out during a hotel fire. Now, he awaits the arrival of some German guests....

CAST

Basil Fawlty	Polly
Miss Tibbs	German Lady
Miss Gatsby	First German
Manuel	Second German
Elderly German	Doctor
The Major	

Basil (*masterfully*) Manuel!

Miss Tibbs Oh, Mr Fawlty!

Basil Ah, good evening.

Miss Tibbs Are you all right now?

Basil Perfectly, thank you. (*to Manuel*) Take this to the room please, dear.

(**MANUEL** *takes the case, somewhat taken aback.*)

Miss Gatsby Are you sure you're all right?

Basil Perfectly, thank you. Right as rain.

(*He makes his way a little unsteadily towards the desk, but misses. He reappears and goes correctly to his position behind the desk.* MANUEL *rushes up.*)

Manuel You OK?

Basil Fine, thank you dear. You go and have a lie-down.

Manuel Que?

Basil Ah, there you are. Would you take my case ... how did you get that?

Manuel What?

Basil Oh never mind...take it...take it upstairs!

Manuel Que?

Basil Take it...take it...

Manuel (*staring*) I go get Polly.

Basil I've already had one. Take it!

Manuel What?

Basil Take it, take it now...(MANUEL *hurries off.*) Tch! The people I have to deal with...

(*He looks up to see a couple approaching the desk. He beams at them.*)

Elderly German Sprechen Sie Deutsch?

Basil ...Beg your pardon?

Elderly German Entschuldigen Sie, bitte, können Sie Deutsch sprechen?

Basil ...I'm sorry, could you say that again?

German lady You speak German?

Basil Oh, German! I'm sorry, I thought there was something wrong with you. Of course, the Germans!

German lady You speak German?

Basil Well...er...a little...I get by.

German lady Ein bisschen.

Elderly German Ah—wir wollen ein Auto mieten.

Basil (*nodding helpfully*) Well, why not?

Elderly German Bitte.

Basil Yes, a little bit tricky...Would you mind saying it again?

German lady Please?

Basil Could you repeat...amplify...you know, reiterate? Come on! Yes?

Elderly German Wir...

Basil Wır?...Yes, well we'll come back to that.

Elderly German ...Wollen...

Basil (*to himself*) Vollen...Voluntary?

Elderly German Ein Auto mieten.

Basil Owtoe ... out to ... Oh, I see! You're volunteering to go out to get some meat. Not necessary! *We have meat here*!

(*Pause; the couple are puzzled.*)

Basil (*shouting very loudly*) Vee haf meat hier...in ze buildink! (*He mimes a cow's horns.*)

Basil Moo. (POLLY *comes in.*)

Basil Ah, Polly, just explaining about the meat.

Polly Oh! We weren't expecting you.

Basil Oh, weren't you? (*Hissing through his teeth.*) They're Germans. Don't mention the war...

Polly I see. Well, Mrs Fawlty said you were going to have a rest for a couple of days, you know, in the hospital.

Basil (*firmly*) Idle hands get in the way of the devil's work, Fawlty. Now...

Polly Right, well, why don't you have a lie–down, and I can deal with this.

Basil Yes, yes, good idea, good idea Elsie. Yes. Bit of a headache, actually...

Miss Tibbs We don't think you're well, Mr Fawlty.

Basil Well perhaps not, but I'll live longer than you.

Miss Gatsby You must have hurt yourself.

Basil My dear woman, a blow on the head like that...is worth two in the bush.

Miss Tibbs Oh, we know...but it was a nasty knock.

Basil Mmmmmmmm...Would you like one?

(*He hits the reception bell impressively.*)

Basil Next please.

(*At this moment four more guests come down the stairs.*)

Basil (*a hoarse whisper*) Polly! Polly! Are these Germans too?

Polly Oh yes, but I can deal...

Basil (*urgent and conspiratorial*) Right, right. Here's the plan. I'll stand there and ask them if they want something to drink before the war...before their lunch...*don't mention the war!*

(*He moves in front of the guests, bows, and mimes eating and drinking.*)

1st German Can we help you?

(BASIL *gives a startled jump.*)

Basil Ah...you speak English.

1st German Of course.

Basil Ah, wonderful! Wunderbar! Ah—please allow me to introduce myself—I am the owner of Fawlty Towers, and may I welcome your war, your wall, you wall, *you all*...and hope that your stay will be a happy one. Now would you like to eat first, or would you like a drink before the war...ning that, er, trespassers will be—er, er,—tied up with piano wire ... Sorry! Sorry! (*Clutches his thigh.*) Bit of trouble with the old leg...got a touch of shrapnel in the war ... *Korean*, Korean War, sorry, Korean.

1st German Thank you, we will eat now.

(BASIL *bows graciously and ushers the party into the dining room.*)

Basil Oh good, please do allow me. May I say how pleased we are to have some Europeans here now that we are on the Continent...

(*They all go in.* POLLY *meanwhile is on the phone.*)

Polly Can I speak to Doctor Fin please?

(*Cue to dining room;* BASIL *is taking the orders.*)

Basil I didn't vote for it myself, quite honestly, but now that we're in I'm determined to make it work, so I'd like to welcome you all to Britain. The plaice is grilled, but that doesn't matter, there's life in the old thing yet...No, wait a moment, I got a bit confused there. Oh yes, the plaice is grilled...in fact the whole room's a bit warm, isn't it...I'll open a window, have a look...And the veal chop is done with rosemary...that's funny, I thought she'd gone to Canada...and is delicious and nutritious...in fact it's *veally* good...*veally* good?

1st German The veal is good?

Basil Yes, doesn't matter, doesn't matter, never mind.

2nd German May we have two eggs mayonnaise please?

Basil Certainly, why not, why not indeed? We are all friends now, eh?

1st German (*heavily*) A prawn cocktail...

Basil ...All in the Market together, old differences forgotten, and no need at all to mention the war...Sorry!...Sorry, what was that again?

1st German A prawn cocktail.

Basil Oh prawn, that was it. When you said *prawn* I thought you said war. Oh, the war! Oh yes—completely slipped my mind, yes, I'd forgotten all about it. Hitler, Himmler, and all that lot, I'd completely forgotten it, just like that. (*He snaps his fingers.*)...Sorry, what was it again?

1st German (*with some menace*) A prawn cocktail...

Basil Oh yes, Eva Prawn...and Goebbels too, he's another one I can hardly remember at all.

2nd German And ein *pickled herring*!

Basil Hermann Goering, yes, yes...and von Ribbentrop, that was another one.

1st German And four cold meat salads please.

Basil Certainly, well I'll just get your hors d'oeuvres...hors d'oeuvres vich must be obeyed at all times without question ...Sorry! Sorry!

Polly Mr Fawlty, will you call your wife immediately?

Basil Sybil!!...Sybil!!...she's in the hospital you silly girl!

Polly Yes, call her there!

Basil I can't, I've got too much to do. Listen...(*He whispers through his teeth.*) Don't mention the war...I mentioned it once, but I think I got away with it all right...(*He returns to his guests.*) So it's all forgotten now and let's hear no more about it. So ... that's two egg mayonnaise, a prawn Goebbels, a Hermann Goering and four Colditz salads ... no, wait a moment, I got a bit confused there, sorry...

(*One of the German ladies has begun to sob.*)

Basil I got a bit confused because everyone keeps mentioning the war, so could you please...

(*The* 1ST GERMAN, *who is comforting the lady, looks up angrily.*)

Basil What's the matter?

1st German It's all right.

Basil Is there something wrong?

1st German Will you please stop talking about the war?

Basil Me? You started it!

1st German We did not start it.

Basil Yes you did, you invaded Poland...Here, this'll cheer you up, you'll like this one, there's this woman, she's completely stupid, she can never remember anything, and her husband's in a bomber over Berlin...

(*The lady howls.*)

Basil Sorry! Sorry! Here, here, she'll love this one...

1st German Will you leave her alone?

Basil No, this is a scream, I've never seen anyone not laugh at this!

1st German (*shouts*) Go away!

Basil Look, she'll love it—she's German!

(*Places a finger under his nose preparatory to doing his Hitler impression.*)

Polly No, Mr Fawlty!!...do Jimmy Cagney instead!

Basil What?

Polly *Jimmy Cagney!*

Basil Jimmy Cagney?

Polly You know...'You dirty rat...'

Basil I can't do Jimmy Cagney!

Polly Please try...'I'm going to get you...'

Basil Shut up! Here, watch—who's this, then?

(*He places his finger across his upper lip and does his Führer party piece. His audience is stunned.*)

Basil I'll do the funny walk...

(*He performs an exaggerated goose-step out into the hall, does an about-turn, and marches back into the dining room. Both German women are by now in tears, and both men on their feet.*)

Both Germans *Stop it!!*

Basil I'm trying to cheer her up, you stupid Kraut!

1st German It's not funny for her.

Basil *Not funny?* You're joking!

1st German Not funny for her, not for us, not for any German people.

Basil (*amazed*) You have absolutely no sense of humour, do you!

2nd German (*shouting*) This is not funny!

Basil *Who won the bloody war, anyway?*

(*The* DOCTOR *comes in, with a hypodermic needle ready.*)

Doctor Mr Fawlty, you'll be all right—come with me.

Basil Fine.

(*Suddenly* BASIL *dashes off through the kitchen, out across into the lobby and into the office. He spots the medical men in pursuit and leaves by the other door into reception. He meets* MANUEL *under the moose's head, and thumps him firmly on the head;* MANUEL *sinks to his knees. The moose's head falls off the wall;* BASIL *is knocked cold. The moose's head lands on* MANUEL. THE MAJOR, *entering from the bar, is intrigued.*)

Manuel (*speaking through the moose's head*) Oooooh, he hit me on the head...

The Major (*slapping the moose's nose*) No, you hit *him* on the head. You *naughty* moose.

1st German (*sadly*) However did they win?

Questions

(1) Discuss how misunderstanding among characters is an important ingredient of the humour of this scene from *Fawlty Towers*.

(2) How does Basil Fawlty manage to create conflict with the German guests almost from the moment of first contact with them?

(3) What kind of humour does Manuel contribute?

(4) Characterization, dialogue and setting work together to produce memorable comedy in *Fawlty Towers*. Explain how each of these adds to the total effect of this kind of comedy.

(5) In your opinion, which is likely to be the more successful medium for the production of this sketch—TV or radio? Give reasons for your choice.

Bookshop

John Cleese and Graham Chapman

The two characters in this TV and radio sketch are played by actors John Cleese (of *Fawlty Towers*) and Marty Feldman.

Cleese Good morning, sir.

Feldman Good morning, can you help me? Do you have a copy of *Thirty Days in the Samarkand Desert with a Spoon* by A.J. Elliott?

Cleese No, we haven't got it in stock, sir.

Feldman How about *A Hundred-and-One Ways to Start a Monsoon*?

Cleese By...?

Feldman An Indian gentleman whose name eludes me for the moment.

Cleese Well, I don't know the book, sir.

Feldman Not to worry, not to worry. Can you help me with *David Copperfield*?

Cleese Ah, yes, Dickens.

Feldman No.

Cleese I beg your pardon?

Feldman No, Edmund Wells.

Cleese I think you'll find Charles Dickens wrote *David Copperfield*.

Feldman No, Charles Dickens wrote *David Copperfield* with two 'p's—this is *David Coperfield* with *one* 'p' by Edmund Wells.

Cleese Well in that case we don't have it.

Feldman Um—funny, you've got a lot of books here.

Cleese Yes, we do have quite a lot of books here, but we don't have *David Coperfield* with one 'p' by Edmund Wells. We only have *David Copperfield* with two 'p's by Charles Dickens.

Feldman Pity—it's more thorough than the Dickens.

Cleese More *thorough*?

Feldman Yes—I wonder if it's worth having a look through all the *David Copperfields*...

Cleese No, no, I'm quite sure that all our *David Copperfields* have two 'p's.

Feldman Probably, but the original by Edmund Wells also had two 'p's—it was after that that they ran into copyright difficulties.

Cleese No, I'm quite sure that all our *David Copperfields* with two 'p's are by Charles Dickens.

Feldman How about *Great Expectations*?

Cleese Ah yes, we have that...

Feldman That's *G-r-a-t-e Expectations*. Also by Edmund Wells.

Cleese Well in that case we don't have it—we don't have anything by Edmund Wells, actually—he's not very popular.

Feldman Not *Nicholas Nickleby*? That's *K-n-i-c-k-e-r, Knickerless*?

Cleese No.

Feldman Or *Christmas Carol* with a 'q'?

Cleese No, definitely not.

Feldman Sorry to trouble you.

Cleese Not at all.

Feldman I wonder if you have a copy of *Rarnaby Budge*?

Cleese No, as I say, we're right out of Edmund Wells.

Feldman No, not Edmund Wells—Charles Dickens.

Cleese Charles Dickens?

Feldman Yes.

Cleese You mean *Barnaby Rudge*.

Feldman No, *Rarnaby Budge* by Charles Dickens—that's Dikkens with two 'k's, the well-known Dutch author.

Cleese No, no—we don't have *Rarnaby Budge* by Charles Dikkens with two 'k's the well-known Dutch author, and perhaps to save time I should add right away that we don't have *Carnaby Fudge* by Darles Tikkens, nor *Stickwick Stapers* by Miles Pikkens with four 'm's and a silent 'q', why don't you try the chemist?

Feldman I have—they sent me here.

Cleese Did they.

Feldman I wonder if you have *The Amazing Adventures of Captain Gladys Stoat-pamphlet and Her Intrepid Spaniel Stig among the Giant Pygmies of Corsica,* Volume Two?

Cleese No, no, we don't have that one—funny, we've got quite a lot of books here.

Feldman Yes, haven't you.

Cleese Well, I mustn't keep you standing around all day...

Feldman I wonder...

Cleese No, no, we haven't—I'm closing for lunch now...

Feldman But I thought I saw it over there.

Cleese Where?

Feldman Over there.

Cleese What?

Feldman Olsen's *Standard Book of British Birds.*

Cleese Olsen's *Standard Book of British Birds?*

Feldman Yes.

Cleese O-l-s-e-n?

Feldman Yes.

Cleese B-i-r-d-s?

Feldman Yes.

Cleese Yes, well we do have that one.

Feldman The expurgated version, of course.

Cleese I'm sorry, I didn't quite catch that.

Feldman The expurgated version.

Cleese The *expurgated* version of Olsen's *Standard Book of British Birds*?

Feldman Yes. It's that one without the gannet.

Cleese The one without the gannet? They've all got the gannet—it's a standard bird, the gannet—it's in all the books.

Feldman Well I don't like them, long nasty beaks they've got.

Cleese Well you can't expect them to produce a special edition for gannet-haters!

Feldman Well, I'm sorry, I specially want the one without the gannet.

Cleese All right! (*Tears out the illustration.*) Anything else?

Feldman Well, I'm not too keen on robins.

Cleese Right! Robins—robins ... (*Tears them out.*) No gannets, no robins—there's your book!

Feldman I can't buy that—it's torn!

Cleese It's torn! So it is! (*Throws it away.*)

Feldman I wonder if you've got...

Cleese Go on, ask me another—we've got lots of books here—this is a bookshop, you know!

Feldman How about *Biggles Combs His Hair*?

Cleese No, no, no, we don't have that one, no, no, funny—try me again.

Feldman Have you got *Ethel the Aardvark Goes Quantity Surveying*?

Cleese No, no, we haven't got—which one?

Feldman *Ethel the Aardvark Goes Quantity Surveying.*

Cleese *Ethel the Aardvark*? I've seen it! We've got it! Here! Here! Here! *Ethel the Aardvark Goes Quantity Surveying*. There! Now—*buy it!*

Feldman I haven't got enough money on me.

Cleese I'll take a deposit!

Feldman I haven't got *any* money on me.

Cleese I'll take a cheque!

Feldman I haven't got a cheque-book.

Cleese It's all right, I've got a blank one!

Feldman I don't have a bank account.

Cleese Right! I'll buy it for you! (*Rings it up.*) There we are, there's your change—that's for the taxi on the way home—

Feldman Wait, wait, wait...

Cleese WHAT? WHAT?

Feldman I can't read!

Cleese Right—*SIT!*...'Ethel the Aardvark was trotting down the lane one lovely summer day, trottety-trottety-trot, when she saw a Quantity Surveyor......'

Questions

(1) Explain how the humour of this sketch comes to the fore in the very first exchange between Cleese and Feldman.

(2) What *type* of person is Feldman portraying in this sketch?

(3) At what point in the sketch does Cleese finally become absolutely infuriated with Feldman?

(4) The ending of a humorous sketch must be funny and satisfying enough to leave an audience laughing, and feeling that they have witnessed a nicely rounded-off piece of fun. Does the ending of *Bookshop* satisfy these criteria? Why or why not?

(5) In your opinion, how is the humour in this sketch mainly achieved?

The Tell-Tale Heart

Based on the story by **Edgar Allan Poe**

> *The Tell-Tale Heart* is a spine-chilling play based on the super-natural story by that master of suspense, Edgar Allan Poe.

CAST

Narrator
Phillip Ranger
Gideon Mansell
Ruth Parry
Inspector of Police
First Warder
Second Warder

Sound-effects note: It would be an advantage to have a tape-recorder, or drum, or some other instrument to produce a muffled, thudding sound like the beat of a human heart amplified many times.

Narrator Midnight ... midnight in Broadmoor Asylum for the criminally insane. A place of echoing corridors, constricting bars, shadows, and half-human sounds and sighs. In a small ante-room at the end of a passage, two stolid, middle-aged warders sit. One smokes quietly; the other reads. Presently the latter puts down his newspaper and speaks...

First Warder Number Fifteen's pretty quiet tonight.

Second Warder The night ain't over yet, Bert.

First Warder Know somethink? It would 'ave been much kinder to let him swing for what he did.

Second Warder We'd have got a more peaceful life, anyway. Just as if this place ain't bad enough—without 'im screamin' his head off all night and wakin'. . .(*Interrupting him comes a long, moaning scream of terror. It breaks into a terrified babbling.*)

Phillip The heart—the beating heart! Stop the beating, for heaven's sake. Stop it! Stop it!

Second Warder (*resigned*) There 'e goes again.

Phillip (*screaming*) It's in my brain. . .inside my head. . .stop it. . .for pity's sake. . .Aaahh! (*His scream of terror dies away.*)

First Warder (*uncomfortable*) Crikey. . .he's even worse tonight.

Second Warder Full moon—that's why.

First Warder Better go down and quieten him. Rouse the whole bloomin' place with them screams he will.

Second Warder I'll go now. (*His footsteps go ponderously down the long corridor.* PHILLIP's *mad babbling comes closer. There is a jingle of keys. A heavy door creaks open.*)

Phillip (*in terror*) Who's that?

Second Warder (*soothingly*) Now, now, it's only me.

Phillip (*relieved*) Warder—thank heaven you've come. It was so loud I couldn't hear you. Listen to it, Warder.

Second Warder Listen to what?

Phillip (*panting*) The heart—*his* heart. Uncle Gideon's. They say I murdered him, but how can he be dead when I can still hear the beating of his heart?

Second Warder There ain't a sound in the place.

Phillip (*slowly*) You're like the rest of them. You think I'm mad, don't you? Like Ruth and the Inspector. But I'm not, I'll swear I'm not. Let me try to convince you—I'll tell you all about it.

Second Warder Now, just a minute. . .

Phillip (*eagerly*) It won't take long, Warder! It's such a simple story, really. You see, I had an uncle, Gideon Mansell, one of the richest men in Surrey. He lived alone, except for his housekeeper, in a ruined old mansion on the downs, where I used to visit him. It was during one of my visits that it happened. In the great library, where the floor boards were rotting away so that you could lift them out quite easily. I remember it was night time and Uncle Gideon sat crouched over the dying embers of a fire as I spoke to him, and I remember his reply...

Mansell (*aged and cantankerous*) No, Phillip!

Phillip (*young and confident*) But Uncle...

Mansell You'll not get so much as a farthing of my money.

Phillip How can you say that with five thousand pounds locked away in that chest.

Mansell (*chuckling*) Ten thousand, Phillip. I know, because I've counted every one of them.

Phillip And for me, fifty pounds might mean the difference between freedom and a prison sentence.

Mansell You need a lesson, Phillip. Do you imagine that just because I've always paid your gambling debts before, I'll go on doing it?

Phillip (*pleading*) But this is the last time. Pay this account for me and I promise I'll get a job somewhere—then—then I'll save and pay back every penny I owe you.

Mansell (*sneering*) Do you expect me to believe that? You *won't* work. I know you. You'd rather sit around waiting for a dead man's shoes.

Phillip (*sullenly*) Even you can't live forever.

Mansell (*thinly*) Come here, Phillip, come closer. Now put your hand on my heart, feel it beating, pounding—strong and vigorous.

Phillip (*softly*) Yes.

Mansell Does that sound like the heart of a man near death?

Phillip There are other things beside sickness, Uncle. You might meet with an accident, like tripping over those rotten floor boards.

Mansell And you think you'd benefit by that? Oh, no. Should I die suddenly, every penny I possess goes to your cousin.

Phillip To Ruth?

Mansell Yes! What's more, she knows it. I've made it my business to tell her.

Phillip (*angrily*) Uncle, it isn't fair.

Mansell That's enough. It's late and the fire's almost out. It's long past my bedtime.

Phillip (*slowly*) You're trembling, Uncle. Is it the cold of this old room? Let me stir the fire for you.

Mansell I can help myself!

Phillip No, the fire-iron is heavy. You mustn't strain that stout heart of yours. Let me use the fire-iron. (*Rattle of fire-iron.*) It is weighty, Uncle. Too heavy for you. This heavy iron poker could quite easily end your life.

Mansell (*afraid*) Phillip...

Phillip (*slowly and cruelly*) It could so easily stop that beating heart, Uncle.

Mansell Phillip, no, put that iron down! (*His voice rises in terror.*) Phillip, don't strike! No! (*There is the thud of a fire-iron, a groan from* MANSELL *and the thud of a body.*)

Phillip (*softly*) Dead! And now for your grave—safe, secret. I know the place, the very place. (*He laughs softly.*) And while you sleep, Uncle Gideon, I shall watch over you.

(*Three days later...*)

Ruth Really, Phillip, I don't understand it at all.

Phillip My dear cousin, it's all so perfectly simple.

Ruth You say that three days ago Uncle Gideon asked you to come here to his house and said he was going away?

Phillip He did.

Ruth He told you to dismiss his housekeeper and the servants, and take care of this house while he was absent?

Phillip Exactly.

Ruth And he didn't even mention where he was going?

Phillip No, he did not.

Ruth What did he say about my (*pause*) financial arrangements?

Phillip He mentioned nothing about those—nothing at all.

Ruth Did you know that Uncle gave me an allowance every month? He used to take it out of a locked chest in his bedroom.

Phillip Then he must have taken it with him. There's certainly no chest in the bedroom now. (*Very softly a muffled, rhythmic thudding begins to sound. Neither* RUTH *nor* PHILLIP *hears it: boom-bup-boom-bup-boom-bup-boom-bup.*)

Ruth I think there's something very wrong here, Phillip. I have the strangest premonition that Uncle is dead.

Phillip (*taken unaware*) What nonsense you talk, Ruth! Why, here in this very room three days ago, he asked me to feel his heart. It was as healthy and strong as my own.

Ruth Phillip...

Phillip Yes?

Ruth That chest I mentioned—there was a fortune in it—ten thousand pounds. My inheritance!

Phillip Uncle told you that?

Ruth Yes.

Phillip Then he was having some game with you. There isn't even a chest, let alone any money. Uncle was really poor—that's why he lived in this mouldy old ruin. He just pretended to be a rich man because he liked to fool...(*He breaks off suddenly.*) Listen! (*The beating is slightly louder: boom-bup-boom-bup-boom-bup-boom-bup. The thudding continues, gradually growing louder as they speak.*)

Phillip Ruth. That sound, that dull, rhythmic thudding...

Ruth (*impatient*) Don't try to sidestep, Phillip. I want the truth about that money.

Phillip (*stammering*) I—I've told you the truth...

Ruth Then why do you falter? Why are you so pale?

Phillip Ruth—that sound! I've recognized it. It's like the beating of a heart!

Ruth I don't hear anything—neither do you. This is a trick to switch the subject.

Phillip Never mind the money. Surely you can hear that sound? It's so plain. It seems to fill the whole room.

Ruth There is no sound in this room.

Phillip But there is! Listen...(*Louder: boom-bup-boom-bup-boom-bup-boom-bup.*)

Ruth No sound at all.

Phillip You're lying, lying. Just saying that to frighten me.

Ruth And why should I want to frighten you, Phillip?

Phillip (*panting*) Because you think I'll confess...

Ruth (*sharply*) Confess what? Phillip, what have you done?

Phillip Nothing.

Ruth Then why talk of confession?

Phillip I—I don't know what you're talking about. I'm confused, I don't know what I'm saying. It's this—this beating in my ears. I can't think. (*Louder: boom-bup-boom-bup-boom-bup-boom-bup.*)

Ruth (*relentless*) Phillip, where *is* Uncle Gideon?

Phillip Ask the housekeeper.

Ruth You dismissed the housekeeper and the servants. You were here alone with Uncle. No one has seen him since! Phillip, don't stand there with your hands over your ears. Listen to me. Where is he? (*Louder: boom-bup-boom-bup-boom-bup-boom-bup.*)

Phillip (*sweating*) Ruth, have pity on me. Stop the sound.

Ruth There is no sound, Phillip. What you hear may be the beating of your own heart, your own—or the heart of an old man. (*Very loud: boom-bup-boom-bup-boom-bup-boom-bup.*)

Phillip (*screaming*) No—no! How can a man's heart beat when he is dead?

Ruth Dead?

Phillip Yes, Ruth—dead. Do you understand—dead? How can a heart live on, even the strongest and most vigorous heart, when the body is already decaying? Yet why can I hear it? Why does it beat and thud in my brain? I must get away from it—away from this room and its hellish owner. (*He rushes out slamming the door. Immediately the thudding ceases. There is complete silence.*)

Ruth (*quietly*) Poor Phillip. What are you—murderer or madman? (*She goes out.*)

(*In the library, several hours later. The door opens;* PHILLIP *shows in a* POLICE INSPECTOR.)

Phillip And this is the library, Inspector. It was in this room that I said goodbye to my uncle.

Inspector I'm sorry to bother you, Mr Ranger.

Phillip Not at all, Inspector.

Inspector It was just that earlier this evening we had a call from your cousin, a Miss Parry. She seemed to fear that your uncle had met with foul play.

Phillip What an extraordinary idea, Inspector.

Inspector (*smiling*) I don't suppose you've been burying any bodies out in the garden, have you?

Phillip Good heavens, Inspector. . .

Inspector Only my little joke, Sir. But this young lady—she—well, she hinted. . .

Phillip That I'd done away with my uncle?

Inspector Well, she did have this funny notion, Sir. I was rather sharp with her, I may say. I told her that before we could arrest anyone for murder, we'd have to have a body. . .(*Boom-bup-boom-bup-boom-bup-boom-bup. The beating starts again—soft at first, then rising to a gradual crescendo. The* INSPECTOR *talks over it.*) . . . and that she was making a pretty serious statement when . . . (*he stops*) Mr Ranger?

Phillip Listen. It's starting again.

Inspector What is, Sir?

Phillip You can hear it, can't you? Ruth said she couldn't, but she was lying. I'm not mad, am I? Tell me I'm not mad.

Inspector Well now, look here, Mr Ranger. (*Boom-bup-boom-bup-boom-bup-boom-bup.*)

Phillip (*eagerly*) You do hear it, don't you?

Inspector Hear what?

Phillip The beating of his heart—the monstrous, pounding thud of a heart that can never be stilled. Listen, it's getting louder and louder. (*Very loud: boom-bup-boom-bup-boom-bup-boom-bup.*)

Inspector There's nothing...

Phillip There is. You *can* hear it! But you won't admit it. No, I don't believe you can. Then ... it's only me. That's his revenge.

Inspector Your uncle's?

Phillip (*wildly*) Yes. I'll confess it now. Anything to stop the pounding—this beating in my brain. I'll confess—I killed him.

Inspector (*concerned*) Mr Ranger, you're not well. (*The beating swells louder—engulfing the entire room: boom-bup-boom-bup-boom-bup-boom-bup.*)

Phillip (*screaming*) You don't believe me? You think I'm mad? I'll show you that I'm sane—sane as anyone. I killed him, I tell you. Killed him and hid him under these rotten floor boards. You think I'm mad, do you? Well, look for yourself. (*With a grinding wrench he tears up the floor boards.*) There he lies, three days dead. Only his heart still lives—that strong, vigorous heart beating eternally, the heart that can never die. Ahhh. (*His scream dies in a moan. A thud as he falls. The beating stops. The door flies open.*)

Ruth Inspector, what's happened?

Inspector (*quietly*) He's collapsed, Miss Parry. Offhand I'd say he's had some kind of a brainstorm.

Ruth And my uncle?

Inspector Murdered. No doubt about that. But this poor devil will never climb the gallows. You see—he's raving mad.

CURTAIN

Questions

(1) Why is the play called *The Tell-Tale Heart*?

(2) Why is the setting at the beginning of the play suitable for the events that are to follow?

(3) What is the attitude of the warders to Phillip?

(4) Describe and comment on the changes that take place in Phillip during the course of the play.

(5) Do you feel Phillip's uncle was justified in not lending Phillip another £50? Why?

(6) In what way was Mansell's attitude to Phillip different from Mansell's attitude to Ruth?

(7) What comments would you make about Ruth's character?

(8) The word 'supernatural' means 'outside the forces of nature'. Can you suggest why *The Tell-Tale Heart* has been called a supernatural play?

(9) What motivated Phillip to kill Mansell?

(10) What sound-effects would be important for the staging of *The Tell-Tale Heart*?

Picnic at Hanging Rock

Screenplay by **Cliff Green**

(based on the novel by **Joan Lindsay**)

The script that follows is the final draft screenplay, the document from which the film *Picnic at Hanging Rock* was made. It is essentially the same script as that used by director, cast and crew on location and by director and editor in the film-cutting room, and finally in the dubbing suite when the sound-track was 'mixed'.

No 'shooting script'—precise list of all shots, including camera angles—was ever prepared.... The detailed treatment of sounds and images, the cutting pattern of the picture, was carried in the director's head.

In writing this screenplay, camera directions and other technical terms were used only when it was felt they were the best and simplest way to express a visualized sound or image.

A guide to technical terms and abbreviations will be found on pages 241−2 of this book.

CHARACTERS

Mrs Appleyard, *headmistress of Appleyard College*
Miss Greta McCraw, *mathematics mistress*
Mlle Dianne de Poitiers, *French mistress*
Miss Dora Lumley, *junior mistress*
Miranda ⎱
Irma Leopold ⎰ *senior boarders, all about 16-17 years*
Marion Quade ⎰
Edith Horton, *about 14*
Sara Waybourne, *about 13*
Rosamund, *about 15*
Blanche, *about 15*
Fanny, *about 14*
Juliana, *about 14*
Cook *at the College*
Minnie ⎱ *maids at the College*
Alice ⎰
Edward Whitehead, *College gardener*
Tom, *handyman at the College*
Mr Ben Hussey, *Woodend livery-stable proprietor*
Doctor McKenzie, *family doctor from Woodend*
Sergeant Bumpher ⎱ *Woodend police*
Constable Jones ⎰
Mrs Bumpher, *Sergeant Bumpher's wife*
Colonel Fitzhubert, *of Lake View, Upper Macedon*
Mrs Fitzhubert
The Hon. Michael Fitzhubert, *the Colonel's nephew, about 18*
Albert Crundall, *coachman at Lake View, about 20*
Maid *at Lake View*
Reporter, *from a Melbourne newspaper*
Schoolgirls
Townspeople, Locals and Assorted Bucolics
Searchers
Police Dog-handler
Policemen, *uniformed and plain-clothes*
Black Tracker
Musicians, Guests, Footman, Maids, *at Lake View garden party*
Father *of one of the schoolgirls*
Mr Hussey's Assistant
Small Boy, *outside Woodend church*
Clergyman

1 **EXT. MIST. EARLY MORNING.**

GREY, EARLY MORNING MIST. LIMBO.

Sound *Practically nothing, except perhaps a faint light whisper of wind—but hardly there—just a zephyr. A distant bird call or two.*

SUPER TITLE:

On Saturday, 14 February, 1900, a party of schoolgirls from Appleyard College picnicked at Hanging Rock near Mt Macedon in the State of Victoria. During the afternoon, several members of the party disappeared without trace.

BEGIN LOSING SUPER.

DISSOLVE THROUGH THE MISTY LIMBO TO:

2 **EXT. HANGING ROCK. EARLY MORNING.**

VWS: *The Rock—strange, haunting—standing up out of the fog-blanketed plain.*

SUPER MAIN TITLES.

LOW-ANGLE SHOT: *The jagged peaks of Hanging Rock, glinting in the early-morning sunlight.*

Miranda (*VO: A whisper*) What we see, and what we seem, are but a dream. A dream within a dream...

3 **INT. COLLEGE—MIRANDA'S AND SARA'S BEDROOM, EARLY MORNING.**

FX *The early-morning bird calls are drifting in closer now.*

A golden head on a lace pillow. In slatted shadow. Miranda.

Her eyes open.

Sound *Throughout this getting-up/titles sequence the natural sounds are separated and accentuated; almost harshly so; almost contrapuntal to the lyrically soft visuals.*

SUPER MAIN CREDITS AND CONTINUE ACROSS THIS SEQUENCE.

Girls' Voices *Whispered verses from old St Valentine cards touch the sound-track through this sequence.*

Nightdressed, frail little Sara is standing in slatted shadow at the shuttered window. Her hand pulls the sliding shutter open: A vertical knife-edged wipe of golden-white light burns horizontally across the screen. Our only relief is the black silhouette that is Sara.

4 INT. COLLEGE—IRMA'S BEDROOM. EARLY MORNING.

Water pours from a jug into a matching white china bowl. Irma begins delicately washing her face in the little alcove off her bedroom.

5 INT. COLLEGE—EDITH'S BEDROOM. EARLY MORNING.

Edith is sitting up in bed counting St Valentine cards.

Edith ...Six and seven and eight and nine and ten and eleven...
Edith smugly smiles.

6 INT. COLLEGE—MIRANDA'S AND SARA'S BEDROOM. EARLY MORNING.

Miranda is sitting on her bed staring out of the window.

FX *The bird call outside is clear and pure and loud and primitive.*
Miranda's golden head is the sun.

7 INT. COLLEGE—MARION'S BEDROOM. EARLY MORNING.

Marion is completing the fastening of her button-up boots—a methodical, mechanical routine. She picks up her glasses, breathes upon them, rubs them with a tiny square of chamois leather, holds them to the light to check that they are sparkling clean, then places them squarely on her face. Ready to face the world.

8 INT. COLLEGE—MIRANDA'S BEDROOM. EARLY MORNING.

A china washing bowl filled with water and floating flowers. Miranda drifts into shot, begins washing her face in the flower-filled water.

9 INT. COLLEGE—BLANCHE'S AND ROSAMUND'S BEDROOM. EARLY MORNING.

Rosamund in a petticoat, posing before a mirror, holding a dress in front of her. Blanche, dressing beyond her, sees what Rosamund is up to, comes across, snatches back her dress.

10 INT. COLLEGE—BEDROOM. EARLY MORNING.

Two beautiful heads of tousled hair fill the frame, reading a St Valentine card.

Two Girls (*Whisper*) 'One for sorrow, two for joy...'

11 INT. COLLEGE—OTHER BEDROOMS. EARLY MORNING.

Junior girls dressing: pulling on stockings, smoothing down bodices, tying ribbons. Gold-flecked shafts of light and tumbled snowy bed linen. Lawn and lace and bare legs and newly budding breasts and shining cascading hair. Joyous, calm, innocent sensuality.

12   INT.   COLLEGE—ANOTHER BEDROOM. EARLY MORNING.

Two beautiful young girls are dressing—one is lacing her bodice, the other is snapping shut her corsets—firm and mechanical and tight. Their bodies are being crushed inside cages of respectable convention.

13   INT.   COLLEGE—MARION'S BEDROOM. EARLY MORNING.

Marion puts fresh blotting paper in a device for pressing flowers, the single delicate wildflower is placed in position. The device is closed— tightly and uncompromisingly.

14   EXT.   APPLEYARD COLLEGE. EARLY MORNING.

LS: The College, glimpsed through the dusty gold and grey-green gums. Foursquare and incongruous. An island of hard stone and English garden, marooned in the bush, dreaming of Europe. Hopelessly.

OPENING TITLES HAVE CONCLUDED.

FX   *The breakfast gong hits the sound-track, bridging to the next scene.*

15   INT.   COLLEGE STAIRCASE. MORNING.

FX   *Breakfast gong bridges from the previous scene.*

In a flurry of pastel muslin, the twenty or thirty girls come tumbling down the broad handsome cedar stairs. Giggling, laughing, chattering, excited.

Miss Lumley   (*VO*) Girls!

The noise is unabated.

Miss Lumley   (*VO*) Girls!

16   INT.   COLLEGE HALLWAY. MORNING.

A hand clap. Miss Dora Lumley is standing at the foot of the stairs. The noise drops a little.

Miss Lumley   Unless you all deport yourselves with rather more grace and considerably less noise, Mrs Appleyard will see to it that none of you go to Hanging Rock today.

The noise stops. Several of the younger girls nod in acquiescent modesty as they move past Miss Lumley, but the other girls— Miranda, Irma and Marion—choose to ignore Miss Lumley. They are almost as old as she is, anyway.

Miss Lumley looks up. Close behind Edith is Mlle Dianne de Poitiers, barely distinguishable from the senior girls, also in her summery picnic frock.

Dianne   (*smiling sweetly*) Bonjour Miss Lumley.

Miss Lumley Good morning, Mam'selle de Poitiers.

Miss Lumley's tight cold smile to Dianne means: 'You were with these girls, Mam'selle, why didn't you keep them quiet?' Dianne's smile back could be interpreted as: 'Today is St Valentine's Day, and besides, we are going on a picnic. Why don't you stop nagging?'

Dianne moves past, on her way to the dining room. The last girl to pass Miss Lumley is also the youngest: sad little Sara Waybourne. She is waylaid by Miss Lumley.

Miss Lumley I believe Mrs Appleyard has decided that you are not to go on the picnic, Sara.

Sara looks at Miss Lumley. She says nothing.

Miss Lumley (*smiling obliquely*) That makes two of us...Off you go.

Sara doesn't answer. Miss Lumley stands to one side, allowing Sara to go through towards the dining room, watches her for a moment, then follows.

17 INT. COLLEGE DINING ROOM. EARLY MORNING.

The girls are moving into the dining room, seating themselves, still excitedly showing their cards.

Isolated in her own pool of golden light, Miranda is gazing dreamily out at the sunlit garden.

The maids—Alice and Minnie—are beginning to serve breakfast.

Miss Lumley enters, moves to the head of the table, holds everyone with her stern gaze.

Miss Lumley For what we are about to receive may the Lord make us truly thankful.

The joyous, expectant meal begins.

18 INT. COLLEGE—MIRANDA'S AND SARA'S BEDROOM. MORNING.

Miranda, sitting in front of a mirror, brushing out her long golden hair.

Miranda (*singing*) See the little horse,
My little horse,
Trotting down the paddock
On his fine white feet.
Black horse, white horse,
Brown horse, grey;
Trotting down the paddock
On a bright sunny day...

Standing open on the dressing-table in front of Miranda is a home-made St Valentine's card. Beyond her, sitting on a bed, staring out of the window, is Sara.

Miranda Some day, Sara, you shall come home with me, to the station—to Queensland—and see my sweet funny family for yourself. Would you like that?

No response from Sara.

Miranda is still brushing her hair. In the mirror, she sees Sara turn her head, watching the slow, methodical brushing. Miranda speaks to the Sara in the mirror.

Miranda You must learn to love someone else apart from me, Sara. I won't be here much longer.

Sara looks at her a moment longer—unblinking—then turns to face back to the window.

Rosamund and Irma come into the room. Sara excludes them.

Rosamund What do you think, Miranda?

Miranda looks up. They see her face reflected in the mirror.

Rosamund Somebody had the nerve to send Miss McCraw a card on a squared paper, covered with tiny sums.

Miranda's face reflected in the mirror. Hold the moment.

19 COLLEGE GROUNDS. MORNING.

The outdoor dunny—a simple timber guard-house set amid garden greenery. The lid inside can be heard to thump down, the door opens, and out comes Miss Greta McCraw, mathematics mistress, stiff, angular and old-fashioned. We follow her as she walks sedately towards the front of the house, dressed in a tatty-formal way for the picnic. She rounds the corner to see the girls, under the slightly excited supervision of Dianne, waiting just off the verandah.

Dianne *(to Irma)* . . . Tais-toi, Irma. . . Miss McCraw vient d'arriver.

Miss McCraw, obviously completely out of her element supervising an excursion, attempts a dignified holiday smile, but it gets lost on the way out. Suddenly an immense, purposeful figure, swimming and billowing in grey silk taffeta, emerges like a galleon in full sail, out of the shadows on to the tiled and colonnaded verandah. The girls are drawing themselves up in a half-circle as Mrs Appleyard takes up her position on the verandah.

Mrs Appleyard Good morning, girls.

The girls curtsy as one.

Girls Good morning, Mrs Appleyard.

Mrs Appleyard Well, young ladies, we are indeed fortunate in the weather for our picnic to Hanging Rock...

Begin a slow, slow pan across the waiting female faces:

Rosamund *Excited.*

Mrs Appleyard (*VO*) ...I have instructed Mademoiselle that as the day is likely to be warm, you may remove your gloves after the drag has passed through Woodend...

Blanche *Impassive.*

Mrs Appleyard (*VO*) ...You will partake of luncheon at the picnic grounds near the Rock...

Irma *Expectant.*

Mrs Appleyard (*VO*) ...Once again let me remind you that the Rock itself is extremely dangerous and you are therefore forbidden any tomboy foolishness in the matter of exploration, even on the lower slopes...

Marion *Bored.*

Mrs Appleyard (*VO*) ...I also wish to remind you that the vicinity is renowned for its venomous snakes and poisonous ants of various species...

Edith *She grimaces.*

Mrs Appleyard (*VO*) ...It is, however, a geological marvel on which you will be required to write a brief essay on Monday morning...

...Miranda. She looks up.

MIRANDA'S POV:

Sara's white face, just visible on the roof, behind the balustrade.

Miranda gives her a sad smile and a tiny secret wave.

Mrs Appleyard (*VO*) ...That is all. Have a pleasant day and try to behave yourselves in a manner to bring credit to the College.

Irma shifts her glance from Mrs Appleyard to Dianne. Their looks lock. They exchange fleeting secret smiles.

Mrs Appleyard I shall expect you back, Miss McCraw and Mademoiselle, at about eight, for a light supper.

20   EXT.   COLLEGE GATES. MORNING.

Mr Hussey's drag, drawn by five spirited horses, is rolling out through the College gates in a cloud of golden dust.

On the box seat beside Hussey (livery-stable proprietor) are Miranda, Irma and Marion.

The drag moves on out of shot, exposing a CU of the gilt-lettered signboard beside the gates:

Appleyard College
Educational Establishment for Young Ladies.

21   INT.   DRAG. MORNING.

TRAVELLING SHOT: *Inside the drag. A sudden transition from light to shade. Shafts of dust-dancing sunlight pierce the canvas sides of the drag, but the heavy black roof keeps the inside gloomy. The civilized girls gently moving about to the motion of the vehicle are chattering animatedly about everything—all of them—all at once — so that none of the spoken, shrilled, laughed, giggled and whispered words are discernible. Miss McCraw and Dianne are sitting together. Dust is seeping in, penetrating to eyes and hair and the air in the enclosed space is beginning to grow stifling. Miss McCraw speaks, ostensibly to Dianne, but in fact to anyone—or no one. Her hard murmur penetrates both the gloom and the noise.*

Miss McCraw   This we do for pleasure. So that we may shortly be at the mercy of venomous snakes and poisonous ants. How foolish can human creatures be!

Dianne doesn't reply, but a tiny smile touches her lips.

22   EXT.   ROAD TO HANGING ROCK. MORNING.

VWS: *Hussey's drag is a tiny moving dot in the vast wheaten-yellow landscape.*

23   INT.   COLLEGE HALLWAY. MORNING.

Mrs Appleyard is moving across the ornate, creamy-gold heaviness that is the lower hallway. Pausing at a small table, brimming with flowers and St Valentine's day cards, she picks up one of the cards and reads it. Her thin lips move incongruously with the lyrical words. The card is thrust back; Mrs Appleyard moves on, towards her study.

24   EXT.   WOODEND MAIN STREET. DAY.

Hussey's drag moving through: small boys chasing, a dog barking; an old man on the pub verandah watches with bored interest.

25 INT. DRAG. DAY.

The girls are pulling off their gloves: Woodend is past; they are pitching and jolting closer and closer to freedom.

26 EXT. ROAD TO HANGING ROCK. DAY.

The drag, passing through more heavily timbered country. The morning is growing hotter. The straining shoulders and rippling rumps of the horses are staining dark with sweat. Hussey pulls out a big spotted handkerchief and wipes his neck. Tiny beads of per-spiration are standing out on the girls' foreheads.

27 INT. DRAG. DAY.

Miss McCraw, jolting serenely amongst the dancing golden dust, her head full of dancing equations. Hussey half-turns back from his seat in front.

Hussey It must be nearly twelve o'clock—we haven't done too badly so far, ladies. I swore I'd have you back at the College by eight.

Miss McCraw There is no reason why we should be late even if we linger an extra hour at the Rock. Mr Hussey knows as well as I do that two sides of a triangle are together greater than the third. This morning we have driven along two sides of a triangle. Am I correct, Mr Hussey?

Hussey nods.

Miss McCraw Very well then—you have only to change your route this afternoon and return by the third side, the return journey will be along the hypotenuse.

Hussey winks at the girls.

Miss McCraw It's Pythagoras, Mr Hussey. Marion, can you hear me up front there? You know what I mean I hope?

Marion has been listening intently but Hussey shakes his head.

28 EXT. ROAD TO HANGING ROCK. DAY.

WS: *The drag, spanking along the dusty, shade-speckled road, approaching Hanging Rock.*

29 INT. DRAG. DAY.

TRAVELLING SHOT: *We see the Rock over Hussey's shoulder, appearing fleetingly between moving trees, then clearly, for several seconds at a time. Dominating the landscape.*

Hussey There she is, girls. Hanging Rock.

Mr Hussey's whip rises to indicate the awesome sight.

Miss McCraw The mountain comes to Mahommed. The Hanging Rock comes to Mr Hussey.

Hussey More than five hundred feet high, she is. Volcanic, o'course...

The girls—and the two teachers—are pushing forward to see.

Hussey ...Thousands o'years old.

Miss McCraw A million years old, Mr Hussey. Or thereabouts.

Hussey Yes, well o'course that'd be right. Thousands, millions... Devil of a long time anyway. After a manner of speakin'...

Miss McCraw (*quietly, almost nostalgically*) Only a million years ago. Quite a recent eruption, really. The rocks all round—Mount Macedon itself—must be all of 350 million years old...

Miss McCraw is away. Only Marion, as seeker of all truths, is really interested. But Miss McCraw continues in her harsh dry murmur, a strange reverential tone in her voice.

Miss McCraw Silicious lava, forced up from deep down below. Soda trachytes extruded in a highly viscous state, building the steep-sided mametons we see in Hanging Rock.

Hussey, almost drowsing, has long been left behind in technicalities.

The drag rattles and jogs along, the great rock itself, clearly visible now, standing high out of the plain, bearing towering witness to the truth of Miss McCraw's monotone.

Miss McCraw And quite young, geologically speaking. Barely a million years.

Irma has been touched by the grandeur.

Irma Waiting a million years just for us...

Miss McCraw says nothing. Her thoughts are hooded now. But there is a strange, unreal gleam in her eyes.

FX *The sound of cicadas—not loud—just insinuating themselves above the pad of horses' hooves on dust and the creak of the wheels. The cicadas bridge to the next scene.*

30 EXT. ROAD TO HANGING ROCK. DAY.

The brooding rock is close, the drag moving towards it—inexorably.

FX *The cicadas—continuing—only a murmur.*

31 EXT. CREEK BELOW HANGING ROCK. MIDDAY.

FX *Cicadas—a touch louder—a constant shrill background but still held low.*

A shining wagonette is drawn up near the creek. An elaborate picnic. A little woman in an elaborate silk dress—Mrs Fitzhubert; a stout, bewhiskered red-faced man wearing a sola topi—Colonel Fitzhubert; a young man in riding breeches—their nephew, the Hon. Michael Fitzhubert; finishing their lunch. Behind them is the magnificent backdrop of Hanging Rock. All three people are drinking tea.

Mrs Fitzhubert More cake, Michael?

Michael No thank you, Aunt.

The tea-drinking continues in total silence from the people, though the constant hum of cicadas populates the hot still air. The long moment of inactivity continues. Seemingly interminable. Finally Michael sets down his cup and saucer, stands.

Michael I think I'll just stretch my legs, Aunt.

Mrs Fitzhubert (*almost drowsily*) Don't go too far. And be careful. There could be snakes.

Michael nods, moves towards the creek. Colonel Fitzhubert has said nothing. He is just sitting there: his eyes beneath the shading pith could be glass.

32 EXT.   TREE NEAR CREEK, HANGING ROCK. MIDDAY.

Michael has reached the creek. Sitting with his back to a large tree, out of view of the picnic party, is Albert Crundall, the Fitzhuberts' coachman. As Michael comes into sight he lifts an opened bottle of beer to his lips, swigs deeply, lowers it back between his knees, then continues eating the large wedge of egg-and-bacon pie he is holding in his other hand.

Albert How's it goin'?

Michael All right.

Michael is standing there a little awkwardly. He feels a touch out of place. Albert indicates the two older people with his head.

Albert Finished eatin', have they?

Michael Pardon?

Albert The colonel and the missus. They've finished eatin', have they?

Michael Er, yes. Yes, they have.

Albert Expect me up there, in a minute, I s'pose. To clear away.

Albert takes another pull on the bottle, Michael's eyes watching its rise and fall.

Albert Can't be more'n midday.

Michael No. (*pause*) I thought it was a little early for lunch, myself.

Albert Yeah.

Albert drinks as before, Michael watching as before. Albert, realizing, proffers the bottle.

Albert Like a drink?

Michael hesitates a moment, then takes the bottle.

Michael Thanks.

Michael wipes the top of the bottle with the palm of his hand, lifts it a touch distastefully to his lips, tilts, tastes, then drinks deeply.

Albert You know, they always allow an hour longer'n it takes to get here. Then they gotta eat straight away...

Michael is returning the bottle.

Michael Thanks.

Albert takes a glug, without wiping the top of the bottle, then hands it back to Michael, who accepts it readily this time.

Albert Well, not that they've got anything else to do. I mean they never go for a walk or nothing.

Michael is about to rub the bottle once more, hesitates, grins, drinks without doing so.

Albert grins.

Albert I sometimes wonder why they bother. The grass back at Lake View is a lot softer an' there's no dust; and a damned sight less insects...

The bottle is passed back. Albert is probing an ants' nest with a stick. He takes a last deep swig from the bottle, then looks up, towards the entrance to the picnic grounds.

FX *The background sound of cicadas, bridging to the next scene, is suddenly intruded upon by the rattle of the approaching drag.*

33   EXT.   PICNIC GROUNDS. MIDDAY.

FX *The sound of cicadas bridges from the previous scene.*

The drag is approaching the gate of the picnic grounds.

Hussey Whoa, there. Whoa!

The drag stops, Miranda climbs down, approaches the sagging gate, now closed.

Miranda skilfully manipulates the heavy, stubborn latch. It falls down, with a sharp clang.

A flock of brilliantly coloured parrots screech out of a tree into the eye of the sun.

The horses rear and plunge wildly.

The parrots are flapping and screeching their way out across the dry sunlit plain, heading and tumbling towards the misty blue-green of Mount Macedon.

FX *The pervading, ever-present shrill of the cicadas; bringing to the next scene.*

34 EXT. HANGING ROCK PICNIC GROUNDS. DAY.

FX *Cicadas—bridging.*

LOW-ANGLE SHOT: *The creamy-white girls, haloed by shining hair; Dianne; Miss McCraw; Hussey; glasses raised above a St Valentine's Day cake.*

Miranda To Saint Valentine!

Glasses clink. Miranda is poised above the cake, knife in hand. She thrusts down. The cake is cut.

35 EXT. PICNIC GROUNDS. EARLY AFTERNOON.

FX *The cicadas—a decibel louder—bridge from the previous scene.*

BIG CU: *Ants are dragging and bowling and rolling great brown and black and pink objects across the sand. Others are hurrying past in the opposite direction, unencumbered. We follow those on their urgent outward journey. Across the grey granulated sand, up and on to a snowy white plain, past shining glittering structures whose purpose can only be guessed at, right up to a great, pink-covered heart-shaped mountain. The ants are making their way into the dark wedge-shaped cavern deep in the side of the mountain and emerging with black-brown and pink burdens—spoils from a quarrying enterprise.*

Hussey (*VO*) Well, now. That's funny...

WIDEN *to see the College picnic party. We know it is a little later. Smoking campfire, horses tethered out grazing beyond the drag, large white tablecloth covered with the remains of lunch: chicken pie, angel cake, jellies, bananas, and a handsome pink-iced cake in the shape of a heart. The two teachers—and the girls—insulated from natural contacts with earth, air and sunlight, by corsets pressing on the solar plexus, by voluminous petticoats, cotton stockings and kid boots. The drowsy well-fed girls lounging in the shade are no more a part of their environment than figures in a photograph album, arbitrarily posed against a backdrop of cork rocks and cardboard trees. Mr Hussey, confident in his surroundings, his backside comfortable on the hard ground, his head in the blue-grey smoke, a pannikin of black tea in one hand, his old chained pocket-watch in the other.*

Hussey ...Blowed if me watch hasn't stopped, dead on twelve o'clock.

Hussey lifts his watch to his ear, shakes it.

Hussey Real funny. (*to Dianne*) You wouldn't have the time I suppose, Miss?

Dianne Miranda—your pretty little diamond watch—can you tell us the time?

Miranda I don't wear it any more. I can't stand hearing it ticking all day long just above my heart.

Irma If it were mine I'd wear it always. Even in the bath. Would you, Mr Hussey?

Miss McCraw (*taking out an old-fashioned gold repeater on a chain*) Stopped at twelve. Never stopped before. Could be something magnetic.

Hussey is squinting at the sun.

Hussey Be well after two, I'd say. We'd better watch it. I promised Mrs Appleyard I'd have you lot back at the College by eight.

The word 'College' touches Irma's eyes with a sliver of ice.

Edith is spooning cake and cream into her mouth.

Edith Except for those people over there...

The wagonette party on the creek can just be seen through the trees.

Edith ...we might be the only living creatures in the whole world.

Belying Edith's words, the battalion of ants continue their crumb-rolling expeditions across the tablecloth, dragging the spoils towards some subterranean larder dangerously situated within inches of Blanche's yellow head, pillowed on a rock.

On the rocks and grass, other diligent ants are crossing miniature Saharas of dry sand, jungles of seeding grass in the never-ending task of collecting and storing food.

Scattered about amongst the mountainous human shapes are heaven-sent crumbs, caraway seeds, a shred of crystallized ginger—strange, exotic but recognizably edible loot.

FX *Cicadas, bridging to the next scene.*

36   EXT.   HANGING ROCK. MONTAGE. AFTERNOON.

FX *Cicadas, bridging from the previous scene.*

Leaves, flowers and grasses glow and tremble under the canopy of light, cloud shadows give way to golden motes dancing above the pool on the creek where water beetles skim and dart.

In the forest and on the slopes of Hanging Rock itself, lizards bask on the hottest stones, a lumbering armour-plated beetle rolls over in the dry leaves and lies helplessly kicking on its back, fat white grubs and flat grey woodlice prefer the dank security of layers of rotting bark. Torpid snakes lie coiled in their secret holes awaiting the twilight hour; in the hidden depths of the thick scrub the birds wait for the heat of the day to pass . . .

FX *And over all shrills the interminable summer song of the cicadas, bridging to the next scene.*

37   EXT.   PICNIC GROUNDS. MID-AFTERNOON.

FX *The cicadas, a touch shriller and louder now, bridge from the previous scene.*

The picnic has been cleared away. The girls, drugged with rich food and sunshine, are sitting and lying about, dozing and daydreaming. Rosamund has produced some fancywork, Blanche is already asleep. One of the girls is sketching Miss McCraw—too easy to caricature sitting bolt upright on a fallen log, her nose deep in a book. Hussey has gone off for a stroll somewhere, Dianne is relaxed at full length on the grass, seemingly asleep, her blonde hair falling about her face. Irma and Miranda are sitting opposite her, Irma delicately peeling an apricot with a small fruit knife.

Marion Excuse me, Mam'selle.

Hussey goes across to the almost dead fire, picks up the two square smoke-blackened water cans by their handles.

Dianne Yes, Marion.

Marion I should like to make a few measurements at the base of the rock if we have time—with Miranda and Irma.

Dianne isn't too sure.

Irma Please, Mam'selle. We'll be back long before tea.

Dianne looks towards Miss McCraw but she is totally engrossed in her book—or appears to be. Dianne looks back; smiles, nods. Suddenly Edith appears.

Edith May I come too? Please...

The three seniors exchange glances, nod. Finally Irma turns to Edith.

Irma So long as you don't complain.

Edith I won't. I promise.

Miranda And don't worry, Mam'selle. We shall only be gone a little while.

Dianne watches as the four girls walk off towards the creek; Miranda a little ahead gliding through tall grasses that brush her pale skirts, Marion and Irma following arm in arm, with Edith bumbling along in the rear. Before they move out of sight Miranda stops, turns her shining head and gravely smiles at Dianne who smiles back and waves.

CU: A page in a book on Dianne's lap—a Botticelli angel.

Dianne Mon Dieu! Now I know...

Miss McCraw's sharp peering face looks up.

Miss McCraw What do you know?

Dianne I know...

Dianne is suddenly embarrassed. But she goes on, nevertheless.

Dianne I know ... (*almost to herself*) I know that Miranda is a Botticelli angel...

Miss McCraw looks at Dianne strangely. Then she glances in the direction taken by the four girls, but her hooked eyes betray nothing. She returns to her book.

Dianne lies down again, on her back staring upwards into the trees. She nibbles a stalk of dry grass. Nothing, for a long, long, minute. She is almost asleep. With a great effort of willpower she turns over on to her stomach. The girl sketching is asleep. Rosamund is asleep over her embroidery. Blanche is still asleep. Everyone is asleep except Dianne and Miss McCraw. Dianne, her sense of responsibility battling her total feeling of languor, begins counting the sleeping girls. Nineteen. Apart from Edith and the three seniors, that is everyone. Dianne lowers her head, relaxes, and falls asleep. Miss McCraw is the only person awake.

FX *The cicadas shrill on—forever—bridging to the next scene.*

38 EXT. FOREST BELOW HANGING ROCK. MID-AFTERNOON.

FX *Cicadas—bridging from the previous scene.*

A burst of wild freedom. The four girls—Miranda, Marion and

Irma, with Edith trailing behind—are running helter-skelter through the ferns. We glimpse them for a moment, beautifully incongruous in their starched and impractical Victorian dresses, then they are gone.

FX *Cicadas—bridging to the next scene.*

39   EXT.   CREEK BELOW HANGING ROCK. MID-AFTERNOON.

FX *Cicadas—bridging from the previous scene.*

The four girls are moving along, following the winding course of the creek. Miranda, Marion and Irma, and—already tagging along a little way behind—Edith. Breathless, excited, pink-cheeked from running, Miranda pauses, looking up the creek, and back.

Miranda We really must find a suitable place to cross over...

The others stop. Edith catches up.

Miranda ...or we shall see nothing at all before we have to turn back.

Irma looks up. The Hanging Rock is tantalizingly hidden behind a screen of tall forest trees. Marion looks along the creek. It is getting wider as it approaches the pool. She gauges the width where they are standing.

Marion At least four feet.

There are no stepping-stones.

Irma I vote we take a flying leap and hope for the best.

Irma gathers up her skirts.

Miranda Can you manage it, Edith?

Edith's frightened little eyes are measuring the gap.

Edith I don't know. I don't want to wet my feet.

Marion Why not?

Edith Because I might get pneumonia and die, and then you'd stop teasing me and be sorry.

Marion and Miranda exchange exasperated glances.

Irma (*kindly*) I'll go first, Edith. Then you can follow. I'll catch you and help you up the bank.

Edith nods. Not too sure, but she'll try. Irma gives her an encouraging smile, gathers her skirts up once more and jumps across, clearing it easily and landing daintily on the other side.

Albert (*VO*) A whistle. Not a wolf-whistle. More like a drover whistling his dog.

PULL BACK VERY WIDE: *Albert and Michael are by the creek further downstream. We realize the previous shot was their POV. Albert is washing champagne glasses in the pool. The Colonel and Mrs Fitzhubert are in the background, asleep. Albert and Michael are watching as Edith is coaxed by the other girls to jump and finally does so—successfully, Irma catching her.*

Albert I thought the fat one was going to take a bath.

Michael grins. Marion jumps across.

Albert Some of 'em are real lookers.

Miranda is about to jump across. Michael is watching intently. He is immediately attracted to Miranda—for some reason he could never explain. Michael holds his breath. Miranda jumps, easily and gracefully, her long golden hair flowing out behind—glinting against the dark water.

Albert Look at the shape of the dark one with the curls. Built like an hourglass.

Michael doesn't answer.

The girls are moving along the other side of the creek, Miranda last.

Albert Have a look at the last one. The blonde. She'd have a decent pair of legs. All the way up to her bum.

Michael is still watching the girls. He speaks without looking at Albert.

Michael I'd rather you didn't say crude things like that, Albert.

Albert I say the crude things. You just think 'em.

Michael looks at Albert, almost angry, blushing. Albert turns, winks, grins. Michael grins back, despite himself. He stands. He is entranced by Miranda.

Michael (*abstracted*) I'll just stretch my legs a bit before we go.

Albert stands watching a moment.

HIS POV: Michael athletically clearing the creek, then disappearing into the forest, following the direction taken by the girls.

Albert grins to himself, then moves off towards the wagonette and out of shot.

JUMP CUT TO: *Michael, emerging from the forest. There is a belt of thick scrub.*

MICHAEL'S POV: The four girls are nowhere in sight. The bush is empty; and silent . . .

FX ...*save for the ever-present shrill of the cicadas, bridging to the next scene.*

40 EXT. HANGING ROCK. MID-AFTERNOON.

FX *The incorrigible cicadas, shrilling the summer away, bridging from the previous scene.*

The four girls are pushing their way through the scrub: Marion, Miranda, Irma, Edith. Twigs and brambles clutch at their clothes as they pass. Underfoot the ground is rough and rocky, soft and mossy by turn; strewn with rotting wood and fallen branches and thick with pockets of decaying leaves. The green and golden light shafts dappled through the trees. Suddenly ahead is a short grassy slope. The girls are concentrating on the obstacles underfoot. Miranda pauses, looks up.

Miranda (*quietly*) Look...

THEIR POV: *Hanging Rock, brilliantly illuminated by the lowering afternoon sun. On the steep southern facade the play of golden light and deep violet shade reveals the intricate construction of long, vertical slabs, some smooth as giant tombstones, others grooved and fluted by a prehistoric architecture of wind and water, ice and fire. Huge boulders, originally spewed red-hot from the boiling bowels of the earth, now come to rest, cooled and rounded in forest shade. The girls are crossing the grassy slope, entering the bracken at the foot of the steepening climb, looking upwards, their feet finding their own way through the ferns, their heads tilted up towards the glittering peaks. Saying nothing, seemingly forever.*

Their feet cushioned in silence, the only noise the all-pervading cicadas.

Finally —

Marion (*VO*) McCraw says the Rock's a million years old.

The girls, their animal senses insulated by civilization, are barely aware of the true nature of their environment...

Edith (*VO*) A million! How can anything be that much?

...of the smells and sounds and textures...

Irma (*VO: Blandly*) My papa made a million out of a mine once—in Brazil. He bought Mama a ruby ring.

...of the structure of Hanging Rock...

Edith (*VO*) Money's quite different.

...the horizontal ledges crisscrossing the verticals of the main pattern...

Marion (*VO*) Whether Edith likes it or not, that fat little body of hers is made up of millions and millions of cells.

...of the hundreds of frail starlike flowers being crushed under Edith's tramp-tramping boots...

Edith (*VO*) Nonsense.

...of the scarlet flash of a parrot's wing, reflected for a moment in Irma's eyes, a flame amongst the leaves...

Marion (*VO*) And what's more, you little goose, you have already lived for millions and millions of seconds.

Marion holds up one hand, two fingers half an inch apart.

Marion In the life of the world a million years is only that much.

Edith, red-faced and hot, is growing angry.

Edith Tell her to stop, Miranda. She's making me feel giddy.

Unaware of the fine details of crenellated crags and lichen-patterned stone, of a mountain laurel glossy above the dogwoods' dusty silver leaves...

Edith Why can't we just sit on this log and look at the ugly old Rock from here?

...of a dark slit between two rocks where maidenhair fern trembles like green lace. Unconscious of the strains and tensions of the molten mass that holds the monolith anchored to the groaning earth...

Edith It's nasty here. I never thought it would be so nasty, or I wouldn't have come.

...of the creakings and shudderings. The wandering airs and currents known only to the little bats, hanging upside down in their clammy cave.

Irma We'll turn around soon. Then it'll be downhill.

None of them see or hear the snake dragging its copper coils over the stones ahead...

Miranda My father once showed me a picture of people in old-fashioned dresses having a picnic at the Rock.

...nor the panic exodus of spiders, grubs and woodlice from rotting leaves and bark.

FX *Cicadas, bridging to the next scene.*

41 EXT. MAZE ON HANGING ROCK. MID-AFTERNOON.

FX *Cicadas, bridging from the previous scene.*

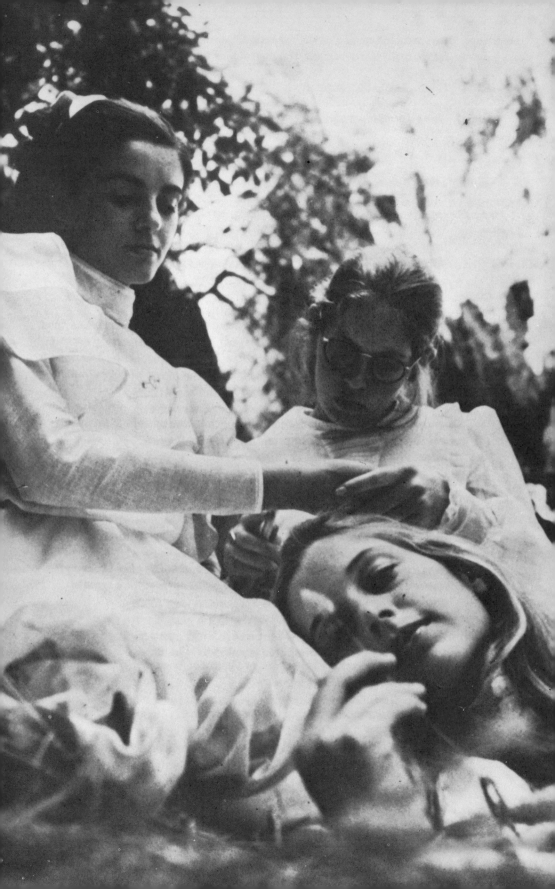

Irma, Marion, Edith and Miranda are weaving their way through a series of narrow crevices high up on the Rock.

Deep, slit-like. From sunshine to shadow, to sunshine to shadow.

Irma has curled herself up in a small hollow—a rock shelf—her legs tucked up under her long dress, her body partly in shadow. She is singing 'Rock of Ages'. The others come into shot, moving past.

Marion and Miranda take up the singing.

Edith stumps past, head down, silent save for her heavy, laboured breathing.

Irma stops singing, climbs out, follows the others.

FX *Cicadas—bridging to the next scene.*

42   EXT.   LEDGE ON HANGING ROCK. MID-AFTERNOON.

FX *Cicadas—bridging from the previous scene.*

A rock ledge. An almost circular platform enclosed by rocks and boulders and a few straight, tall saplings. Miranda appears, then Marion, Irma, finally Edith—exhausted.

Miranda We can't go much further. We promised Mademoiselle we wouldn't be long away...

The three older girls explore the ledge. Edith sits down in the shade, hot and huffy. Irma discovers a sort of a porthole in one of the rocks.

IRMA'S POV: The picnic grounds, down below. As if through a telescope, the little scene stands out with stereoscopic clarity between the trees: the drag with Mr Hussey busy amongst his horses, smoke rising from the fire, the girls moving about in their light dresses, Dianne's parasol open like a pale-blue flower.

Irma If only we could stay out all night and watch the moon rise.

Miranda has come up beside Irma and is watching the scene below.

Edith Blanche says Sara writes poetry. In the dunny. She found one, all about Miranda.

Miranda (*gently*) She's an orphan.

Irma Sara reminds me of a little deer Papa brought home once. I looked after it, but it died. Mama said it was doomed.

Edith Doomed. What's that mean, Irma?

Irma Doomed to die, of course...

        'The boy stood on the burning deck,
          Whence all but he had fled, tra, la...'

Edith I think I'm doomed, I'm not feeling at all well.

Marion (*to Edith*) I do wish you'd stop talking for once.

Irma kneels down and strokes Edith's burning forehead, and lays her hand on the back of Edith's hand. A tear trickles down Edith's face.

Irma We'll go back soon. It's downhill.

Irma has taken off her shoes and stockings, and, clutching shoes in one hand and stockings in the other, shakes out her ringlets, springs up on to a flat-topped rock and begins to dance, like a ballerina, with curls and ribbons flying and bright, unseeing eyes. She blows kisses to her admirers in the wings, tossing a flower from her bouquet into the stalls.

As Irma has been dancing, Marion and Miranda have pulled off their shoes and stripped off their stockings and are moving off uphill, away from the ledge.

Irma at last sinks into a full-blown curtsy to the Royal Box halfway up a gum tree. Edith, standing now, points uphill.

Edith Irma! Look at them! Where in the world are they going? Without their shoes...

Irma looks, laughs mischievously and follows, still holding her shoes and stockings at the end of outstretched arms. Edith watches for a moment, distressed, then sets off after them.

Edith Irma! Irma, wait for me...wait!

The three older girls are almost out of sight. Sobbing quietly to herself, Edith drives her pudgy little legs to follow.

FX *The cicadas shrill on—bridging to the next scene.*

43   EXT.   HIGHER LEDGE ON HANGING ROCK. LATE AFTERNOON.

FX *Cicadas, louder now, bridging from the previous scene.*

A semi-circular shelf, higher up, much the same as the lower one. Irma is peering down...

IRMA'S POV: *...at the plain below: just visible, infinitely vague and distant. The glint of water and tiny figures coming and going through drifts of rosy smoke, or mist.*

Irma (*VO*) Whatever can those people be doing down there? Like a lot of ants...

Marion is leaning over Irma's shoulder, looking down.

Marion A surprising number of human beings are without purpose ...Although it's probable that they are performing some function unknown to themselves.

Irma is looking out now, not down. Out across the golden, mystic plain...

Miranda has joined them.

Miranda Everything begins—and ends—at exactly the right time and place.

The distance is still. Totally. Not a breath of wind moves Irma's hair. Suddenly—

FX *A sound as of a distant roll of drums approaching across the plain, insinuates itself under, into and above the constant shrill of the cicadas —and is as suddenly gone.*

If Irma heard the noise, she made no reaction.

Miranda (*VO*) Look!

The girls turn. Miranda is pointing further up ahead.

THEIR POV: *The monolith, rising up ahead. A single outcrop of pock-marked stone, a monstrous egg perched above a precipitous drop to the plain.*

The girls, still carrying their shoes and stockings, begin moving upwards again. Edith sighs resignedly to herself and follows. But there is no excitement, now, just a great drugged lassitude. Whether the result of physical exhaustion or whatever, the girls have no way of knowing. They drag their leaden limbs up the slope—all of them, Edith included, and fall down on the gently sloping rock in the shelter of the monolith and are instantly in a deep sleep.

A horned lizard emerges from the black shadow and approaches them, finally lying without fear in the hollow of Miranda's outflung arm.

FX *Suddenly the cicadas stop. Hold the silence for a long moment.*

44   EXT.   PICNIC GROUNDS. LATE AFTERNOON.

FX *The cicadas are hard at it again. The golden silence was short-lived.*

The picnic grounds are in deep shadow now, the solid black presence of the Hanging Rock spreading across the lower slopes and beyond the creek. Dianne and the girls are still asleep. The wagonette down by the creek has gone. The big square billies are steaming over a good fire. Hussey is not around, but there could be someone moving among the horses on the grassy stretch beyond the drag. Only Miss McCraw is still awake, her long nose still deep in her book. She looks up, up at the Rock. Hold.

FX *The cicadas are still shrilling—inevitably. But the new sound insinuates itself. A low wordless murmur, almost like distant voices. With now*

*and then a sort of trilling that might be little spurts of laughter—but
very distant.*

Miss McCraw is still looking up at the Rock.

FX   *The murmuring trilling has gone. The shrilling sound of the cicadas lifts
in volume—perceptibly so—bridging to the next scene.*

45   EXT.   HANGING ROCK. LATE AFTERNOON.

FX   *The cicadas—all-pervasive and insistent—bridging from the previous
scene.*

*The light is strange and beautiful. Golden yellow against a dark
background as though a thunderstorm is imminent.*

*HIGH-ANGLE SHOT from the monolith. An unknown POV,
framed in leaves, peering through foliage.*

*CU: Miranda's shapely bare leg. A procession of queer-looking
beetles in bronze armour is making a leisurely crossing of her ankle.*

FX   *The shrilling cicadas are joined by the low wordless murmur—closer up
here—by the trilling singing and laughing. Once, twice, gone. The
cicadas are harshly triumphant.*

*Widen to see Miranda waking, opening her eyes, looking down at the
beetles without the slightest expression of fear or apprehension—or
indeed any expression at all. Miranda hauls herself up on to her
elbow, her leg moves a fraction, the beetles tumble off, Miranda
watching as they scuttle off to safety under some loose bark.*

*Miranda looks about. In the colourless twilight every detail stands
out, clearly defined and separate.*

Marion's torn muslin skirts, fluted like a nautilus shell.

Irma's ringlets, framing her face in exquisite spirals.

*Edith, flushed and childishly vulnerable in sleep. Edith awakes, sits
up, shocked and confused. She looks around, sees Miranda is also
awake.*

Edith   Oh, Miranda, I feel awful. Really awful.

*Miranda has stood. Marion and Irma are waking up and staggering to
their feet. They look about. Past, beyond, through each other. Edith
is still sitting there.*

Edith   I feel perfectly awful, Miranda. When are we going home?

Miranda doesn't answer. No one answers.

Edith   When are we going home?

Miranda begins moving away, up the rise. Marion and Irma are

*moving away with her. Barefoot, across the sharp stones without a
stumble—or a word. Seeming to glide along. Uphill. Up.*

Edith watches them: Puzzled...

Edith (*she croaks it*) Miranda...

   ...frightened...

Edith Miranda!

   ...terrified

Edith Miranda!

FX *The shrilling of the cicadas is now a terrible roaring scream.*

The girls are fast moving out of sight behind the monolith.

Edith Don't go up there! Come back!

*Edith turns, looks about. She sees something. Her eyes dilate with
horror. She screams.*

FX *The cicadas and Edith's screaming blend into an inextricable nightmare
of sound, 'peaking' the audio.*

46   EXT.   FURTHER DOWN THE SLOPE. LATE AFTERNOON.

Steep-pitched forest.

FX *The cicadas, continuous.*

*Edith is coming, her screaming heralding her panic-stricken approach
long before she is in shot. Suddenly she is here, rushing wildly
distraught across the field of vision; stumbling, pitching, running,
running, running—and screaming.*

47   INT.   COLLEGE HALLWAY. LATE AFTERNOON.

Sound *Blessed relief. The screaming has gone. Miraculously. Only silence
... Then, slowly, the ticking of a clock insinuates itself.*

The College hallway—empty.

48   INT.   COLLEGE—HEADMISTRESS'S STUDY. LATE AFTERNOON.

*Mrs Appleyard—not a pomaded wisp of her elaborate pompadour is
out of place. Thin, late-afternoon light, dappled green from the
garden outside, falls across the top of the big, handsome, dark-stained
desk at which she is sitting.*

A fly is crawling across the window.

*Mrs Appleyard sits staring at nothing for a long moment. Then she
stands, walks across to the window and looks out, staring through and
past the fly.*

MRS APPLEYARD'S POV: *Young turkeys, virginal white, stalking and scrabbling around a flower bed. The garden is warm and green and living. Momentarily, for no apparent reason, something troubles her. She moves towards the door, opens it, goes through, closes the door in our face.*

49   INT.   COLLEGE HALLWAY AND CORRIDORS. LATE AFTERNOON.

TRACKING SHOT: *Mrs Appleyard in full sail through the hall-way and along the corridors of the College. Past dark-stained doors and under carved and tortured wooden arches, past plants in pedestal pots and hallstands embellished with a thousand winking tiddling mirrors.*

Mrs Appleyard, moving through browns and mauves, greys and bottle-greens, blacks and maroons; through the occasional shaft of translucent red and blue from a stained-glass window or fanlight or the watery gold of light filtering down from a stairwell above.

Mrs Appleyard, in full control of herself, her College and her emotions, even on this fading holiday afternoon.

She has reached the closed door of the schoolroom. She pauses a moment, sets a composed, tolerant, summer-holiday-afternoon expression firmly on her face. Grasps the floral ceramic doorknob, turns it and opens the door.

50   INT.   COLLEGE—SCHOOLROOM. LATE AFTERNOON.

MRS APPLEYARD'S POV: *The schoolroom. A long simple room of bare boards and stark walls. Ink-stained desks, benches, a few charts and maps on the walls, a high teacher's desk, an easel black-board, a photograph of Queen Victoria. Sitting at a desk, an open book in front of her, her back to the door, facing the window in a pool of golden-green light from the garden beyond, is Sara.*

Mrs Appleyard (*mock kindness*) Sara . . .

Sara, unaware until now of Mrs Appleyard's presence, turns, scrambles clumsily to her feet, pulling her desk lid up and letting it fall crashing as she does so.

Mrs Appleyard is still standing in the doorway.

Mrs Appleyard I hope you have learned your poetry, Sara.

No answer from Sara.

Mrs Appleyard Stand up straight, child. Hold your shoulders back. You are getting a dreadful stoop.

No reaction from Sara.

Mrs Appleyard Well? Have you got your lines by heart?

No answer from Sara. Mrs Appleyard moves a little way into the room.

Mrs Appleyard Well, have you?

Finally—

Sara I can't...I...It doesn't make sense.

Mrs Appleyard Sense? You little ignoramus! Evidently you don't know that Mrs Felicia Heymans is considered one of the finest of our English poets.

A long pause. Finally Sara plucks up some sort of courage. There is a tiny flicker of excitement in her face.

Sara I ... I know another piece of poetry by heart. It has ever so many verses. Much more than 'The Wreck of the Hesperus'...

Mrs Appleyard is watching her—hard.

Sara ...Would that do?

Mrs Appleyard What is the name of this poem?

Sara 'An Ode to Saint Valentine.'

Mrs Appleyard I am not acquainted with it.

Mrs Appleyard is being cautious.

Mrs Appleyard Where did you find it?

Sara I didn't find it. I wrote it.

Mrs Appleyard You *wrote* it?

Sara (*begins; hesitantly*) 'Love abounds,
　　　　　　　Love surrounds...'

Mrs Appleyard No thank you, Sara. Strange as it may seem, I prefer Mrs Heymans.

Sara's expression closes; her eyes glaze over.

Mrs Appleyard Give me your book and proceed to recite to me as far as you have gone.

Nothing from Sara. Mrs Appleyard comes closer, holds out her hand.

Mrs Appleyard Your book please, Sara.

Sara hands the open book to Mrs Appleyard.

Mrs Appleyard Go on.

Sara (*finally*) I can't...

Mrs Appleyard Not one line?

> *Sara's eyes are filling with tears. She shakes her head. Mrs Appleyard, just under control, slaps the book back on the desk, moves away.*

Mrs Appleyard I shall leave you now, Sara. I expect you to be word perfect when I send Miss Lumley in half an hour.

> *Sara is staring at her, through tears, seeing nothing.*

Mrs Appleyard Otherwise I am afraid I shall have to send you to bed instead of letting you sit up until the others return from the picnic.

> *Mrs Appleyard has reached the door. Without giving the hateful girl one more glance she glides through and slams it shut. The key turns in the lock.*

> *Sara turns her face from the door, stares out at the darkening garden for a moment, then rests her head on the scarred, ink-stained lid of the desk and begins to sob.*

Sara Bertie...Bertie—Jesus where are you?...Miranda...

51   EXT.   COLLEGE ROOF. DUSK.

*A tense, expectant Mrs Appleyard appears on the roof; almost adrift
in the muted dusk light.*

She looks out, watching for the drag.

Nothing.

52   INT.   COLLEGE—MINNIE'S BEDROOM. EVENING.

*A tiny lamplit room, the attic window deep in shadow, tumbled
bedclothes lying on the floor. Minnie and Tom lie naked under the
sheet, embracing in the yellow light.*

FX   *The distant jingling of a bell shatters the mood.*

*Minnie leaps out of bed, making a vain attempt to hide her naked-
ness.*

Minnie   I gotta go! That's Mrs Appleyard.

Tom laughs at Minnie's panic.

Tom   Let someone else.

Minnie   They won't. I'm on.

*Minnie dressing behind a screen, attempting at speed to put on corsets,
camisole and other Victorian armour, Tom chuckling all the while.*

Minnie   Mrs Appleyard'll skin me.

FX   *The bell again. Commanding.*

Minnie reaches the door. She opens it, turns to face Tom.

Minnie   You better go.

*Tom smiles at her. Minnie smiles back, kisses across space, goes
through the door, closing it.*

53   INT.   COLLEGE—HEADMISTRESS'S STUDY. NIGHT.

FX   *A clock ticking.*

*Mrs Appleyard sits rigidly behind her desk, listening to time slipping
by.*

Mrs Appleyard   *(almost under her breath)* Why are they so late?

*Minnie has come in. Nervously she starts to clear away the remains
of a half-eaten supper, trying all the while to be as quiet as a mouse.*

A long moment. Suddenly—

Sound Off   *Shouting in the hall, the sound of the approaching drag.*

Mrs Appleyard   God be praised.

Mrs Appleyard is at the door of the study before Minnie has put down her tray.

54   EXT.   COLLEGE—FRONT VERANDAH AND GROUNDS. NIGHT.

Mrs Appleyard's cheeks, under the unshaded porch light, are the colour of tallow.

Sound Off *Hooves on the highroad—approaching. The drag is close.*

Tom has already bounded off down the drive. He pulls back the big iron gates as the twin headlamps of the drag swing around, the wheels scrape as they turn, the lamps momentarily light the handsome gold-lettered sign-board. The drag moves through the gateway and crunches slowly up the gravel drive.

Mrs Appleyard is maintaining her position of dignity on the top verandah step. Behind her in the lighted doorway stand the rest of the household—Cook, Minnie, Alice, Miss Lumley, the other maids, Mr Whitehead.

Hussey   (*hoarsely*) Whoa, there. Whoa...

The panting horses stand steaming in the cooling night air, Hussey jumps wearily down from his box, and from the dark mouth of the drag the girls come straggling out one by one. Some crying, some sodden with sleep, all hatless, dishevelled, incoherent. Dianne comes stumbling towards Mrs Appleyard, up the steps, into the yellow light.

Mrs Appleyard Mademoiselle. Why are you so late?

Dianne I...Mrs Appleyard...something terrible...has happened!

Mrs Appleyard What...What do you mean?

Dianne I...I can't...

Mrs Appleyard And where in Heaven's name is Miss McCraw?

Dianne We left her behind...At the Rock.

Mrs Appleyard Left her behind? Has everyone taken leave of their senses?

At that moment, Tom, seeing Dianne teetering on the second step, rushes forward and catches her just as she faints. The silence bursts into wild activity. Cook, Minnie, Alice are immediately there, loosening clothing, helping Tom to carry her inside.

One of the girls is carrying three straw hats. Edith—ashen-faced staring, wrapped in a blanket—is led through the pool of lamplight.

No one notices Sara in a nightdress, as she pushes frantically through the milling girls, searching for Miranda. Suddenly she sees the three hats. She stares at them, haunted.

Mrs Appleyard takes immediate control.

Mrs Appleyard Miss Lumley, get these girls to bed immediately. And Cook—hot soup, please, for them all.

Hussey, dusty and weary-eyed, is suddenly beside Mrs Appleyard, his big hand cradling one arm.

Hussey Mrs Appleyard. I must speak to you alone.

Mrs Appleyard nods, her eyes full of terror.

55 INT. COLLEGE—HEADMISTRESS'S STUDY. NIGHT.

Mrs Appleyard is seating herself behind her desk. Hussey sits opposite.

Hussey Well now ... aah ... Ma'am ... the strength of it is this aah ...three of your young ladies, and ... and Miss McCraw ... are missing ... on the Rock.

Mrs Appleyard looks at him for a long silent moment.

Mrs Appleyard (*finally*) What happened?

Hussey Well, now, Mrs Appleyard. That's the trouble. Nobody *knows* what happened.

56   EXT. WOODEND MAIN STREET. NIGHT.

People—men, women and children—are moving out of houses, pubs, shops; emerging from side lanes; gathering in little excited groups or standing silently alone—apprehensive.

Voices Schoolgirls—Lost on the Rock—and a teacher—Three of 'em—kids—from the College—Hanging Rock—No knowin'...

The words are muttered, murmured, shouted, whispered; carried on the night wind, now gently stirring.

Some of the people are beginning to gather on the roadway. A vehicle comes into shot: the police buggy driven by Sergeant Bumpher. The people move aside as the vehicle passes, heading for Appleyard College.

57   EXT. COLLEGE—FRONT DOOR. NIGHT.

CU: *Hussey.*

Hussey Well, all three of 'em are good big girls...

Widen to see Hussey facing Sergeant Bumpher. Minnie is hovering in the hallway beyond.

Hussey (*confused*) ...Mature, like. Seniors.

Bumpher Old enough, yer mean...

Hussey can't meet Bumpher's eyes.

Bumpher And the mistress...The mathematics mistress...

Hussey Forty if she's a day.

Bumpher How soon after the girls did Miss McCraw leave?

Hussey Don't know. No one knows. No one saw her leave. All asleep.

Bumpher And the little one...

Hussey Edith Horton. Like I said. She came tearin' out of the bushes, dress all torn, screaming fit to...(kill).

Bumpher's eyes flick.

Hussey When we'd shushed her screaming all we could get from her was that she'd left the other three somewhere up on the Rock.

FX *Dogs barking, bridging to the next scene.*

58   EXT. HANGING ROCK AND SURROUNDS. MORNING.

Sound Over *Dogs barking, bridging from the previous scene.*

A VISTA SHOT FROM THE ROCK: *Men down below, moving about, tethered horses, buggies and traps. Dogs are running about, yelping excitedly.*

SEQUENCE OF SHOTS: *A full-scale search taking place on Hanging Rock and through its surrounds.*

Men—locals and policemen—moving up the steep slopes of the Rock.

A policeman traversing the length of a deep crevasse.

A black tracker in his comic-opera uniform; searching for tracks—without success.

A line of locals and policemen moving methodically across a stretch of open ground beneath the Rock.

Men moving slowly through the shadowy forest. Occasionally the name of a missing girl is called. The words ring eerily through the trees.

A policeman with a hurricane lamp probing the depths of a dark dank cave.

59   INT.   COLLEGE—EDITH'S BEDROOM. MORNING.

Dianne's drawn face: tense and strained.

Dianne Try and remember Edith, chérie...

Edith is sitting up in bed, the sulky heroine of the moment. Standing on one side of the bed is Dianne, on the other side is Bumpher. Dr McKenzie is just behind Bumpher.

Dianne ...what it was that frightened you up on the Rock?

Edith sniffs, continues looking straight ahead. Bumpher is watching her closely. Dianne moves nearer, sits on the edge of the bed, her face close to Edith's.

Dianne (*quietly*) Think carefully, darling. Carefully. There must have been something.

No reaction from Edith. Dianne looks at Bumpher; shrugs. Bumpher's face betrays nothing. Edith is still staring straight ahead. She sniffs petulantly.

Bumpher Did you speak to anyone? Was there a man?

The doctor turns to Dianne.

Doctor I hope you don't blame yourself. No one can be held responsible for the pranks of destiny. And besides, it may turn out to be a storm in a teacup.

60 INT. COLLEGE—HEADMISTRESS'S STUDY. MORNING.

Mrs Appleyard is closing her study door. Dr McKenzie is standing in the middle of the room.

Doctor Her legs are quite severely scratched. From running through brambles, I should imagine.

The doctor sits—uninvited.

Mrs Appleyard Nothing else?

Doctor Nothing I could detect.

Mrs Appleyard She hadn't been...

The doctor looks at her, not prepared to help.

Mrs Appleyard (*finally*) ...molested?...

Doctor (*realizing*) Ah...No, no. Nothing like that. I have examined her. She is quite intact.

The doctor is looking at her, quite openly. Mrs Appleyard looks away.

61 INT. COLLEGE—SCHOOLROOM. AFTERNOON.

The girls are sitting at desks, working—or pretending to—in the drowsy afternoon warmth. Miss Lumley is seated behind the high teacher's desk at one end of the long plain room.

Sound Over *A knock at the door.*

The eyes swivel towards the door: Rosamund; Blanche; Sara.

The girls watch as Miss Lumley stands, moves across to the door, opens it. Bumpher is standing there.

Miss Lumley and Bumpher *An inaudible murmur.*

The girls exchange glances, whispering together.

All except Sara—she is excluded.

Miss Lumley turns back to the class.

Miss Lumley Blanche...

Blanche stands.

Miss Lumley You first.

Blanche nods, moves self-consciously, importantly, towards the door. The other girls are whispering excitedly together. Blanche has gone through the door, Miss Lumley closes it.

Miss Lumley On with your work please, girls.

Heads down, the girls are working again—sort of. Except Sara.
She is staring at the wall; at nothing.

62   EXT.   OUTSIDE LAKE VIEW HOUSE. DAY.

Bumpher is questioning Michael on the driveway outside Lake View.
Constable Jones is standing beside him—self-conscious—trying to
take notes as inconspicuously as possible.

Bumpher When you saw these girls crossing the creek did you
recognize any of them?

Michael How could I? I've only been in Australia about three weeks
and I haven't met any young ladies.

Bumpher I see. Did you have any conversation with any of these
girls—either before or after they crossed to the opposite
bank?

Michael Certainly not! I've just told you Sergeant, I didn't know
them. I simply noticed these three young ladies crossing the
creek. There's no offence in that, surely.

Bumpher What did they look like?

Michael is unsure of his meaning.

Bumpher The girls. Describe them to me.

Michael The first one was tall and dark, then there was the little
dumpy one, then a girl with glasses. The last one was slim and
fair.

Bumpher That's four.

Michael Pardon?

Bumpher A few minutes ago you said there was only three of 'em.

Michael smiles, a touch embarrassed.

Michael Oh, yes, of course. That's because the slim one was back a
little.

Jones writes on. Nothing from Bumpher.

Michael They moved off into the trees and that's the last we saw of
them.

Bumpher Did they know you were watching them?

Michael colours.

Michael I . . .

Bumpher is watching him—hard.

Michael I couldn't be sure. They made no sign. But Albert did whistle at them...

Bumpher makes no reaction.

63   INT.   LAKE VIEW STABLES. DAY.

Albert is shovelling muck.

Bumpher (*VO*) What sort of a whistle?

Bumpher is questioning Albert. Jones is taking notes.

Albert Well I dunno. Just an ordinary sort of whistle.

Bumpher Show me.

Albert grins, looks at Bumpher, then Jones, then back at Bumpher, then he controls his face and whistles—exactly as he did that afternoon by the creek below Hanging Rock.

No reaction from Bumpher. Jones scribbles on.

Albert (*to Jones, grinning*) Get that down all right, did yer?

Jones scribbles on. Nothing from Bumpher.

Albert Yes, well they was worth a whistle. Two of 'em was, anyway.

Bumpher (*flatly*) What did you do then?

Albert shrugs.

Albert Nothin'. We stood around yarnin' for a bit, then the Colonel and the Missus woke up, so I packed up.

Bumpher waits.

Bumpher (*finally*) Where was Michael Fitzhubert?

Albert thinks; adjusts.

Albert How do you mean?

Bumpher Well, where was he?

Albert The Colonel and the Missus was in the wagonette. I was drivin' and young Mr Michael followed on behind on the Colonel's white Arab.

Bumpher There all the time, was he?

Albert Who?

Bumpher Michael Fitzhubert.

Albert Well I reckon he was. He was there when we left and he came up alongside every now and then. He was there when we got back.

Jones is scribbling on, interminably.

Albert ...So I suppose he was there all the time. But not havin' eyes in the back of me head...

No reaction from Bumpher. None at all.

64 **INT. SERGEANT BUMPHER'S HOME. NIGHT.**

Sergeant Bumpher and Mrs Bumpher in their parlour. Bumpher sitting in his chair, deep in thought.

Mrs Bumpher crochets in a chair close by the lamp. She occasionally throws a glance in his direction.

Bumpher Well, Mrs Bumpher?

A long pause.

Mrs Bumpher Since you won't tell me *all* details how am I to give an opinion, Lionel?

Bumpher There *are* no details.

Mrs Bumpher People don't just disappear, my dear. Not without good cause.

There is a long pause. Finally he asks his question.

Bumpher There's talk, is there?

Mrs Bumpher Not just gossip. People have theories.

Bumpher Go on.

Mrs Bumpher It couldn't be a local.

Bumpher What couldn't?

Mrs Bumpher No one around here would do a thing like that.

Bumpher just looks.

65 **EXT. COLLEGE GROUNDS. MORNING.**

An ancient 'Al-Vista' panoramic camera is slowly panning, its tiny clockwork motor humming, operated by a young man—a newspaper reporter—complete with push-bike.

THE CAMERA'S POV OF THE COLLEGE: *A slow pan across the face of the building; Bumpher's buggy stands by the steps. Through the front door comes Mrs Appleyard, followed by Bumpher, Dianne, Edith, Minnie and a couple of the girls.*

Mrs Appleyard notices the reporter and immediately begins hustling the girls back into the College.

Bumpher assists Dianne and Edith into the buggy, climbs up himself and drives off.

The reporter has emerged from behind his camera.

Reporter (*calls*) Good morning.

Mrs Appleyard beckons Minnie to her.

Mrs Appleyard (*she hisses it*) Send that reporter packing! (*calls*) Girls! Get inside at once.

Minnie is approaching the reporter.

Reporter Good morning.

Minnie Git off!

The reporter is hurriedly packing his camera and trying to mount his bike as Minnie comes closer.

66   EXT. HANGING ROCK. LATE MORNING.

The upper slopes of the Rock.

Perhaps we glimpse—in high-angle LS—Bumpher's buggy, standing in the picnic ground far down below, the horse peacefully cropping grass nearby.

The rocks. Dominant. Dianne moves between two rocks, then emerges; Edith is with her, Bumpher close behind, they have been climbing hard.

Dianne Which way now, Edith?

Edith looks about her: left, right, ahead.

Edith I...I don't know.

Dianne Think darling. You have done very well so far.

Edith is getting upset.

Edith I don't know. It all looks the same.

Dianne glances towards Bumpher, but he is watching intently.

Edith I wasn't looking. I was tired. I wanted to go back.

Dianne Perhaps if we went a little higher...

Edith I was tired. I sat down on a log.

Dianne Which log, Edith? This one? Look around, chérie. See if you can see it now.

Edith looks around, sees a log close by, goes and sits on it.

Dianne Is that the one? You went that way?

   Edith shrugs.

Edith I don't know. I was tired. I'm tired now.

Dianne Chérie...

Edith But there is one thing I remember...

Dianne (*quietly*) What do you remember, Edith? Tell us...

Edith It was when I was coming down—when I was running...

   Dianne and Bumpher are watching her—totally absorbed.

Edith It was a cloud.

Bumpher (*quietly*) What sort of cloud?

Edith It was red.

   Dianne is puzzled. Bumpher is just looking at Edith—a totally
   bland expression on his face.

Edith I remember it clearly. It was just after I passed Miss McCraw.

   Bumpher is down on his knees, right beside the child.

Bumpher (*quietly, holding his excitement*) Who did you say you
   passed?

   Edith looks at him. Stares right into his face.

Edith Miss McCraw. She was going uphill as I was coming down.

Bumpher Did she stop? Did you speak?

   Edith shakes her head. She is staring straight ahead now, dredging
   down into her memory.

Edith She was too far away. She was as far away as those dead trees
   over there.

   Edith points. Bumpher measures the distance with his eyes. Edith is
   looking at Dianne. She giggles.

Edith She was funny.

Bumpher Funny? How?

   Edith turns to Dianne. She giggles again.

Edith I'd rather not say.

Dianne You must, Edith. It could be very important.

Edith It's rude.

Dianne and Bumpher exchange glances. Dianne goes right up to Edith, bends down, Bumpher steps back a pace or two. Edith looks at him, shrugs, smirks, covers her mouth, whispers in Dianne's ear. An expression of horror crosses Dianne's face. She stands, faces Bumpher.

Dianne Les pantalons. She had no skirt. Just...les pantalons.

Edith is watching the two adults—her eyes glistening. Suddenly Bumpher has Edith by the shoulders, looking right into her face.

Bumpher Drawers...You mean she was just wearing...drawers.

Edith nods. Her smirk disappears, her lower lip trembles, her eyes fill with tears.

67 EXT. VERANDAH AT LAKE VIEW. AFTERNOON.

Seated on wickerwork chairs on the verandah, looking out across the beautiful dreaming garden are Bumpher and Michael. They each have a drink. It is almost a social occasion.

Jones is hovering in the background.

Bumpher turns to Michael, half-smiles.

Bumpher The first time we spoke to you, Mr Fitzhubert; why didn't you tell us you followed the four girls?

Bumpher is watching him. Bland.

Michael I didn't exactly 'follow' them.

Bumpher is just looking.

Jones begins taking out his notebook—almost surreptitiously.

Michael I...I just jumped across the creek and walked towards the Rock for a little way.

Nothing from Bumpher. Jones is taking notes—almost secretly.

Michael I was curious. In England young ladies like that wouldn't be allowed to go walking in the forest. Not alone, anyway.

Michael realizes the ambiguity of his last words; but he presses on.

Michael But they'd gone by the time I was out of the trees; so I turned back.

Bumpher says nothing for a long moment. Michael is uncomfortable.

Bumpher (*on another tack*) As the girls were jumping the creek. What were you thinking about?

Michael looks from one to the other.

Michael I...

Bumpher Yes...?

Michael I...(*shrugs*) Well, how they all did it differently, as it were.

Bumpher Speak up. How do you mean 'differently'? Ropes, vaulting poles...?

Michael With different degrees of gracefulness.

Bumpher Did you say anything?

Nothing from Michael.

Bumpher To Crundall, I mean.

Michael No. No, I don't think so.

Bumpher Did Crundall say anything?

Both policemen are waiting for Michael to answer.

    68   **EXT. OUTSIDE LAKE VIEW STABLES. AFTERNOON.**

Jones is reading stiffly from his notebook.

Jones 'He said, "Look at the shape on the dark one..."'

    WIDEN A LITTLE *to see Bumpher standing there; watching.*

Jones '"Built like an hourglass."'

    BUMPHER'S POV: *A grinning Albert.*

Jones (*reading*) 'And then he said, "And the blonde one on the end. She'd have a decent pair of legs..."'

Albert knows what's coming, and he's a touch embarrassed now.

Jones (*reading*) '"...They'd go all the way up to her bum."'

Bumpher Is that what you said?

Albert Something like that.

Bumpher So you followed them. So you could have a proper look.

Albert turns on Bumpher, angry.

Albert No. I didn't.

Bumpher says nothing. Jones says nothing.

    69   **INT. COLLEGE—MIRANDA'S AND SARA'S BEDROOM. AFTERNOON.**

Miranda's room, still full of her possessions—and her presence. Her tennis racket; her photograph in a small oval frame; her home-made St Valentine card.

Sara looks up as Dianne and Bumpher come in.

Dianne opens the drawer, searching. She pulls out a lacy petticoat.

Bumpher (*to Dianne*) One last go. For the bloodhound.

Sara has been watching—horror touching her eyes. Bumpher (carrying the petticoat) and Dianne are about to go out. Dianne throws Sara a 'be brave' smile. Sara blinks, turns her face back to the window. An isolate, in her own tiny hell.

Sara (*to herself*) Miranda...

Hold the moment.

70   EXT. HANGING ROCK. AFTERNOON.

Policemen (including Bumpher and Jones) are searching crevices in the rock, looking under heaps of leaves and bark, probing bushes with long sticks—obviously looking for bodies. They find nothing.

71   EXT. CREEK BELOW HANGING ROCK. AFTERNOON.

A police party (Bumpher and Jones among them) dragging the dark green water of the creek with grappling hooks. Again and again. Nothing.

72   EXT. HANGING ROCK. DAY.

The bloodhound, attended by Bumpher and the police dog-handler, snuffling obscenely among the dust and dry leaves.

There is a moment of excitement when, on an almost circular platform of rock towards the summit, the bloodhound suddenly growls and bristles. But at what?

They search the rocks surrounding the platform and find nothing. They have difficulty, however, in coaxing the still-growling hound away from the area.

73   EXT. COLLEGE GROUNDS. DAY.

The main College building. Standing on the roof, behind the balustrade, is Sara.

Sara (*whispers*) Miranda...

74   EXT. LAKE VIEW GARDEN AND LAKE. AFTERNOON.

Sara (*VO: A sob breaking up the word*) Miranda...

A beautiful white swan, sailing serenely across the lake, concentric ripples spreading out and out across the dark still water.

Sound *The music of a small ensemble.*

CU: Michael. We realize the swan was his POV.

Albert (*VO*) The old man hired me to look after horses...

Albert and Michael are sitting on the tiny verandah fronting the little rustic boathouse overlooking the lake, a bottle of beer in front of them; Albert in working clothes, Michael in morning suit, his grey topper on the small table beside the bottle.

Albert ...so I'm buggered if I'm gunna be a lackey at a bloody garden party.

A carriage rolls up the drive, stops. A footman opens the door, a distinguished-looking couple alight, the carriage drives off.

On the lawns beyond the boathouse a garden party is in progress. Mrs Fitzhubert is entertaining the State Governor and his wife and a number of distinguished guests. A hired footman, three musicians from Melbourne, the maids serving strawberries and cream, plenty of French champagne. Colonel Fitzhubert, with a selected group of male cronies, has retreated with tumblers of Scotch and soda, under a weeping elm beside the lake, round from the boathouse.

Albert So that's what I bloody-well told him. More or less.

Michael is still watching the swan. Albert takes a swig on the bottle.

Albert burps.

Albert They had the bloodhound out the other day.

A silence between them. Music from the garden party drifts across.

Michael I wake up every night in a cold sweat, wondering if they're still alive.

Albert The way I look at it is this. If the bloody cop, the bloody abo tracker and the bloody dog can't find 'em, no one bloody can ... People have got 'emselves bushed before today, and as far as I'm concerned, that's the stone end of it.

Michael is suddenly angry. Angry at this Australian complacency. Angry because he can't forget the face of that girl as she crossed the creek. On an impulse he pushes his beer away from him, towards Albert. The glass overturns, spilling the remains of his drink.

Michael It's not the end of it as far as I'm concerned. They may be dying of thirst on that infernal rock. ... While you and I sit ... drinking cold bloody beer!

Albert eyes this 'new' Michael. His intensity has genuinely surprised, even shocked Albert. He smiles.

Albert That's where you and me's different.

A silence between them. Music from the garden party drifts across.

Albert If you take my advice, the sooner you forget the whole thing the better.

Michael I can't forget it. I never will.

Sound Off *Strains of the ensemble playing 'God Save the Queen'.*

Albert The Governor must be leaving—hey?

Michael, preoccupied, stares at the swan.

Albert Your Aunt'll raise hell if you're not on show...

Michael Albert! I want to go back to the Rock. To look for them. Will you come with me?

Albert lights a cigarette, looks out towards the lake, and the swan.

Albert Beautiful birds, them swans...A week in the bush...They'd be dead by now.

MICHAEL'S POV: *The white swan, flapping its wings, moving out across the water, its pink feet trailing behind, struggling to get airborne.*

Michael (*VO*) Then I'll go alone.

75 **EXT. LAKE VIEW KITCHEN DOOR/BACK VERANDAH. EARLY MORNING.**

Michael, sneaking out through the kitchen door, almost guiltily, carrying his boots. He pauses, reacts to Albert who is standing waiting with the horses, then moves towards him.

76 **EXT. LAKE VIEW DRIVE AND LANE. EARLY MORNING.**

Albert and Michael, riding down the Lake View drive. Out through the gates on to the steep, tree-shaded lane. Lush, verdant, civilized, affluent, lyrical. Smoke spiralling up from breakfasting kitchens beyond high-hedged gardens.

77 **EXT. MACEDON FOREST. MORNING.**

On a ridge above the plain, Albert and Michael rein in and pause. Hotter now; the horses sweating, the two men hanging in their saddles, saddle-bags packed with provisions, half-bags of chaff tied on behind—well prepared.

THEIR POV: *Hanging Rock, floating in splendid isolation on a sea of pale grass, in full sunlight, its jagged peaks and pinnacles more sinister than ever.*

78 **EXT. RIDGE. MORNING.**

Heels into flanks and the horses are moving off through the hot still air, down the ridge and out of shot. The Rock: waiting.

79 EXT. HANGING ROCK. EARLY AFTERNOON.

FX *The buzzing of blowflies.*

Michael is pushing his way through the thick scrub: it scratches his body, clutches at his clothes, the ground treacherous underfoot.

Out of the scrub. Ahead a grassy slope, merging into bracken. Fronds of curled brown velvet snap under his touch, his boots tread down the neat abodes of ants and spiders, his hand brushing against a streamer of bark dislodges a writhing colony of caterpillars in thick fur coats, brutally exposed to the strong light.

From a loose stone a lizard awakes and darts to safety at the clumping monster's approach. The rise grows steeper, the undergrowth denser. Gentle Michael, sweating freely now, pushes on through the waist-high bracken, every step cutting a swathe of death and destruction through the dusty green.

80 EXT. HANGING ROCK. MID-AFTERNOON.

FX *Blowflies.*

Mid-afternoon. Higher up. Michael looking way down below: the plain. Looking up: the vertical facade of the Rock drawing nearer, massive slabs and soaring rectangles, outcrops of prehistoric rock and giant boulders forcing their way to the surface above layers of rotting vegetation and animal decay: bones, feathers, birdlime, the shed skins of snakes, rocks with jagged horns and jutting spikes, obscene knobs and scabby carbuncles; others smoothly humped and rounded by the passing of a million years. The only sound the buzzing of flies.

81 EXT. HANGING ROCK. LATE AFTERNOON.

FX *Blowflies.*

Late afternoon. Michael, higher up still. Stumbling, climbing, seemingly without purpose. Suddenly—

Albert *(VO) A distant, faint coo-ee.*

Michael pauses, looking down.

MICHAEL'S POV: *The picnic ground diminished to a patch of pink and gold light between the trees.*

Albert *(VO) The distant coo-ee comes again.*

Michael looks upwards. The Rock goes upwards, seemingly forever. Taking a tiny pigskin-covered notebook from his pocket, he tears out a number of leaves and spikes them on to the twigs of a mountain laurel. Taking one last look around, Michael moves off downhill and out of shot, leaving fragments of paper hanging like little flags in the calm evening air. The only sound is the buzzing of blowflies.

82   EXT.   CREEK BELOW HANGING ROCK. EVENING.

Albert and Michael share a cup of tea by a brightly burning fire.

Albert   I followed that old overgrown track up—seemed like miles
—on me stomach. Nothing 'cept animals' bones.

   Michael says nothing.

Albert   (*almost in explanation*) People stop usin' tracks, but animals
don't.

   Michael is sipping the hot tea, preoccupied.

Albert   We'll have to be goin' soon. It'll be dark before we get back.

Michael   (*suddenly*) I'm staying here.

Albert   You're what?

Michael   I'm staying here.

Albert   (*almost incredulous*) You mean here? On the Rock?

Michael   Yes.

Albert   What the hell for?

   Michael doesn't answer.

Albert   You're mad.

Michael   (*losing his temper*) Perhaps I am. But I'm still staying. Someone has to. Just...just because you lot are Australians...

Albert   (*quietly*) You're a funny bugger...

   *Albert looks at him: hard. He realizes there is no use his arguing.
   But he has another worry.*

Albert   What the hell am I gunna tell 'em when I get back without
yer?

Michael   Tell them anything you like.

   Albert looks at Michael's implacable face: probing, without success.

83   INT.   LAKE VIEW—COLONEL FITZHUBERT'S STUDY. NIGHT.

*Colonel Fitzhubert, in his shadowed study, staring into a glass of
port, lamplight flickering on the fine glassware. Worry touches the
colonel's eyes. He looks up.*

Colonel   Woodend?

   Albert is standing awkwardly near the door.

Albert   At the Victoria, sir. The little pub near the corner. Mr

Michael was pretty knocked up, so he's sleeping there. At the pub.

Colonel Hmmm. Well I'm dashed if I know how his aunt will take it.

Albert breathes out.

The Colonel gives one last look . . .

Colonel Hmmm . . .

. . . then takes a good draught of port.

Colonel All right; carry on, Crundall.

Albert (*VO*) Thank you, sir.

Sound Over *Albert going out.*

The Colonel is staring at nothing.

84   EXT.   CREEK BELOW HANGING ROCK. NIGHT.

FX *Bush night sounds.*

The bush—black. We pan to find Michael on a bed of bracken, asleep, uncovered. He moans a little and moves—but he sleeps on.

85   INT.   LAKE VIEW—ALBERT'S ROOM ABOVE THE STABLES. NIGHT.

FX *A horse snuffling and stamping—somewhere close.*

Albert's truckle bed in his little box of a room above the Lake View stables. Albert is lying there, his eyes wide open, staring into the darkness.

86   EXT.   HANGING ROCK—LOWER SLOPES. NIGHT.

FX *Bush night sounds.*

Someone is coming, as quietly as possible, pushing through the bracken and the spiky scrub. Closer. Almost stealthily. Closer. Heavy breathing. Closer. The branches part. A white face looms up to the lens. Michael. He pushes past, a straining, haunted blur. The branches whip back and sting our face.

87   EXT.   HANGING ROCK. DAWN.

FX *Magpies—early morning birds.*

Michael comes into shot, pushing his chilled body through the dew-wet, waist-high bracken.

Higher up, the scraps of paper on the mountain laurel, now limp with dew. Michael touches one of them, looks up ahead, then pushes on, upwards.

88 EXT. HANGING ROCK. MID-MORNING.

Higher up still. Mid-morning, now. No bird songs. Michael spikes a page from his notebook on a twig, marking his route. He is wearying. He stumbles, his foot caught in a cleft. Slowly, carefully, he extricates it. He looks up.

MICHAEL'S POV: *He is staring straight into the gaze of a wallaby, some twenty feet away, looking down at him from a ledge of rock. The wallaby watches him for a moment, then bounds off slowly on a zig-zag course, following an animal track through the undergrowth.*

Michael (*to himself*) People stop using tracks; but animals don't...

Michael pulls himself up on to the ledge, sets off along the wallaby's path, spiking another scrap of paper as he goes.

89 EXT. HANGING ROCK. LATE AFTERNOON.

Even higher. Hot, now. And still. Michael emerges from the scrub on to a higher ledge, a natural platform of striated rock ringed with stones, boulders and clumps of wiry fern, shaded by straggling eucalypts. Michael pauses, looks about for a moment. Totally weary, his legs like lead. A sloping rock offers meagre shade. He lowers himself down and falls asleep.

FX *Sneak in the buzzing of blowflies.*

Hold Michael, in the thin ragged sleep of exhaustion.

90 EXT. LAKE VIEW STABLES/DRIVE/GATEWAY. MIDDAY.

Outside the stables. Albert swings his legs over his horse, mounts. A half-bag of chaff tied behind the saddle, the saddle-bags packed. Albert rides off, past the house, down the drive, out through the gate, on up the lane.

91 EXT. HANGING ROCK. MIDDAY.

Michael, still asleep beneath the overhanging rock. His face moves, twitches.

FX *The blowflies have gone, replaced by a low distant wordless murmur, almost like distant voices, with now and then a sort of trilling that might be little spurts of laughter.*

Michael opens his eyes, looking straight up.

HIS POV: *Eucalypts, their long pointed silver leaves hanging motionless on the heavy air.*

Miranda (*VO: A little way off*) *Laughing.*

Michael is on his feet, looking upwards.

Miranda (*VO*) *The laughter comes again...*

Michael Miranda?

No answer.

Michael (*louder, almost feverish*) Miranda?

No answer.

Michael sets off, uphill. Running, as best he can, up the steep slope. Prickly grey-green dogwood tears at his fine English skin. Huge rocks and boulders block his path, each a nightmare obstacle to be somehow got around, clambered over, crawled under. They grow larger and more fantastic.

Michael (*calling*) Miranda! Miranda!

He pauses, and somehow in his feverish state he spears a scrap of paper to a bush, then moves on.

Michael lifts his eyes for a moment from the treacherous ground underfoot.

HIS POV: *The monolith, black against the sun.*

Michael crawls towards the monolith, towards what looks like hair growing weirdly out of the side of the rock.

92 **EXT.   CREEK BELOW HANGING ROCK. MID-AFTERNOON.**

The Arab pony, tethered, feeding. The pony lifts its head, whinnies.

Albert, his horse in a lather of sweat, is riding into the camp-site. He notes the pony, dismounts, tethers his horse, kicks the fire, looks about.

Albert *Coo-ees.*

No answer.

Albert *Coo-ees again.*

No answer.

Albert moves off towards the creek and out of shot.

Albert, leaping the creek, moving off through the forest; urgently.

93 **EXT.   HANGING ROCK. MID-AFTERNOON.**

Albert is following leaves of paper spiked on bushes. From one to the next, to the next. Hot, tired. It's been a long hard climb.

FX *A blowfly begins buzzing—suddenly.*

Albert looks up. Ahead; sees something. Runs forward; stops. Michael is lying on his side, slumped over a tussock, one leg doubled

up under him, facing awkwardly downhill, unconscious, deathly pale, but breathing. Badly scratched face and hands. Beset by ants and flies.

Albert reacts.

94   EXT.   ROAD TO HANGING ROCK.

TRAVELLING SHOT: *Albert on the Arab pony, riding madly towards Hanging Rock, followed by the careering police buggy, driven by Bumpher, Dr McKenzie beside him: dust and the rolling, flashing eyes of horses hard-driven.*

95   EXT.   HANGING ROCK—PICNIC GROUND. LATE AFTERNOON.

HIGH-ANGLE LS: *Albert on horseback, followed by the buggy with Dr McKenzie and Bumpher aboard, move at speed through the open gateway and into the picnic ground, pulling up at the camp-site.*

Albert has dismounted, the two men have scrambled down from the buggy. Albert is leading them towards the creek and the Rock.

96   EXT.   HANGING ROCK. LATE AFTERNOON.

Bumpher and Albert, scrambling downhill as best they can bearing between them a makeshift stretcher fashioned from the all-weather buggy rug and two sapling poles, Michael's inert body jogging and sliding perilously about on the stretcher. Close behind is Dr McKenzie, clutching his black bag.

97 EXT. PICNIC GROUND. LATE AFTERNOON.

Bumpher and Albert are about to lift the stretcher up on to the buggy. The doctor takes Albert's end off him.

Doctor I'll take it, young feller. I've had thirty years experience fitting 'em in so they don't spill out on the road.

Michael is being hoisted into the buggy. Suddenly his eyes snap open. He is staring beseechingly into Albert's face. His eyes tilt downwards, looking at one hand: the hand unclenches. In the palm is a fragment of torn, dust-soiled lace. Albert sees the lace. Bumpher and the doctor are otherwise engaged. Albert takes the lace, nods at Michael. Michael's eyes close over once more.

Albert begins moving away from the buggy.

98 EXT. LOWER SLOPES OF ROCK. LATE AFTERNOON.

Albert, thrusting uphill, determination just holding his panic under. Upwards.

99 EXT. HANGING ROCK. LATE AFTERNOON.

Albert, at the point where he found Michael. He sees the paper leaf spiked to the twig. Looks uphill, sees another one in the distance, begins moving towards it.

Another piece of paper; Albert moving on, upwards.

Another.

And another; the monolith is straight up ahead.

FX *The buzzing of flies invades the sound track.*

A slip of paper, speared through by a thorn. Albert looks to the left—the way Michael had gone, moving level with the monolith, the sawtooth ridge of the topmost peaks glittering like gold against the sunset.

FX *The buzzing of flies is loud, now.*

Up ahead are the two 'balancing boulders'. Albert pushes on towards them, following the brave little paper flags.

100 EXT. HANGING ROCK—MONOLITH. LATE AFTERNOON.

Immediately below the balancing boulders Albert pauses, moves forward, hesitates, then drives himself towards it. A shred of fine paper is lying at the entrance to the tiny cave beneath the monolith.

FX *The buzzing of flies is almost intolerably loud.*

A girl, lying face downwards on a ledge of sloping rock, half in a tiny cave beneath the monolith, one arm flung out over her head, like a child fallen asleep on a hot afternoon. Ants everywhere. Busy. To Albert, a dead thing; hated; corrupted. He stretches out his leg, catches his elastic-sided boot under one shoulder and tips it over—as he would a dead calf in the paddock. The eyes are closed, the dark ringlets matted with dust and dried blood. A big blow-fly crawls out of a nostril. Albert gags, is almost sick, he forces himself to touch and hold one severely scratched wrist.

Albert Christ!

Suddenly, as Albert stares at the hated thing, there is a flick of life from Irma. Perhaps an eyelid moves. Albert's horror is now overwhelming.

Albert Jesus bloody Christ!

Albert starts back, takes one last look, then moves off, as the darkness, stored all day in fetid holes and caves, seeps out into twilight. The girl is left once more alone; to the ants and the harshly celebrating flies.

101   EXT. HANGING ROCK. LATE AFTERNOON

LOW-ANGLE LS: *Albert, way up on the top of a cliff-face. Silhouetted. He cups his hands around his mouth.*

Albert (*a long terrible wail*) Ahhhhh...! Ahhhhh...!

102   EXT. WOODEND MAIN STREET. NIGHT.

Woodend main street, fitfully lit by a few flaring lamps. Little knots of people are gathering, almost spontaneously.

Into shot comes the buggy, driven by Bumpher, Dr McKenzie seated beside him. In the buggy are the inert, unconscious forms of Michael and Irma, wrapped in blankets: children. A grim-faced Albert rides beside the buggy. The buggy stops outside the dispensary. The doctor tumbles out, hurries into the dispensary. Three or four locals gather round, peering into the black, closed buggy.

103   INT. COLLEGE—DIANNE'S BEDROOM. NIGHT.

Dianne, illuminated by a guttering candle, just beginning to wake.

Minnie (*VO*) Mam'selle...!

Dianne begins sitting up.

Minnie is standing by the bed, holding a candle.

Minnie (*unable to contain herself any longer*) They've found Irma!

Dianne What did you say?

Minnie They've found Irma. And she's still alive.

Dianne exhales—a long pent-up sigh of relief.

Dianne No one else?

Minnie looks at Dianne, shakes her head, her eyes filling with tears.

104   EXT.   WOODEND MAIN STREET. NIGHT.

A group of men—all armed, several carrying flaring torches—come clattering along the street, moving in the direction of the Rock.

Suddenly Constable Jones confronts the armed men, holding up one hand. They slow to a walk, then stop.

Jones The search has been called off.

Local We won't be searchin'. Not for bodies.

Jones notes the weapons.

Jones Go home. There's nothing you can do.

Another Local It's gone on long enough.

Jones Go home. It's a police matter.

Jones and the locals stare at each other for a long hard moment. The tall policeman, unarmed, is a symbol of authority they are not prepared to defy. One man hesitates.

Jones Well go on, get off. You too.

They slowly, reluctantly drift away.

Jones stands there in the near-darkness watching them, his thoughts hooded.

105   INT.   BUMPHER'S HOUSE. NIGHT.

A very tired, confused-looking Bumpher closes the front door of his house. He lets out a sigh and loosens the top buttons of his jacket.

Outside, various shouts and the sound of running feet momentarily distract him.

Mrs Bumpher has been standing near the kitchen door all the while, observing her husband. She looks frightened. Bumpher avoids her eyes.

More shouting and the sound of men and horses breaks the spell. Bumpher moves to the door.

106   INT.   COLLEGE SCHOOLROOM. MORNING.

Mrs Appleyard addressing the pupils: formally pious.

Mrs Appleyard We can thank the Lord for this merciful deliverance of our dear classmate, Irma...

The girls—all of them—sitting at desks: stunned, wide-eyed.

Mrs Appleyard ...and pray that Marion and Miranda...

The two teachers are standing at the back of the room: Dianne— pleased; Miss Lumley—trying to assimilate the truth of it.

Mrs Appleyard ...and our beloved Miss McCraw, will be likewise spared. It has been seen fit that our dear Irma should convalesce at the home of Colonel Fitzhubert on Mount Macedon...

The girls are still staring at Mrs Appleyard, barely able to believe the news.

Mrs Appleyard So, although you will be delighted by these good tidings, I would ask you to remember please, that of the three remaining lost members of the party there is, as yet, no trace.

The girls are still taking it in. Mrs Appleyard looks over their heads towards the back of the room.

Mrs Appleyard You may carry on, Mademoiselle.

Dianne moves to the front of the class, Mrs Appleyard and Miss Lumley go out. As soon as the door closes the girls go wild with hysterical joy: laughter, tears, fond embraces, two girls dancing a fevered jig around the room; and Dianne watching them: a smile on her lips and tears in her eyes.

107   INT.   COLLEGE—HEADMISTRESS'S STUDY. MORNING.

Miss Lumley is standing in the middle of the room, Mrs Appleyard is closing the door—shutting out the world.

Miss Lumley (*a touch timidly*) Wonderful news, Mrs Appleyard.

Mrs Appleyard is sitting down behind her desk.

Mrs Appleyard Don't be so foolish, woman. If all of them had been found—but only one. That will make it worse. Far worse.

Miss Lumley is struck dumb by her tone.

Mrs Appleyard This tragedy is little more than a week old, and already three—three, mark you—sets of parents have written advising me that their daughters will not be here next term.

Miss Lumley is about to say: 'How inconsiderate', but she doesn't get a chance.

Mrs Appleyard ...Now the newspapers have something further to sensationalize about. Newspapers all over the world have headlined our morbid affair, Miss Lumley; I mean, you realize that, I suppose?

Miss Lumley nods, quivering with the sheer thrilling horror of it.

Mrs Appleyard has the big ledger on the desk. She opens it, begins flipping through the pages.

Mrs Appleyard The three who have been withdrawn, plus the three missing on the Rock...

Miss Lumley Two, Mrs Appleyard. Only two, now. I'm quite sure Irma will be coming back next term.

Mrs Appleyard is looking down the current column of names and figures.

Mrs Appleyard In addition there are several sets of tuition fees impossibly overdue.

Miss Lumley is enjoying herself now, being taken into the headmistress's confidence like this.

Mrs Appleyard Sara Waybourne, for instance.

Miss Lumley Most inconsiderate, if I may say so, Mrs Appleyard.

Mrs Appleyard stands.

Mrs Appleyard Yes, well I expect we shall see our way through, somehow.

She glances at the clock.

Mrs Appleyard Don't let me detain you, Miss Lumley. You have a class in a few minutes, I believe...

Miss Lumley stands.

Miss Lumley Senior needlework.

Mrs Appleyard Just tell the Waybourne girl to call in and see me, will you please. Straight after luncheon will be convenient.

Miss Lumley Yes, Mrs Appleyard.

Miss Lumley is about to go.

Mrs Appleyard Oh, and Miss Lumley...

Miss Lumley pauses.

Mrs Appleyard Do your best to forbid morbid and idle chatter about this whole wretched business.

Miss Lumley Yes, Mrs Appleyard, I will.

Miss Lumley goes out, closing the door on Mrs Appleyard, who is now reaching for the brandy decanter.

108   INT.   LAKE VIEW HOUSE—IRMA'S SICKROOM. MORNING.

Irma—white-faced, unconscious, lying in the immense double bed with its patchwork quilt, seemingly afloat in a sea cave. The venetian blinds are drawn against the green garden light that ripples on the whitewashed walls.

Suddenly we realize that Michael is standing there, his face still bearing some evidence of his ordeal on the Rock. He is looking at Irma, his eyes expressionless.

FX *The sound of a horse-drawn vehicle outside—wheels on gravel.*

Michael goes to the window, parts the slats of the venetian blind, peers out.

A moment, then Michael moves away from the window, takes one last look at Irma, goes out, closing the door behind him.

We hear the unmistakable sound of the door being locked from the outside.

109   EXT.   LAKE VIEW HOUSE. MORNING.

LS: *Michael moving along an upper balcony, close to Irma's sickroom. He ducks down out of sight as the police buggy rattles past, towards the front door. Bumpher is driving, Dr McKenzie beside him.*

110   INT/EXT.   LAKE VIEW HOUSE FRONT DOOR. MORNING.

The maid has opened the door. Bumpher and Dr McKenzie, their silhouettes against the light outside, move through and past, into the house. The door closes.

111   INT.   LAKE VIEW HOUSE—IRMA'S SICKROOM. MORNING.

Bumpher and Dr McKenzie standing close together. In the foreground is Irma—in bed—still unconscious.

Doctor (*professional murmur*) Remarkable. Nothing more serious than shock and exposure. No broken bones. A few cuts and bruises on the face and hands. Hands, especially.

Dr McKenzie clinically picks up the small limp hand that has been lying outside the coverlet.

Doctor Scratched. Fingernails torn and broken.

Bumpher digests the verbal and visual evidence. But he says nothing. Dr McKenzie lets the hand drop.

Doctor Several other unusual factors. Head quite badly bruised. Probably concussion. A blow, perhaps. Or a fall. But if she fell, why isn't she injured elsewhere? Her body is quite unblemished.

Nothing from Bumpher.

Doctor And her feet are unmarked. That's very strange, because she wasn't wearing shoes or stockings when she was found.

Bumpher We found no trace of 'em up there.

Doctor No...(*almost as an afterthought*) She is quite intact.
Bumpher nods.

Doctor (*musingly*) I'd give my head to know what happened to her.

> *The door to Irma's room opens and a maid tiptoes in. She moves to a small table near the bed and picks up a bundle of soiled clothing. Poor Irma's picnic dress and underclothes.*

> *The doctor and Bumpher leave the room watched by the maid. She seems a little nervous. As the door closes she unravels the pile of clothing, momentarily holding up the crushed dress. She then looks as if she is about to follow the doctor and Bumpher; almost as though she wants to tell them something.*

112 INT. HALLWAY. LAKE VIEW HOUSE. MORNING.

> *Mrs Fitzhubert, in whose care Irma has been placed, is showing Bumpher and the doctor to the door.*

> *The maid from the preceding scene hurries into the hall holding Irma's clothes. Bumpher hesitates for a moment, wondering if the girl is going to say something. She doesn't. Mrs Fitzhubert turns and stares at her. The maid lowers her eyes. With a nod Bumpher leaves. Mrs Fitzhubert turns to the maid.*

Mrs Fitzhubert What is it, my girl?

Maid Well, Ma'am, it's Miss Irma.

Mrs Fitzhubert Yes?

Maid Well, it's about her clothing...

Mrs Fitzhubert What is it, my dear?

Maid Well, I didn't know like if the Sergeant should be told. There wasn't any corset...Miss Irma's corset, like...It's missing...

Mrs Fitzhubert (*reassuringly*) You did right, my dear. It can't possibly be of any interest.

> *As the maid moves through towards the back of the house Mrs Fitzhubert crosses to the window and stares after the Sergeant's buggy, disappearing through the front gate.*

Tom, sitting on an upturned tub in the green-brown gloom of the hot-house having a quiet smoke—well out of sight of everyone.

Tom   Any number of unsolved murders there are. Take Jack the Ripper, for instance.

Mr Whitehead is planting out seedlings—from a small seed-box into a larger one. He carefully lifts a seedling out of a smaller box, pokes a hole in the soil in the larger box, places the seeding in position, pushes the grey sandy soil in around it with his fingers.

Tom is watching Whitehead through his smoke, noting how slowly and methodically the older man is going about his task.

Tom   The police are up there again. Thick as flies.

Nothing from Whitehead—just fingers probing mucky soil.

Tom   Someone reported seein' a light flashin' around a pigsty on a place about a mile from the Rock.

Whitehead stands, wiping his soil-stained fingers on his trousers.

Whitehead   There's some questions that've got answers and some haven't...

Tom doesn't follow this line of Mr Whitehead's at all.

Whitehead picks up a watering can.

Tom   No. There'll be a solution turn up d'reckly, more'n likely.

He glances back at Whitehead. Whitehead is watering the trans-planted seedlings.

Tom   ...Like kidnapping or...you know...something like that... They could've fallen down a hole! Oh, there'll be a sol-ution somewhere, all right. There's gotta be.

Whitehead puts down the watering can. He smiles at Tom; a slightly mocking smile.

Whitehead   Come over 'ere. Come on. Over 'ere.

Tom, a little mystified, follows Whitehead to a corner of the hot-house. Whitehead looks about as if to make sure he won't be over-heard. He then speaks softly but dramatically to a wide-eyed Tom.

Whitehead   Did you know, lad...Did you know that there are plants that...that can move?

Tom   No!

Whitehead, with beautiful timing, reaches for a leaf on a plant close by. He delicately touches the leaf with his earth-stained finger. As if touched by the withering rays of the sun, the leaf suddenly closes.

The demonstration has a chilling effect on Tom, even if he doesn't quite know why.

Whitehead has made his point about nature and he moves away, a trace of a smile on his lips. Tom is left staring at the still crimped leaf.

114   EXT.   HANGING ROCK UPPER SLOPES. DAY.

A LOW-ANGLE VIEW *of the strange twisted stone peaks of Hanging Rock. The air is still, the sun high overhead casts shadows in hollows on the Rock. Some of the massive boulders seem almost to have twisted human features: here a gnarled old woman, there the visage of a hooded monk.*

From the Rock's POV. We look down, down on to Sergeant Bumpher. He stares up at the rock-pile, his eyes squinting in the harsh glare of the sun.

Bumpher Jim! Jim!

Constable Jones emerges from a clump of trees. Bumpher takes off his jacket and rolls up his sleeves, all the while keeping his eyes on the Rock. Jones joins him, wondering a little at the strange manner of his superior.

Bumpher I'm not giving up, Jim. (*a pause*) If they're not *on* it... then maybe they're *in* it.

115   EXT.   COLLEGE FRONT DRIVE. DAY.

Hussey, sitting aboard one of his buggies, waiting outside the front entrance to the College. One of the girls, accompanied by her father —carrying luggage—emerges. Hussey climbs down to help with the luggage. The girl and her father climb aboard.

Four girls are watching the buggy driving off: desolate; left behind.

116   INT.   COLLEGE—HEADMISTRESS'S STUDY. EARLY AFTERNOON.

Sara is standing in the open doorway.

Sara (*scared*) Miss Lumley said you wanted to see me, Mrs Appleyard...

Mrs Appleyard looks at Sara for a long hard moment. The anger and frustration that Mrs Appleyard feels as she sees her College sinking before her eyes seems somehow represented in the frail melancholy figure of Sara. She struggles to control the irritation and bitterness inside her.

Mrs Appleyard That is correct. Come in.

Sara comes in—just.

Mrs Appleyard (*with terrible mock patience*) Close the door.

> *Sara closes the door.*

Mrs Appleyard I have written Mr Cosgrove several letters but I have not been favoured with a reply thus far.

> *Nothing from Sara.*

Mrs Appleyard In fact it is all of six months since I received a letter or a cheque. I therefore have no alternative but to cancel all your extras.

> *Nothing from Sara.*

Mrs Appleyard This means that as of today you can no longer partake of dancing or drawing lessons.

> *Sara's eyes flick; drawing is her life; but she says nothing.*

Mrs Appleyard And unless all your outstanding fees are paid by Easter, we shall have to make other arrangements.

> *Nothing from Sara.*

Mrs Appleyard You know what that means, don't you Sara?

> *Sara shakes her head.*

Mrs Appleyard You will have to go away.

> *Nothing from Sara.*

Mrs Appleyard (*as though offering her an attractive alternative*). There are places for girls in your predicament. Institutions, Sara. . .

> *Sara is holding it in—just.*

Mrs Appleyard Now, off you go.

117 INT. COLLEGE—BACK CORRIDOR AND STAIRS. EVENING.

FX *The sound of a bell clanging—distant.*

> TRACKING SHOT: *Miss Lumley, snooping along a gloomy back corridor. She stops, looking down.*

Miss Lumley Sara, what's wrong with you?

> WIDEN *to see Sara, fitfully lit by a hanging lamp overhead, sitting on the stone floor at the foot of a narrow staircase leading upwards.*

Miss Lumley Are you feeling ill?

> *Sara could have been crying, we can't be sure. She doesn't answer.*

Miss Lumley People don't sit on cold steps in the dark unless they're weak in the head.

Sara doesn't answer.

Miss Lumley You heard the bell. Go and wash for supper.

Nothing from Sara.

Miss Lumley Aren't you hungry?

Sara shakes her head.

Miss Lumley Then you had best go straight to bed. Quickly.

Sara stands, staring straight ahead, her gaze going right through Miss Lumley.

118 EXT. COLLEGE. NIGHT.

LS: *Appleyard College. The clumsy two-storey mansion etched black against the dark indigo sky. Only one light is burning. A square of yellow in an upper-storey window. Possums are scuttling around the roof.*

FX *We hear the rattling snoring noise possums make.*

119 INT. COLLEGE—DIANNE'S BEDROOM. NIGHT.

Dianne is in bed, reading a French novel by lamplight. She looks up, staring at the black rectangle that is the window.

FX *Possums.*

120 INT. MINNIE'S BEDROOM. NIGHT.

Minnie and Tom together in Minnie's little bed. Naked under the covers. No lights, save the faint glimmer from the attic window. Minnie and Tom are holding each other.

Tom (*a crooning whisper*) I love you, Minnie, I love you, darlin'..

Tom is looking into Minnie's eyes, but Minnie is staring at the window.

Minnie I feel sorry for them kids.

Minnie has broken the spell.

Tom The ones on the Rock, yer mean?

Minnie Yes, them too.

Tom is watching her, his eyes full of love.

Minnie I was thinkin' of all them poor little devils. Here at the College.

Tom Them. They're all right. Rollin' in cash, most of 'em. Or at least their mothers and fathers are.

Minnie Some of 'em are orphans—or wards—or, you know.

Tom isn't happy. Minnie's love is being diverted elsewhere—for the moment. But Tom is patient.

Minnie And the ones with parents? They could be anywhere in the world. The kids don't seem to know themselves, half the time.

Tom is waiting.

Minnie Nobody cares for 'em. Any of 'em.

Tom pulls Minnie closer.

Tom (*gently*) Minnie...

Minnie is looking at Tom, now.

Minnie (*quietly*) What?

They kiss—a long, long, kiss—secure in their deep mutual love.

121 INT. COLLEGE—BLANCHE'S AND ROSAMUND'S BEDROOM. NIGHT.

The camera begins a slow exploration of the bedroom that Blanche and Rosamund share. A bed—empty—the covers pulled back. A second bed: Rosamund and Blanche in together, holding each other—asleep. Nothing sensual. Just children; lonely and frightened.

122 INT. COLLEGE—MRS APPLEYARD'S BEDROOM. NIGHT.

A large, high-ceilinged room, an elaborate canopied bed in the centre. Mrs Appleyard in the bed, covers up to her chin, her head a hedgehog of heavy steel curling-pins. Her eyes are open, staring at the windows. She tosses over, irritably, and is now staring at the wall.

123 INT. COLLEGE—MIRANDA'S AND SARA'S BEDROOM. NIGHT.

Sara, wide awake, staring into the dreadful dark.

FX *Possums.*

The room is a shadowed cavern of memories of Miranda: her cedar cupboard, her hats in their hatboxes, her tennis racket, her St Valentine cards, a photograph in its oval frame: hold the gently smiling image.

124 INT. LAKE VIEW—MICHAEL'S BEDROOM. NIGHT.

The white swan seems to be sitting on the brass rail at the end of Michael's bed. Michael is lying there, watching it, a feverish glint in his eyes. Michael and the swan look at each other for a long moment.

125   EXT.   HANGING ROCK. DAY.

Suddenly the Rock is alive with people once more:

Bumpher, standing talking with three senior plain-clothes policemen —probably from Melbourne.

Journalists...

Searchers...

Sightseers.

Someone incongruously even eating a picnic lunch.

Irma has been found; why shouldn't the others be likewise discovered alive, or—with a bit of luck—dead?

126   EXT.   HANGING ROCK UPPER SLOPES. DAY.

A searcher calling through a megaphone down into a chink in the rock; try anything. The voice echoes weirdly.

A searcher, stamping his feet on a shelf of rock: hollow.

127   INT.   LAKE VIEW—IRMA'S SICKROOM. AFTERNOON.

Dianne, standing at the open door.

Dianne   Hello, Irma.

WIDEN to see Irma in bed. Dianne closes the door; suddenly, impulsively, moves towards Irma.

Dianne   Madame Fitzhubert showed me in. How do you feel?

Irma lifts herself up on her elbow. Dianne is sitting on the edge of the bed, looking at Irma, eyes full of love.

Dianne   Oh, Irma...

They hold each other.

Dianne   Oh, Irma. We thought you had gone forever.

Both girls are weeping now, abandoning themselves to the silent luxury of sorrow shared. The shadow of the Rock lies with an almost physical weight upon their hearts. The thing is beyond words; almost beyond emotion.

Dianne is first to return to the tranquil reality of the summer afternoon. She draws up the blinds, letting in the peace of the garden beyond.

Dianne   Let me look at you, chérie.

Irma smiles through her tears.

Dianne   So pale. But prettier than ever. The handsome nephew; has he paid you a visit yet, the one who found you?

Irma (*almost choking on it*) And the police...

Dianne And could you...(*tell them anything?*)

> *Irma's eyes are filling with tears once more.*

Irma I remember...Nothing!

> *She bursts into deep, heartfelt tears of anguish and sorrow.*

128   EXT.   LAKE VIEW GARDEN. MORNING.

> *Michael sitting on the lawn in a deckchair reading a book—or trying to.*

Sound Over   *The tinkle of falling water.*

> *He looks up, out across the lake. Then he turns his head a little.*
>
> MICHAEL'S POV: *A giant clamshell bird-bath in the shade beneath a great old oak tree. Beyond, in a small man-made grotto, a vision of Miranda appears, for a brief instant.*
>
> *Michael's eyes shift.*
>
> HIS POV: *A white swan, floating on an ornamental pond.*
>
> *Michael's eyes follow the swan as it becomes airborne and flies away.*
>
> *Michael sits there watching. Across the lawn some distance away Irma approaches with Dianne. Albert Crundall crosses the lawns carrying a box of pheasants. Dianne moves away.*
>
> *Irma calls to Albert.*
>
> *Michael watches, a faint smile touches his lips.*

Irma Albert...

> *Albert's eyes flick but he pretends not to have heard.*

Irma Albert?

> *He pauses. She approaches closer. He focuses on some invisible object of interest above her head.*

Albert Miss?

Irma You know who I am don't you, Albert?

Albert Yes, Miss.

Irma Well...?

Albert Well what, Miss?

Irma I would like to thank you.

Albert Pardon Miss?

Irma To thank you. For rescuing me. On...the Rock.

Irma is very aware of Michael sitting just out of earshot. She has been trying not to look in his direction. Albert has sensed this. He glances towards Michael, then back again.

Albert That was nothin'. Besides, it weren't me. It was Mr Michael. He found yer.

She can now legitimately sneak a look in Michael's direction.

Irma But you *rescued* me.

An awkward pause.

Irma Aren't we going to shake hands?

Albert wipes his huge paw on his trousers and takes her hand.

Albert (*picking up his box*) Tell you the truth, I never give it another thought. I mean after the Doc and the Sergeant got you on the stretcher...Well...

They are joined by Dianne.

Albert I'd better be getting back to work.

He moves off, Irma watching; then Dianne joins her and together they approach Michael. He rises to greet them.

We watch the introduction in wide shot then cut in for a close-up of both Michael and Irma.

It is obvious that Irma is in love with Michael. Dianne can hardly restrain a display of the pleasure she feels at this beautiful match— this 'pairing of birds'.

Several shots follow of the trio walking in the garden, Irma and Michael, obviously getting on well together. Dianne as chaperone noticeably hangs back, finding various plants in the garden of particular interest.

129 INT. ALBERT'S ROOM ABOVE THE STABLES. NIGHT.

FX *A horse, stamping and snuffling, close by.*

A trapdoor in the floor opens and Michael emerges from the stables below carrying two bottles of beer wrapped in a wet chaff-bag. It is raining outside.

Albert (*VO*) How are they?

Albert is lying on his bed, almost naked.

Michael Beautifully cool.

Michael is fetching two mugs from a shelf.

Albert Best place I know for keepin' beer cold—that pond.

Michael snaps the top off one of the bottles.

Michael It's hot up here.

Michael is pouring beer into the mugs.

Albert Always is. Right under the roof.

Michael hands Albert a brimming mug.

Albert Ta.

Albert quaffs about half a mugful of the cold beer—which he obviously appreciates.

Michael It's a wonder you can get any sleep at all.

A silence.

Albert You've been seein' a lot of that Miss Leopold. Hey?

Albert's attempt at a joke. It fails.

Michael Yes.

130   EXT.   LAKE VIEW LAKE. LATE AFTERNOON.

A few yellow, brown and red leaves are floating between the reeds. The little lake, looking a touch chilling under the lengthening shadow. The small punt comes into shot, Michael expertly poling it among the closing waterlilies, Irma relaxing in the bows.

Irma Summer will soon be over.

Michael sits opposite her.

Michael Probably just as well. I don't think this old punt will be safe to take out again.

Irma rests her hand lightly on Michael's.

Irma *(her thoughts adrift)* It's sad, really. Like someone dying.

Michael looks at her. The chill in his glance brings her back.

Irma I mean the summer...The end of summer...is like...

Michael is looking out across the lake again.

Irma *(quietly; almost blundering on mock-innocently)* Miranda said everything begins and ends at exactly the right time and place...

It is almost as though Irma has pushed Michael too far—almost intentionally. He has removed his hand, stood once more, is now punting slowly—smoothly—mechanically. His figure, almost back against the lightening sky, is high above her, almost standing over her, almost threatening her, almost...

Michael (*still looking away*) Irma, what happened on the Rock?

Now Michael looks at her. His face is anguished, almost cruel. All traces of innocence have gone.

The colour has drained from Irma's face. She is deeply shocked. She looks away.

Nothing from Michael. He is staring over Irma's head at the haunted lake. His eyes are empty. The reeds stir mournfully.

DISSOLVE TO: *Michael, pulling the punt up to the boathouse. Irma watching.*

Michael (*finally*) I'm going away. North. To Queensland.

Irma takes a long moment to react. Finally she understands. Turning, she clatters off the little jetty, runs along the edge of the lake, her skirts flying...

Michael Irma! Irma!

...and into the bush.

131   EXT.   HANGING ROCK LOWER SLOPES. LATE AFTERNOON.

The search for the missing girls and their governess has been abandoned. A desolate feeling. Signs of the recent activity: the remains of some bales of hay, a broken cartwheel, lunch papers, a poster nailed to a signboard: 'Missing presumed dead'; above a detailed description are three extremely bad photographs of Miranda, Marion and Miss McCraw. Below this Bumpher has attached another sign.

> 'WARNING!
> No progress beyond this point due to police investigations.
> (Sgd) L. BUMPHER
> Sergeant of Police.'

132   INT.   MIRANDA'S AND SARA'S BEDROOM. EVENING.

The room is dimly lit, Sara lying in bed, facing the wall, her back is to Minnie, who is standing there, a supper tray in her hand.

Sara Tell Mam'selle I don't want it. (*an afterthought*) Thank you.

Minnie But you must eat. You'll be sick if you don't.

Sara turns to face Minnie, hair framing her pale face.

Sara I'm sick already. If I eat that I'll be even sicker.

Minnie Nonsense. Now come on, Miss...

Sara cuts across her, suddenly.

Sara (*flatly*) Do you know what, Minnie?

Minnie No, what?

Sara I was in an orphanage, once.

Minnie (*quietly*) Were you, Sara . . .

Sara (*dreamily*) I had a brother then . . . called Bertie . . . I told the matron I wanted to be a lady circus rider on a white horse, in a spangled dress . . .

Minnie is watching, and listening.

Sara She was afraid I'd run away. So she shaved my head.

Sara is looking at Minnie, daring her to disbelieve her. Minnie doesn't.

Sara (*simple innocence*) So I bit her arm. It bled. So she painted my head with gentian violet.

Minnie looks at Sara for a long moment, her eyes full of compassion. Then she leaves.

133 EXT. COLLEGE GROUNDS. MORNING.

Green and gold peace. Sara is sitting on a garden seat staring at nothing.

The young white turkeys stalk past.

Sara stands, moves slowly across and into the College.

FX *A piano playing—a child with reasonable competence—Bach's Prelude No. 1—bridging to the next scene.*

134 INT. COLLEGE HALLWAY/DRAWING ROOM. MORNING.

Rosamund is sitting at the piano, practising. The music, bridging from the previous scene, captures the melancholy mood of the College.

Sara, carrying her little flower-basket, drifts into the hallway beyond, pauses a moment, listening, then moves on.

FX *The piano bridges to the next scene.*

135 INT. COLLEGE—MIRANDA'S AND SARA'S BEDROOM. MORNING.

FX *The piano playing bridges from the previous scene.*

Sara is at the marble washstand, pouring water from the big china jug into a long glass vase. She places the single flower in the vase and carries it across to her dressing table, setting it down in front of the oval-framed photograph of Miranda.

Sara There you are, Miranda, dear. You like these best.

FX *The piano music concludes.*

Sara stands there for a long moment, staring at the vase and the photograph, gravely serious.

Suddenly, with a start, Sara turns to face the door. Dianne is standing there. Perhaps she has been there for some time. Sara smiles.

Sara She likes daisies best of all.

Dianne kneels beside Sara and takes her in her arms.

Dianne Sara, Sara, you do know that Miranda might not come back.

Sara looks at her for a long moment.

Sara (*finally*) Miranda knows lots of things other people don't know. Secrets... She knew she wouldn't come back.

Dianne stares at this strange frail child for a moment before again embracing her.

Sound Off *The scrape of wheels on gravel and the clip-clop of hooves— continuing...slowing...*

Hussey (*VO: Distant*) Whoa, there!

Sound Off ...*stopping*

Sara goes quickly to the window, looks out.

SARA'S POV: *One of Mr Hussey's cabs pulled up out in front of the College. Mr Hussey is helping Irma alight. She pays him.*

Sara still looking out.

Sara (*a shouted whisper*) Irma! Irma!

Sara runs across the room past Dianne, heading for the door...

Sound Over *Cab horse clip-clop—receding.*

...*opens the door, hurries out, leaving the door open.*

136   INT.   COLLEGE—HEADMISTRESS'S STUDY. MORNING.

Mrs Appleyard has been standing at her study window, watching Irma coming up the steps, hatred in her eyes. A changed Mrs Appleyard. Although not one wisp of her elaborate coiffure is out of place, and her clothing is as impeccable as ever, her back is not as iron-rod erect as before and her tallow-yellow face is now a suet-grey mask with sagging cheeks and age-ringed eyes.

Mrs Appleyard moves across the room to her desk like a sleepwalker in a mobile nightmare. She glances once more at a letter lying open on her desk, sits, opens her big ledger. Some of the names have been ruled off. She picks up her ebony ruler, dips her steel-nibbed pen in the red inkwell and neatly rules off yet another pupil's name. The red line goes through the copperplate script like a straight bleeding incision. Mrs Appleyard sits there, staring at nothing: her carefully structured world is falling apart—decomposing like a rotting organism.

FX *A piano, hammering out 'Men of Harlech'—hideously. Bridging to the next scene.*

137   EXT.   COLLEGE GROUNDS. MORNING.

FX *'Men of Harlech'—bridging from the previous scene.*

Dianne and Irma, delighting in each other's company once more, are walking through the College grounds, towards the detached gymnasium.

FX *'Men of Harlech' bridges to the next scene.*

138   INT.   COLLEGE GYMNASIUM. LATE MORNING.

Miss Lumley on the little raised dais at one end of the room, thumping out 'Men of Harlech' on the upright piano, the hideous music bridging from the previous scene.

The gymnasium, known to the girls as 'the Chamber of Horrors', is a long narrow building lit only by a row of barred skylights. On its bare lime-washed walls various instruments for the promotion of female beauty and health have been set out. There is, as well, a rope ladder suspended from the ceiling, a pair of metal rings and a set of parallel bars. A pair of iron dumb-bells and a set of weights complete the equipment.

Three rows of girls—fourteen in all—dressed in black serge bloomers, black cotton stockings and white rubber-soled canvas shoes, listlessly dip and rise in time to the music, performing a lunatic ritual with wooden indian clubs. One two, one two, one two: interminably.

Miss Lumley (*in time with her playing*) Fanny! You are ridiculously out of step! Pay attention to the music, please!

One two, one two, one two...

Suddenly the door opens, Miss Lumley stops playing in the middle of a bar.

Everyone is looking towards the door.

Irma and Dianne are standing in the doorway.

Dianne Excuse me, Miss Lumley...

Nothing from Miss Lumley.

Dianne Voilà, mes enfants, see whom we have with us today! Our dear Irma is going to stay with us for but a few hours. Soon she leaves to join her parents in Europe. Alors, mes enfants, for ten minutes you may talk as you please...

Dianne looks towards the dais.

Dianne Providing you approve, Miss Lumley.

Nothing from Miss Lumley.

Not a stir, not a murmur from the girls. They are standing there, silent, transfixed. Then each head, as one, looks upwards, over Dianne and Miss Lumley, through the lime-washed wall of the gymnasium, up, out and beyond.

FX *Suddenly the room is alive with the sound of cicadas—loud, oppressive, all-pervading.*

The girls break rank, silently, their rubber-soled feet shuffling on the sawdust floor. They are moving a little closer to Dianne and Irma. Their gaze is the inward stare of people who walk in their sleep.

The girls are moving closer.

The girls are moving closer still.

The girls are moving closer yet.

The girls are coming closer, inexorably closer.

The girls are close, so close. Irma and Dianne have been separated. Irma is pressed against the wall, the pressing girls a close semi-circle around her.

FX *The cicadas have gone. Suddenly. The silence is terrible.*

Edith (*shrilly*) Tell us, Irma, tell us!

A snub nose hugely out of focus with an exposure of bristling hairs...

Fanny Yes Irma, tell us.

...a cavernous mouth agape on a gold-tipped tooth...

Juliana Tell us, Irma, tell us!

...the moist tip of a drooling tongue...

Rosamund What happened to Miranda, Irma?

...heated bodies pressed against Irma's sensitive breasts...

Blanche You *know* what happened! Tell us.

...hot fetid breath on Irma's face.

Voices Miranda! Marion! Where are they? Tell us, Irma! Tell us! Men did it, didn't they? It was a man! Tell us! Tell us!

Irma (*now angry*) How can I tell you? I can't remember.

Edith has pushed right to the front.

Blanche Why can't you remember? Tell us Irma!

Edith They're dead! All dead as doornails in a filthy dirty cave full of bats on Hanging Rock. Dead—and going rotten.

Slap! Dianne has somehow pushed forward and slapped Edith across the face.

Edith pushes back through the others—shocked and frightened— her hysteria gone, her face livid and stinging. The others fall back, the hysteria under control. Dianne is holding a shocked and sobbing Irma. Suddenly Rosamund comes forward, takes Irma's arm.

Irma moves away with her. Blanche takes the other arm. Irma tries to smile. The Rock has changed everything. No one involved is left untouched and for these girls there is no going back to the innocence that should have been theirs for several years yet. They leave in ones and twos, ashamed and saddened.

Dianne lets out a deep sigh, looks up towards Miss Lumley, still sitting at the piano, seemingly immovable.

Sound Over *A faint whimper.*

Dianne turns, hurries towards a dim corner of the gymnasium, behind a vaulting horse. A padded horizontal board, fitted with leather straps: Sara is strapped to the board—rigid.

Dianne looks up. Miss Lumley has come down from the dais and joined them. Her lips are smiling.

Miss Lumley It's for her own good. To cure her terrible stooping.

Dianne's eyes are full of an inexpressible hatred.

139 INT. COLLEGE—HEADMISTRESS'S STUDY. LATE AFTERNOON.

Mrs Appleyard is seated at her desk, the big ledger open before her. Mrs Appleyard glances at a recently opened letter, picks up her pen, dips it in the red ink and rules another pupil out of existence. Only nine names are left.

Sound Off *A knock at the door.*

Mrs Appleyard is staring at nothing.

Sound Off *Knocking—again and again.*

Mrs Appleyard (*finally*) Come in.

The door opens. Miss Lumley is standing there.

Mrs Appleyard Well, come in.

Dora Lumley is suffering an agony of indecision. She finally summons up courage, strides to Mrs Appleyard and hands an envelope across the desk.

Miss Lumley My notice, Ma'am.

140 INT. COLLEGE STAIRCASE. EVENING.

Mrs Appleyard, slowly descending the lamplit staircase, exhausted. The events of the past month are taking their toll. She meets Minnie, on the way up, carrying a tray set out with a lace-trimmed cloth and fine Japanese china: a boiled egg, bread and butter, jelly and cream.

Mrs Appleyard Oh? And have we an invalid in the house?

Minnie is not frightened of flaccid old Mrs Appleyard now.

Minnie Miss Sara's supper, Ma'am. Mam'selle asked me, seein' the child's feelin' poorly.

Mrs Appleyard Hmmm...

Minnie smiles, moves past and up. Mrs Appleyard continues descending, then suddenly stops and turns.

Mrs Appleyard Minnie...

Minnie pauses, almost at the top.

Mrs Appleyard Kindly tell Miss Sara not to put out her light until I have had a word with her.

Minnie Yes, Ma'am.

141 INT. COLLEGE—HEADMISTRESS'S STUDY. NIGHT.

The door opens, Mrs Appleyard comes in. She stands there in front of her desk for a long moment—looking slowly around the room— as though for the first time.

It is all there—her life—on display: photographs, trophies, knick-knacks, faces. Glass, china, ebony, ivory, silver, bronze. Solid, respectable, blameless, arrogant, dead. A museum.

She sits down at her desk.

FX *The clock ticks on, forever.*

Mrs Appleyard's face is an empty mask. She turns her chair away from the faces on the wall. They must not see.

We hear nothing, but her lonely body is shaking with deep stifled sobs.

Mrs Appleyard (*a whisper*) God help me.

142   INT.   COLLEGE—MIRANDA'S AND SARA'S BEDROOM. NIGHT.

Sara is in bed. The supper Minnie brought her untouched. She hears someone approaching along the corridor. A shiver passes through her body as the door opens, revealing Mrs Appleyard; but she summons all her silent sulky courage and stares coolly at the hateful woman.

Mrs Appleyard's face stiffens. How she detests this unbreakable bastard child. She glances at the uneaten food.

Mrs Appleyard You recall our recent discussion, Sara?

Nothing from Sara.

Mrs Appleyard Answer me when I address you, child!

Sara (*finally*) Yes.

Mrs Appleyard I have considered your situation carefully. I have searched my mind—and my conscience—for a solution.

Sara blinks. The woman may as well be speaking Bantu.

Mrs Appleyard But this is not a charitable institution, and as your fees have not been forthcoming I have been forced to make certain arrangements on your behalf.

Still Sara says nothing. But she knows what Mrs Appleyard is on about now.

Sara awaits sentence.

Mrs Appleyard You will be returned to the orphanage.

Even battle-hardened Mrs Appleyard, with years of monstering children behind her, is momentarily disturbed by this strange haunted child. Sara's face is all eyes—enormous black eyes, burning into her own.

143   INT.   COLLEGE—MRS APPLEYARD'S BEDROOM. NIGHT.

Mrs Appleyard, fully dressed, sits on the edge of her bed. She seems disturbed by her interview with Sara. She stands, makes to leave the room, then changes her mind and returns to the edge of the bed.

144   EXT.   APPLEYARD COLLEGE. NIGHT.

WS: *The school, shrouded in a fine mist. Silence. Lights pierce the gloom, but only just. A painted ship adrift on a painted sea.*

FX *The faint distant sound of breaking glass.*

145   EXT.   LAKE VIEW HOUSE. MORNING.

The Fitzhubert carriage is drawn up outside the front door of the house. Luggage is being passed by a maid to a footman who stacks it on the back of the vehicle.

Lake View is being closed for the winter.

146   INT.   LAKE VIEW—ALBERT'S ROOM ABOVE THE STABLES. MORNING.

Albert, soon to drive the carriage to the station, is partly dressed in his coachman's uniform. He has been pouring whisky into two mugs. He picks them up, we track with him as he moves to where Michael is standing by the tiny open window. Albert offers Michael a mug.

Albert   Here. Farewell drink.

Michael takes the mug, but says nothing for a long moment.

Michael   Later...when things are settled...Why not come up north with me...?

Albert   Well...I dunno. There's the Colonel...

Michael   I want to look at a big cattle station. Goonawingi.

Finally Albert grins.

Albert   Yes, I reckon I could. Be a change...

Michael is staring at his whisky. Albert lifts his mug.

Albert   To us, then. And Queensland.

Michael lifts his mug. But he is a touch preoccupied.

Michael   Lately I find whisky's quite a help when I can't sleep.

Albert   You still thinking about that bloody Rock?

Michael   I can't help it. It comes back at night. In dreams.

Albert   I had a funny dream last night!

Michael drinks.

Albert   There was this smell. Real strong.

Michael fills Albert's mug.

Albert   It was like I was wide awake.

Albert drinks.

Albert   Pansies. That's what it smelt like. And the place was all lit up. Bright as day. But pitch-black outside. And there she is. Standing there. Right there. At the end of the bed.

Michael   Who? Who was it?

Albert   It was only a bloody dream.

Michael: intent.

Albert It was me kid sister. I haven't seen her...not since the orphanage. She always liked pansies...Then she went sort of misty.

Michael (*almost a whisper*) Translucent.

Albert I calls out, 'Sara! Don't go!' 'Goodbye Bertie', she says. 'I've come a long way to see you, but I must go.' And then she went. Clean through that wall.

Nothing from Michael.

Albert You reckon I'm batty...

Nothing from Michael for a long moment.

Michael (*finally*) No. Of course not.

Albert's face tells us he will accept Michael's offer.

147 EXT. APPLEYARD COLLEGE—MAIN GATE. MORNING.

FX *Distant church bells.*

Michael stands near the main gate, staring towards the school. The big Georgian structure is bathed in morning sunlight. Several girls emerge from the building. Michael thinks of Miranda, of the picnic, of all that has happened.

Behind him, Albert is approaching from the waiting Fitzhubert carriage.

Albert Mike?

With a last look Michael turns and walks back towards the carriage.

148 INT. WOODEND CHURCH. MORNING.

The College girls—and Dianne—in church. The organ playing, everyone is singing 'Rock of Ages', everyone is ignoring everyone else.

The tiny church is comfortably full, but there is an empty pew in front of the one occupied by the College party, and another empty pew behind them.

Rosamund (*VO*) *weeping.*

PAN to find Rosamund, tears streaming down her face. The singing continues—remorselessly.

149 EXT. WOODEND CHURCH. MORNING.

Church is over. A knot of locals in their Sunday best are standing in the front grounds of the little building, talking, gossiping. A few worshippers are still emerging, the clergyman is saying his farewells.

Someone looks up towards the church door. The talking has stopped. The party from Appleyard College is emerging: nine girls, followed by Dianne. Each exchanges a good-morning with the clergyman, moves down the steps and along the path. The locals move to one side —well to one side. It's as though the girls have got the clap or something. Pairs of eyes follow the scandal-infected party as they approach the gate. A small boy is standing by the gate. He hisses, just as Blanche turns; her tongue comes straight out and straight back in again, neither breaking stride nor losing her dignity. The silent non-approvers watch as the party approaches the two Hussey buggies —Mr Hussey and his assistant sitting stiffly on their seats—looking straight ahead, disowning their clients—just doing a job. No one gets down to help anyone—the College girls are on their own.

150   INT.   COLLEGE HALLWAY. LATE MORNING.

The party of schoolgirls, returned home from church, is filing in through the door, talking quietly and pleasantly together. They look up, see Mrs Appleyard standing in the study doorway and are quiet. They continue on up the stairs, seemingly cowed into silence. Dianne is the last to come in. She closes the front door.

Mrs Appleyard Mademoiselle. . .

Dianne looks up.

Mrs Appleyard I would like a word with you, please.

151   INT.   COLLEGE—HEADMISTRESS'S STUDY. LATE MORNING.

Dianne follows Mrs Appleyard into the study. Mrs Appleyard closes the door, sits down behind her desk.

Mrs Appleyard Sit down please, Mademoiselle.

Dianne Merci.

Dianne sits.

Mrs Appleyard (*working hard to appear normal*) We were speaking last night about the Waybourne child. You expressed concern about the state of her health.

Dianne nods.

Mrs Appleyard We have been relieved of any further responsibility. Her guardian, Mr Cosgrove, arrived this morning and took her away with him.

Dianne But was she fit enough to travel?

Mrs Appleyard Apparently.

Dianne I should have been here. To supervise her packing.

Mrs Appleyard I myself helped Sara put a few things she specially wanted in her little covered basket. Mr Cosgrove was in a hurry to get away.

Mrs Appleyard stands—the interview is concluded.

Mrs Appleyard I shall not be coming in to luncheon. Kindly tell them not to lay a place for me.

Dianne (*unaccountably*) Nor for Sara.

Mrs Appleyard Nor for Sara.

Dianne has moved to the door, opens it.

Mrs Appleyard (*a touch of ice*) Is that rouge I see on your cheek, Mademoiselle?

Dianne Powder, Madame. I find it becoming.

Dianne goes out, with a delicate swish of her skirts.

Mrs Appleyard stands—slowly—then moves across to the door, closing it and turning the key in the lock.

The cupboard under her desk is open a little. She pushes it with her foot—it closes, and springs open again. Impatiently she attempts to close it again. To no avail. She bends down, opens it, takes out the little covered basket that has been resisting the door, re-positions it in the cupboard, closes the door properly this time, and locks it.

152 INT. COLLEGE—UPPER HALLWAY. LATE AFTERNOON.

Dianne walks along the upper corridor toward her room. She glances in the direction of Sara's room.

The door is slightly ajar. A shadow from a figure in the room is cast on the wall. Dianne pauses.

Dianne (*a whisper*) Sara . . .?

She hurries to the room, hesitates a moment at the door, then enters.

153 INT. COLLEGE—MIRANDA'S AND SARA'S BEDROOM. LATE AFTERNOON.

The shadow belongs to Minnie.

Minnie Young Sara certainly left in a terrible hurry. She's a funny little thing.

Sara's dressing-gown is over the back of a chair, a pair of bedroom slippers on the washstand. Minnie begins stripping the sheets off Sara's bed. Dianne has moved across to the mantelpiece. She picks up the photograph of Miranda.

Minnie looks up for a moment, then returns to her bed-stripping: saying nothing.

Dianne replaces the photograph. Miranda is smiling at her.

154   EXT.   COLLEGE GROUNDS. MORNING.

Sound *The sudden noise of chattering, laughing, excited schoolgirls bursts on to the sound-track.*

Mr Hussey is pushing the last trunk into position on a buggy already overloaded with luggage and schoolgirls—in their travelling clothes.

Hussey That's that...

Hussey climbs up on to his seat.

Hussey Stand clear, ladies, please. All clear to go? Right, take hold of it.

Dianne is watching as the buggy begins moving away.

Girls Goodbye, Mam'selle! Goodbye!

Dianne is waving.

Dianne Au revoir.

Dianne stands watching and waving as the buggy, its cargo of girls —their sentences suddenly commuted—waving back, clip-clops down the drive, through the gate and out of shot.

The girls are singing 'Frère Jacques'.

155   INT.   COLLEGE HALLWAY. MORNING.

Dianne, suddenly very weary, comes through the front door and walks slowly across the hallway towards the stairs.

Mrs Appleyard (*VO*) Mademoiselle, have the last of them gone?

Dianne stops, turns. Mrs Appleyard is standing in the doorway to her study, fighting to control her twitching face and jumping limbs.

Dianne Yes, Madame.

An ironic smile touches Mrs Appleyard's lips.

Mrs Appleyard Well, we have the entire place to ourselves.

Dianne doesn't answer.

Mrs Appleyard I wonder if you would care to join me at dinner tonight. To celebrate the vacation.

Dianne Of course, Madame.

Mrs Appleyard You will be leaving early in the morning?

Dianne Yes, Madame.

The last traces of an elegant dinner on a small, beautiful table, intimately lit. Mrs Appleyard is drunk, but she has herself under control; the twitchings and shakings have gone and only the heavy-lidded eyes and the slight slurring of speech betray her condition.

Mrs Appleyard Arthur—my late husband—and I always took our annual holidays at Bournemouth.

Dianne is sitting opposite her. Tired, bored stiff, a touch embarrassed by the totally novel intimacy of it all—and just a little frightened.

Mrs Appleyard Delightful place. Absolutely delightful. Nothing changed. Ever. Not in forty years. The pier, the sands, the people, the guest-house, dependable. Completely and utterly dependable.

Mrs Appleyard reaches for the almost-empty brandy decanter.

Mrs Appleyard A little more, Mademoiselle?

Dianne clasps her elegant stemmed brandy glass—half-full. She smiles—with some difficulty.

Dianne No thank you.

Mrs Appleyard As you wish.

A silence. Mrs Appleyard is staring ahead, as though working out the solution to some difficult problem. Suddenly she strikes the table with her fist, causing Dianne and several cups, saucers and plates to jump.

There is another silence. Finally she speaks, as though to herself. Dianne is now plainly frightened.

Mrs Appleyard I came to depend so much on Greta McCraw. So much masculine intellect. I came to rely on that woman. Trust her. How could she allow herself to be spirited away?

She turns to Dianne as though expecting an answer. There is none.

Mrs Appleyard Lost. Raped, murdered in cold blood like a silly schoolgirl. On that wretched Hanging Rock.

The last words are spoken with a hint of the bitterness and hatred she has now transferred to the picnic ground. Suddenly aware of exposing herself to Dianne, she smiles sweetly and resumes her earlier mood.

Mrs Appleyard (*glancing at Dianne's glass*) Yours is still half-full, Mademoiselle.

Dianne attempts to communicate her satisfaction at the state of her glass with a half-smile.

Mrs Appleyard pours the last of the brandy into her previously empty glass. She reaches for the bell cord.

Minnie appears.

Minnie Yes, Ma'am?

Mrs Appleyard Is there more brandy, Minnie?

Minnie I wouldn't...(*think so, Ma'am*)

Mrs Appleyard Yes, there is! I remember. We opened a bottle the day the Bishop of Bendigo came to lunch. It should be in the pantry. *

Minnie Yes, Ma'am.

Minnie stalks off, disapproval in every movement.

Mrs Appleyard Providing that lecherous creature Tom hasn't drunk it all, of course.

Dianne is somehow preoccupied.

Dianne Will Sara Waybourne be back next term, Madame?

Mrs Appleyard stares at her. Blinks.

Mrs Appleyard Now, where was I? Ah, yes. Bournemouth.

157 INT. MIRANDA'S AND SARA'S BEDROOM. NIGHT.

The room is empty. Slowly the door opens and an old woman comes in. An old woman carrying a nightlight. An old woman with head bowed under a forest of curling-pins, with pendulous breasts and sagging stomach beneath a flannel dressing-gown. Mrs Appleyard: without her battledress of steel and whalebone.

The big double bedroom, feebly lit, is now in perfect order. The blinds are all drawn to the same level, disclosing identical rectangles of moonlit sky and the dark tops of trees. The two beds, each with a pink silk eiderdown quilt neatly folded, are immaculate. Putting the nightlight on a bedside table she opens the cedar cupboard.

The old woman's scrawny be-ringed talons scrabble through Miranda's beautiful dresses; they go methodically through the shelves —shoes, tennis rackets; through the bureau: the stockings, handkerchiefs, those ridiculous Valentine cards—dozens of them. But no letters, no documents. The dressing table; the washstand. Lastly, the mantelpiece. Nothing of significance. Then suddenly—Miranda: the photograph—watching her every move, glowing somehow in the moonlight.

The old woman steps back, picks up the nightlight and shuffles out, closing the door.

For a moment we are alone with the room, its memories and its ghosts.

158   EXT.   COLLEGE GROUNDS. MORNING.

FX   *The humming of bees—a peaceful noise—just insinuating itself on to the sound-track.*

Mr Whitehead trundles into shot, slowly pushing a wheelbarrow along the path beside the hot-house. He reaches the entrance to the hot-house, stops, takes two potplants off the barrow and goes inside.

FX   *The humming of bees, bridging to the next scene.*

159   INT.   COLLEGE HOT-HOUSE. MORNING.

FX   *The humming of bees bridges from the previous scene.*

Whitehead, carrying the potplants, coming through the green mouldering gloom of the hot-house.

Something crunches underfoot. He pauses, looks down, broken glass. He looks up.

HIS POV: *A couple of glass panes in the roof have been broken ahead of where he is standing. Not dramatically—one whole pane seems to have been removed in its entirety, another has broken cleanly. The patch of sky beyond is beautifully blue.*

FX   *The humming of bees is a fraction louder.*

Mr Whitehead sniffs the air—wrinkles his nose. Something doesn't smell too good.

Mr Whitehead begins moving purposefully towards the place beneath the broken panes—towards the back of the hot-house. The plants have been placed more thickly back here, and are bigger. A veritable tropical jungle in miniature.

FX   *The humming is a touch louder.*

Mr Whitehead continues moving through the light-slated greenery, the going becoming more difficult as the plants become even thicker and larger.

FX   *The humming is very loud, now.*

Suddenly he sees it—a small body in a nightdress soaked with dried blood. One leg bent under the tangled body, lying twisted on a long

*slate slab. Only one pot has been smashed, one plant unearthed—
the bare roots obscenely touching the other thin leg. Feet bare, head
crushed in, the small white face across which a stream of ants is
moving—unmistakably Sara's.*

FX *The humming is hideously, totally loud.*

*Mr Whitehead gags, is almost sick, then begins moving hurriedly
backwards through the greenery, no thought now of what damage he
is causing the plants. The dead girl is left alone with the gloom, the
ants and the roaring bees.*

160 **INT. COLLEGE—HEADMISTRESS'S STUDY. MORNING.**

*The skeleton of taffeta that is now Mrs Appleyard, sitting hunched
over her desk, staring at nothing. Her luggage, packed ready for
departure, is stacked between the desk and the door.*

Sound Over *A knock at the door.*

Mrs Appleyard doesn't stir.

Sound Over *The knock comes again.*

Not a flicker from Mrs Appleyard. Suddenly the door flies wide open, as though of its own accord. Mr Whitehead is standing there, his face ashen, damp black soil clinging to the knees of his sagging trousers and the front of his unironed shirt. He doesn't move from the doorway.

Mrs Appleyard's eyes: waiting for it.

The camera begins a slow track in on Mrs Appleyard as she stands rigidly by her desk, her eyes fixed on some point beyond the old gardener. There is a silence, as if her very look has stifled the words in his throat.

All sound on the track fades to a heavy leaden silence.

As the camera reaches its end position, holding the headmistress in close-up, we see on her face a hint of madness.

DISSOLVE TO:

161 EXT. PICNIC GROUNDS. AFTERNOON.

The picnic. The schoolgirls moving against the shadowed textured background that is Hanging Rock in jerky slowmotion: clockwork dolls.

Miranda, Irma, Marion, Edith. Dianne, Miss McCraw, Mr Hussey.

Voice Over *The body of Mrs Arthur Appleyard, principal of Appleyard College, was found at the base of Hanging Rock on Friday, March 27, 1900. Although the exact circumstances of her death are not known, it is believed she fell while attempting to climb the Rock. The search for the missing schoolgirls and their governess continued spasmodically for several years without success. And to this day their disappearance remains a mystery.*

Dianne, waving.

Miranda, waving. Hold her image, frozen forever.

FADE SOUND AND VISION.

END CREDITS.

Picnic — Looking Back

Note: Numerals given in brackets are page-numbers.

(1) How is an atmosphere of mystery and enigma established from the very beginning of the film?

(2) The second sound-direction in the script states: '*Throughout this getting up/titles sequence the natural sounds are separated and accentuated; almost harshly so; almost contrapuntal to the lyrically soft visuals.*'

Why do you think there is this contrast so early in the film, between the natural sounds of the bush and the lyrically soft visuals—which, at this stage of the film, depict the young girls in their College rooms? [143−4]

(3) Turn to page 146 and read the description under 14 EXT. In this long shot of the College, the incongruity of the traditional and conventional College building in its bush setting is emphasized. Give other examples of similar incongruities that have already been written into the script.

(4) Conflict is an essential ingredient in any piece of vital drama. What kind of conflict is quickly discovered in the film among the teachers (or mistresses), and between the teachers and their students? [147]

(5) Referring to going home to Queensland, Miranda says to Sara: 'You must learn to love someone else apart from me, Sara. I won't be here much longer.'

What other meaning is concealed within these words of Miranda's? [148]

(6) Look at page 148.

...Suddenly an immense, purposeful figure, swimming and billowing in grey silk taffeta, emerges like a galleon in full sail, out of the shadows on to the tiled and colonnaded verandah. The girls are drawing themselves up in a half-circle as Mrs Appleyard takes up her position on the verandah.

(a) Why is this a wonderful description of the headmistress?
(b) What aspects of her character are revealed in it?

(7) What warnings does the headmistress, Mrs Appleyard, give to the girls who are assembled for their day's outing to Hanging Rock? [150]

(8) Are any of her warnings relevant to what really happens? Give reasons for your answer.

(9) Miss McCraw's geological analysis of Hanging Rock [153] should have been boring—except that an added comment by Irma produces a powerful feeling of suspense, and of rather fearful anticipation.
    What is Irma's comment and how does it produce suspense?

(10) Read the following description of the picnickers. [157—8]

> ...The two teachers—and the girls—insulated from natural contacts with earth, air and sunlight, by corsets pressing on the solar plexus, by voluminous petticoats, cotton stockings and kid boots. The drowsy well-fed girls lounging in the shade are no more a part of their environment than figures in a photograph album, arbitrarily posed against a backdrop of cork rocks and cardboard trees. Mr Hussey, confident in his surroundings, his backside comfortable on the hard ground, his head in the blue-grey smoke, a pannikin of black tea in one hand, his old chained pocket-watch in the other.

In what way does this description of the girls at their picnic present them as an *intrusion* into the bush environment? Why isn't Mr Hussey presented in the same way?

(11) What would you say is the deeper purpose of the above description?

(12) What difficulties do you think a director would have in interpreting the above description? In your answer, consider (a) the actors, and (b) the film crew.

(13) Mr Hussey's and Miss McCraw's watches have stopped, both on twelve o'clock. How would you expect a film audience to react to this? [157—8]

(14) What do the detailed studies of the ants and other creatures around the picnic area and on the Rock contribute in the way of *symbols* to the film? [157—9]

(15) The frantic sound of cicadas (and sometimes of blowflies) forms an auditory background in many scenes in the film. Why do you think the film-makers have selected these particular sound-effects for the most dramatic scenes?

(16) To what extent does the following description of Hanging Rock capture the awesomeness of the monolith? [164]

> THEIR POV: Hanging Rock, brilliantly illuminated by the lowering afternoon sun. On the steep southern facade the play of golden light and deep violet shade reveals the intricate construction of long, vertical slabs, some smooth as giant tombstones, others grooved and fluted by a prehistoric architecture of wind and water, ice and fire. Huge boulders, originally spewed red-hot from the

boiling bowels of the earth, now come to rest, cooled and rounded in forest shade. The girls are crossing the grassy slope, entering the bracken at the foot of the steepening climb, looking upwards, their feet finding their own way through the ferns, their heads tilted up towards the glittering peaks. Saying nothing, seemingly forever.

Their feet cushioned in silence, the only noise the all-pervading cicadas.

(17) What kind of warning do you think is signalled by the statement that '*The girls, their animal senses insulated by civilization, are barely aware of the true nature of their environment...*'? [164]

(18) Contrast the characters of Marion and Edith as they are revealed in the dialogue between the two on pages 164–5.

(19) Interpolated in the girls' conversation as they climb the slopes of the Rock are descriptions of the intricate environment that probe the fundamental forces at work on the Rock. The signs of these forces—mostly unseen and unfelt by the girls—are urgent and menacing. What kind of menace seems to be threatening and imminent? [164–5]

(20) As Miranda, Marion and Irma climb towards the summit of the Rock, Edith screams [171]:

EDITH   Miranda!

FX   *The shrilling of the cicadas is now a terrible roaring scream.*

    The girls are fast moving out of sight behind the monolith.

EDITH Don't go up there! Come back!

    Edith turns, looks about. She sees something. Her eyes dilate with horror. She screams.

FX   *The cicadas and Edith's screaming blend into an inextricable nightmare of sound, 'peaking' the audio.*

Do you find this an effective climax? Why or why not?

(21) What new insights into Mrs Appleyard's character are revealed in the scene in which she demands that Sara recite the poetry of Mrs Heymans? [172–4]

(22) Explain how suspense is developed in the scene in which Mrs Appleyard waits for, then meets, the drag carrying the girls back from the picnic. [175–7]

(23) Look at the description of the Rock on page 192, under 8o EXT. In this description the emphasis is placed on corruption and decay. What would you say is the reason for this emphasis?

(24) The first climax occurs in the scene where the three senior girls seem to vanish as they climb—or are drawn—towards the

summit of the Rock. At what point does the second climax occur?

(25) What is the hated and corrupted 'thing' that Albert finds near the two balancing boulders on the upper slopes of Hanging Rock? What surprise does this 'thing' have in store for Albert? [198—9]

(26) What other aspect of Mrs Appleyard's character becomes evident from her reaction to Miss Lumley's timidly put comment, 'Wonderful news, Mrs Appleyard'? [201]

(27) Tom, the handyman at the College, seeks a rational explanation for the disappearance of the girls. But Edward Whitehead, the College gardener, smiles at Tom in a slightly mocking manner. ('Did you know, lad...Did you know that there are plants that...that can move?') He then confronts Tom with a mysterious demonstration [205—6]:

Whitehead, with beautiful timing, reaches for a leaf on a plant close by. He delicately touches the leaf with his earth-stained finger. As if touched by the withering rays of the sun, the leaf suddenly closes.

The demonstration has a chilling effect on Tom, even if he doesn't quite know why.

Whitehead has made his point about nature and he moves away, a trace of a smile on his lips. Tom is left staring at the still crimped leaf.

What do you think this demonstration might symbolize?

(28) Mrs Appleyard, in her study, *'sits there, staring at nothing: her carefully structured world is falling apart—decomposing like a rotting organism.'* [219]
    What is Mrs Appleyard's carefully constructed world and why is it falling apart?

(29) How is horror created in the scene in which the girls in the gymnasium press around Irma, demanding 'Tell us, Irma, tell us!'? [220—22]

(30) What horrible discovery does Dianne make in the gym? [222]

(31) Why does Mrs Lumley hand in her notice of resignation to Mrs Appleyard? [222—3]

(32) Mrs Appleyard comes to hate Sara and thinks of her as *'this unbreakable bastard child'* [224]. How does her hatred finally manifest itself?

(33) Do you think that the conclusion of *Picnic at Hanging Rock* is a satisfying one? Give reasons for your answer.

General Questions

(34) Some of the characters in *Picnic at Hanging Rock* are 'rounded' characters, in the sense that they develop or change as the plot or story-line of the film unfolds. Other characters are 'flat'—they do not substantially develop or change as the story unfolds.

Briefly, say how each of the following 'rounded' characters develops as the story unfolds: Sara, Irma, Mrs Appleyard, Michael, Dianne.

(35) To what extent is Mrs Appleyard herself responsible for her own and her school's downfall? Where else must blame for this downfall lie?

(36) 'The strength of the film *Picnic at Hanging Rock* over the novel from which it is derived lies in the way the period, the atmosphere and the mood can be conveyed with true-to-life impact to an audience.' Comment on this view of the film.

(37) Explain the part played by sound-effects in the creation of atmosphere in *Picnic at Hanging Rock*.

(38) The fact that the climax—the girls' disappearance on the Rock —comes quite early does not detract from the suspense and mystery that pervade the rest of the story. Explain why this is so.

(39) Read the glowing account of *Picnic at Hanging Rock* below.

> '*Picnic* proves to be our wonder movie,' wrote the Adelaide *Advertiser* when the film had its world premiere on 7 August 1975. 'It is any country's most beautiful movie in a very long time.'
>
> Lady Joan Lindsay's powerful short novel has been adroitly adapted by screen playwright Cliff Green into a script which the famous British playwright, Harold Pinter, summed up as very impressive.
>
> *Picnic at Hanging Rock: A Film* captures the lines, sounds, shots and scenes of this menacing story of the Victorian era. A comparison of the script and the finished film will demonstrate something of the complexity and creativity of the final editing and sound-mixing stages. Whilst this will be of great interest to the student, the mysterious tale itself will excite all who read it. Moreover, David Kynoch's photographs remain a stunning reminder of the magnificent stylized imagery.

Do you agree or disagree with these opinions on the film? Why?

(40) What 'message' does the story contain for you?

Technical Terms

BIG CU Big close-up. The image — usually a small detail — is very large on the screen.

BRIDGING The sound is continuous from the end of one scene through to the beginning of the next.

CU Close-up. The camera is, or appears to be, very close to the subject. Head and shoulders only in the case of a human figure.

DISSOLVE The image gradually changing from one shot to the next. The two sections of negative are overlapped, the end of the first being faded out and the beginning of the second being faded in.

EXT Exterior.

FINE CUT A film-editing term. Practically the final version of the film, prior to adding music, additional sound-effects, titles, etc.

FRAME One single picture in a strip of film. In this screenplay it is used to suggest the farthest edges of the picture; the full extent of the screen.

FX Effects. In this screenplay, sound-effects.

HIGH-ANGLE SHOT The camera is set in a high position, pointing down.

INT Interior.

INTO SHOT Into camera range.

JUMP CUT A seemingly jarring transition from one shot to the next, justified if the shock-effect heightens the dramatic impact. Alternatively, a cut within a scene, during which 'natural' time has been artificially condensed.

LOW-ANGLE SHOT The camera is set low, pointing upwards.

LS Long shot. The camera is distanced from the subject being filmed. For example, it could be far enough away to include all of a group of people, or a building and its immediate surroundings.

MONTAGE A series of shots dissolving or cutting from one to the next to suggest a passage of time, journey, visual mood, etc.; or to cover a briefly stated piece of story-development.

MOVIOLA A miniature projector, used by editors when cutting and assembling film.

OUT OF SHOT Out of camera range.

PAN The camera swivels from left to right, or right to left, during a shot.

'PEAKING' THE AUDIO The audio level goes 'into the red' on the sound recordist's instrument; a technical flight of fancy by the writer in an endeavour to indicate the excruciatingly high pitch of sound required.

POV Point of view.

SUPER Superimpose. Usually titles. White or coloured lettering appearing on a shot or sequence of shots.

TRACKING SHOT Similar to a travelling shot, except that the camera is mounted on a 'dolly' (trolley), probably moving along a set of tracks or rails, laid to provide a smoother movement.

TRAVELLING SHOT The camera is moving with the object being filmed. It may be mounted on a camera-car or it may be mounted on the object — usually a vehicle — being filmed. Alternatively, it may be filming a moving point of view of a static object.

VO Voice-over. Dialogue can be heard, but the speaker is not in shot.

VWS Very wide shot. Full advantage is taken of the panoramic quality of the wide cinema screen.

WIDEN The camera pulls or zooms back, revealing a wider view. Alternatively, a cut to a wider shot of the same scene.

WIPE Strictly speaking, an alternative to a dissolve; as though an invisible roller passed over the screen, wiping out one image and replacing it with another. Used in a less literal sense in this screenplay.

WS Wide shot. Similar to a long shot, but with the composition of the shot stressing width rather than depth.

ZOOM The image grows larger ('zoom in') or smaller ('zoom out'), almost as though the camera were moving in or out. In fact, the effect is achieved by using a lens of variable focal length.